Kent's Contribution

KENT'S CONTRIBUTION

Richard Church

ADAMS & DART

PEOPLE OF ENGLAND SERIES is a new approach to local history.
Each volume will contain short biographies of 12–15 personalities
intimately connected with a particular county, each of whom
achieved eminence or notoriety in a wider historical context. In
this way the strands of our national heritage can be traced back to
their local roots. Further volumes in preparation are: WILT-
SHIRE PORTRAITS *by Kenneth G. Ponting*; and PEOPLE OF
DEVON *by Professor Jack Simmons*.

© *1972 by Richard Church*
First published in 1972 by Adams & Dart, 40 Gay Street, Bath, Somerset
SBN *239 00111 7*

The text is set in 'Monotype' Plantin and printed by
W & J Mackay Limited, Chatham

Printed and bound in Great Britain

Contents

'Hear me but speak, and bear me where you will.
Kent, in the Commentaries Caesar writ,
Is term'd the civil'st place of all this isle:
Sweet is the country, because full of riches;
The people liberal, valiant, active, wealthy,
Which makes me hope you are not void of pity.'

(SHAKESPEARE *Henry VI*. Part 2, Act IV. Sc. vii).

An Introduction

AN INTRODUCTION is needed today from a writer who is so old-fashioned as to write about heroes and heroines, thereby inferring that there is such a thing as inequality in human society. George Orwell got over this embarrassment by the use of irony, saying 'that all men are equal, but some are more equal than others'. That has a touch of genius about it, worthy of Swift.

I can only blunder on, obstinate in the belief that hitherto no two individuals, animal or vegetable, have ever been exactly alike or equal. I say *hitherto*, because we are constantly being threatened nowadays, by scientists, technologists, politicians and the organisers of vaster and vaster industrial combines, that it has become necessary for all men to be equal in order to face the cosmic problems of the future, both as a human race, and in view of the growing inadequacy of Mother Earth to house us. A great deal of hysteria is prevalent amongst the peoples in the more crowded parts of the world, as we foresee our future when there is 'standing-room only' where climate and other conditions make life worth living. The most recent threat from the scientists is that an invention called 'cloning' is in process. Lord Ritchie-Calder has stated that (and I quote significantly from *The Financial Times* of 17 September 1971, likely to be an epoch-making date), 'within fifteen years it might be possible to grow from a nucleus of an adult cell a new organism with the same genetic characteristics as the person donating the cell nucleus. The human copies would be more identical than identical twins. Their mental processes would be the same, so that they would have the same psychic awareness amounting to telepathic identity.'

How marvellously this would fit in with the requirements of future politics in its efforts to control vaster and vaster communities. How welcome it would be to the economists who will have to plan the feeding, housing, education and general maintenance of the masses, who in the not so distant future will be bred with a single identity, to respond without demur to the simplest form of control.

The more one thinks about this dire prophecy, the more one sees in it a kind of travesty of Plato's *Republic*, and all subsequent Utopian concepts of a world-state ruled by a specially bred aristocracy of intellect and moral excellence.

In reaction against such dreadful forebodings, we can argue that they are mathematical in origin, and that mathematics always begin with an hypothesis, an assumption of certain axioms. But nature has never conformed to those axioms, and therefore mathematics are an artefact of the human mind. So we may escape after all, and future generations may continue to be comparatively equal, but with some just a little more equal than the others, as Orwell so bitterly remarked.

Yes, reply these computer-bewitched prophets, but the human mind is evolving from out and above the so-called behaviour of nature, and making it reliably subservient to our future needs, which will have to be so economised that there will be no room for variants, such as heroes and geniuses. This argument can further be refuted, *ad infinitum*, as philosophy and physics become so heated in their headlong collision that they incandesce, to make a new theology rather of the kind predicted early in the twentiety century by Olaf Stapledon in his book *First and Last Men*, an imagined history of the human race dating forward from the end of the first world war.

Meanwhile, there is quite a large number of people interested in variety, and all that it implies in the nature and conduct of things, from spiral nebulae down to microscopic biological organisms. Somewhere between those two extremes the scale focuses down to human nature, a manifest of life still various, still unaccountable, still capable of evolving surprise, drama, and readable history.

In that belief, I have framed up a certain selection of men and women, within a geographical enclosure, rather as an archæologist stakes out a bit of ground which he fancies may reveal something relative to his particular interest. My particular interest is my fellow mortals, as individuals rather than as communities. And I make no apology for again referring to the fact that I am probably swimming against the tide, in which mass psychology comes rolling in like oil pollution, reducing the infinite variety of organic life to a lubricated extinction, as our technological expertise is doing over the oceans of the world.

Hitherto, wherever mankind has settled, he has produced certain characters of distinction whose idiosyncracies, for good or evil, have dominated both their environment and their fellow creatures. The most primitive of tribes have had their chieftains, and even today, in communities as vast as those of Russia and China, we see the same process in operation; a substantial denial of the horrifying prophecies of the few scientists who are also imaginative enough to foresee the possibilities of their technical experiments, their tinkerings not only with the formations of material nature, but also with the mysterious energies from which it has emerged and whose volitions have controlled its evolution. There may be some of us so old-fashioned that we call those energies by a specific name, God, who is outside number, time and space.

But I become metaphysical, and may give a wrong impression of the book I have written and am trying to introduce. My folly in doing this is to forestall a certain kind of attack which is fashionable today. It is that of a condescending dismissal of past excellencies and achievements, because of their seemingly slow *tempo*: 'All that is clumsy, ponderous, archaic' is the snide remark. But in fact, life has always moved at lightning pace, and the poets, the philosophers and other observant persons, in their own ages, have never ceased to say so. I say so now; but it wants more than a book of this quiet, reminiscent nature, to prove that 'there is nothing new under the sun'.

I have been content, however, to tell the life-stories of a few outstanding characters born in the county of Kent, whose achievement has made their names survive the anonymity of time and death.

I have not gone far back into the past, for individuality becomes almost impossible to assess as time defaces it, as it does the features of statues chiselled in primitive and pre-historic times. Character is dissolved in myth. I would not care to analyse the personality of Jack the Giant-killer, nor an individual such as Jack Cade, who emerged momentarily out of the rank and file of the anonymous community, to gesticulate awhile and then disappear, leaving no personal record, as he had produced no family history on which the biographer might work to make a convincing portrait.

In addition to this difficulty, there is the larger social problem created by the time lapse. It is a persistent one, and very powerful. The changes of modes of thought, of day-to-day details in human habits, speech, the utensils used in the home and in public life, all these factors play a formative part in the making of a character, the way a person acts and thinks. That person is partly conditioned by his environment; and it includes details so small as the shape of the knife with which he cuts up his food, or whether or not he uses a fork, or gropes his way to bed by candle-light or by turning on a switch. These mechanics of daily life are like the little threads that bound Gulliver to the ground, and set him thinking and trying to move in directions that would have been different had the threads not detained him, physically and mentally.

People alive today who were born toward the end of the nineteenth century are greatly amused when they watch, on the television, the present-day simulacrum of the old music-halls, both the stage and the auditorium. What they see is a complete fantasy, a picturesque caricature of the original scene. And that failure in focus is caused by the veil of no more than some eighty years. When the obscuration is some eight hundred years thick, the historian, and the biographer especially, are bound to grope almost blindly after the reality of the period into which they are trying to make their way. How is it possible, for example, to see the Kentish scene which confronted Julius Caesar, though he described his experience lucidly enough, and in doing so revealed, permanently, certain aspects of his personality. But I know that were I to try to complete the portrait, my inability to bring in the background, with the necessary corrections of our false conventional conceptions about the appearance and sophistications of Caesar's British opponents, would be an impossible task. The more readable a historian becomes, the more his work has been illustrated by imaginative conjecture. Much of the 'glory that was Greece', much of the 'splendour that was Rome', have been added by the artistry of the time-spirit; for time is creative as well as obscurant.

Working within the small frame of Kent, I have realised that these influences, of this spirit standing always at hand, are likely to be more conspicuous because of the geographical confinement, and that is why I have not dared to go back far enough into the past for the features of individuals who lived then to become wholly distorted. But the individuals were there, and we are sure of this not only through the evidence of the archæologists, who today continue to bring to light more and more of the subtleties and sophistications of a past formerly presumed to be primitive, but also by our self-criticism during the correction of our mistaken view of that past.

We know, with greater evidence, that man has always been an ingenious animal, both in practical matters connected with daily life, and also in mental ventures in speculating about his ever widening experience, and deducing therefrom his religions and mythologies. The poet, the priest, the engineer, have been members of the human community for many thousands of years, and this signifies that individual personality and social environment have had parallel differentiation. Here then, is an argument that cuts both ways: for a belief in the value of an aristocracy, implying leadership; and of a democracy, implying co-operation of the many. Greatness is comparative. Historians and biographers who ignore this truth are liable to bias and distortion.

My handful of characters, picked more or less at random out of the procession of Kentish history over the past six hundred years, cannot be representative of any point of view, any philosophy of history. H. A. L. Fisher, in his *History of Europe*, came to the conclusion that no philosphy can be deduced from history, and that seems to me to be wrong, because if he is right, then time and space have no function in the evolution of the family of man. But we know that they do, and our certainty comes not only from religious imagination, but also from our discoveries in science, which today is both physical and metaphysical. And this power which we call 'imagination' appears to be a fundamental on which we have built our civilisations, and are still using toward seemingly unlimited enlightenment, even though by way of disasters. That makes the story of mankind, as presented in every religious system from tribal totemism to the superb formulations of the great religious creeds which survive today, to influence even scientists, and restrain even materialists.

What I am anxious to emphasise, is that in telling the life-stories of these few historical figures, I have not forgotten the vast numbers who comprise 'the pilgrimage of eternity', the beloved and loving folk who are the body of mankind, even though by much of their conduct, their stupidity and superstitions, they have made *homo sapiens* the most destructive and most cruel of all living creatures on earth. I think of the families, the mothers especially, who are the links of the chain of civilization through the centuries. My book ends with the words 'Here is rest!', a quotation from a Kentish writer of light verse in the nineteenth century. But that phrase is the key to life. It unlocks the door to what comes after.

For life goes on, and society goes on, constantly producing men and women whose only perpetuation is through their children, and further generations. Life also produces outstanding individuals, of various talents, and occasionally creatures possessed by genius, a faculty for which we still cannot account. Even as I write these words, there are some such, of every degree, in their infancy, growing up toward their private destiny, with here and there some who will put their permanent mark upon society, to pronounce the further history of the human race. Such appear in every generation, and survive even those periods when wars decimate a whole generation and destroy a whole culture, as we have seen in the twentieth century. The power of the revival of the human spirit is incalculable, even in terms of the calculations of the astronomers.

I think of the people I might have picked out from this procession of Kentish folk, and I realise, with dismay, how arbitrary I have had to be, because of the mechanical limitations imposed by this book, as a medium of communication, and also by the limitations of knowledge and vitality which I share with every other individual. I have neglected some people whom I have known personally, whose Kentish contribution I believe to be perpetual. Only one of them have I described, Victoria Sackville-West, a friend and neighbour. There have been others, now also dead, but their work survives. One can say, with justifiable hyperbole, that if you turn a stone in Kent, you start a poet, or some other imaginatively conceived relic of the history of the county. One poet, still living, I cannot mention, because he was born in London. His large contribution of poetry is of such a rare quality that the late Robert Bridges (of Kentish origin), while Poet Laureate, wrote a pamphlet about the remarkable vocabulary and use of archaic words used by this younger artist in words, whose verse is largely coloured by the environment of west Kent, where a conjunction of two tributaries with the Medway make a riparian labyrinth.

Not far from Edmund Blunden's boyhood home at Yalding, two other poets of the same generation, the one born at Mereworth, and the other near Goudhurst, met each other while returning home on a troop-ship from Palestine at the end of the 1914–1918 war. They struck up a friendship, and subsequently became professional men of letters, and thus into my acquaintance. Their contribution to Kent is most intimate, not only in their verse, but particularly in their respective books about their childhood in the county.

C. Henry Warren, whom I have described elsewhere as the Richard Jefferies of the twentieth century, because of his almost over-heated love of nature, was born at Mereworth in 1895. He worked editorially for the British Broadcasting Corporation for some years during the nineteenth-twenties, but later preferred economic uncertainty as a free-lance writer, living alone in a country cottage, almost a hermit, without the burden of family life, in order to be in constant contact with his major interest: Earth's 'rocks, and stones and trees', as Wordsworth summed up the structure of mother nature.

Let me quote an example of Warren's innocent sensuality, which has made me compare him with the physically sick Richard Jefferies. The paragraph is taken from the book about his childhood at Mereworth, on that picturesque, hilly hinterland of the mid-Weald between Tonbridge and Wrotham. He is writing about a typical Kentish fruit orchard, or rather, the path to it. 'Our favourite orchard was one that had to be approached through a long avenue of walnut-trees; and it was there, I am sure, that I first experienced what is still for me one of the most characteristic of all spring scents, the scent of young walnut-leaves bruised and broken in the hand. By jumping up I could just manage to reach the lowest branches, snatching at the tender brown leaves that sprouted from their tips. When I had crushed them in my hot, clenched palm, I would hold them against my nostrils, inhaling the bay-like scent of their oily sap. Here, too, it was that I would come again, later in the year, to see them 'bash' the autumn trees and bring to the ground the last of the ripened nuts. Kicking through the crisp layers of leaves, I would join in the search till evening came and it was no use trying to look any longer, and I must go home with fingers so stained that for days no amount of pumice would fetch them clean. But walnuts, much as I liked them, greedily as I broke away the shucks to get at the bitter, crinkled kernels, could never give me a keener pleasure than the scent of those week-old leaves that I loved to hold against my eager nostrils by the sheer suction of indrawn breath. That scent, sucked as it were into my very being, is now part and parcel of the English spring'. That stretch of upland in mid-Kent has long been famous for its nut copses: the 'Kentish cobs', each nut in its little puckish green helmet.

Warren did not long survive the death in 1959 of his slightly older

friend, Frank Kendon, who was born in 1893 at a boarding school for boys
founded by his grandfather in 1866 in a tiny hamlet, Curtisden Green,
two miles north of Goudhurst, a hill-top village with a view to all points
of the compass. But for its rose-red cosiness, it might be one of those
citadels that crown most of the heights in the Italian Apennines.

As a writer, Kendon was of larger stature than Warren. He was a
consummate craftsman, both in prose and verse, as well as being a good
engraver. After some years in Fleet Street, he went to the Cambridge
University Press as deputy secretary, and was responsible for the format of
the books put out by the Syndics. He put his personal mark even on that
austere and excellent imprint. The mark was one of simplicity. This rare
virtue was signified in all his work, as in his life, in the later years of which
he became a member of The Society of Friends, thus returning full circle
to the religious faith of his family, after a personal excursion into a field
of passionate devotion to the arts, and like Warren, into a love affair with
nature. Also like Warren, he wrote a short book about his childhood, in
prose that reminds me of a glass of water drawn from a deep spring, so
fresh, so cold, that a mist gathers round the outside of the glass. Curtisden
Green is seen through the eyes of this small boy, already a secular saint,
and it becomes another Assisi.

The Small Years was published by the Cambridge University Press in
1930, and it was through this book that I met him, for I was so enchanted
by it that I wrote a leader, I think in *The Spectator*, after Walter de la
Mare, who wrote a preface to it, had drawn my attention to this miniature
masterpiece. It continues to be reprinted, and is likely to survive alongside
The Natural History of Selborne, and Jefferies' *The Story of my Heart*.

Kendon published several collections of poetry, but characteristically
made no such effort as a formal *Collected Poems*. I remember that John
Masefield once said to me that this procedure was absolutely necessary
if a poet was to enter for the immortality stakes. Thus Kendon's poetry,
non-fashionable at all times, and especially today in the latter half of the
twentieth century, has been woefully neglected. Maybe time and posterity
will enhance it, and bring yet unborn readers even to the longer poems
such as *The Life and Death of Judas Iscariot*, whose familiar story is enriched
by the poet's first-hand evocation of the scenery of Palestine, where Kendon
served in our army during the first world war.

He had the subtle gift of understatement, carrying an anguished appeal
in a calm phrase, as in the last line of the following tiny lyric, called

The Immigrant

When Ruth was old
She'd take her children's children on her knee.
They never wearied to be told
Tales of her girlhood in a far country.

For though her eyes grew dim,
Men said of her, 'Her heart is always young',
And Boaz, while she spoke to him,
Loved the faint accent of a foreign tongue.

Another artist of similar nature was a man ten years younger than Kendon. Thomas Hennell was born in 1903 at his father's rectory, in Ash, near Wrotham, near Warren's birth-place. His skill as a draughtsman was so outstanding that Sir George Frampton persuaded the boy's father to send him to art schools rather than to a university. So he evolved as a craftsman, singularly devoted, in almost a medieval way, to his art. Like Warren, he never married. The modern world became too much for him, and for three years in early manhood he lost control of his reason, but in 1938 he recovered and resumed his ever-maturing craftsmanship. But his destiny remained dark, for during the second world war he was sent out to the far East as a war artist, and was killed by bandits in October, 1945. He had found recognition earlier with wartime pictures made for the War Office in Iceland in 1943, which were exhibited in the National Gallery. In that year also he became a member of The New English Art Club. Concurrently with his real vocation, he also wrote several books, including a collection of poems in 1936, put out during his illness, and two books about the Kentish way of life, *Change in the Farm* and *The Countryman at Work*, the last being introduced by the distinguished naturalist-author Harold J. Massingham, who sums up Hennell's contribution to Kent: 'It is quite meaningless to pigeon-hole Hennell into the man, the artist, the writer. The key to them all is the English countryman. Hennell belonged to Kentish fields and orchards in exactly the same sense as Hardy and William Barnes belonged to Dorset, Gilbert White to Selborne, John Clare to Northamptonshire and Jefferies to Wiltshire. He was so Kentish that, as Mr Delmar Nabber told me, "he did not enter into mountain nature". Hennell was so dyed-in-the-wool a countryman, so direct a descendant of the English water-colourists in his art and of the old self-supporting independent craftsmen of our villages and market towns by character, blood and inclination (his grandfather was a silversmith), so completely the scholar-gypsy in his intimacy with every phase of country life and inexhaustible knowledge of our rural culture as it was in its flower and survives in its eclipse, so utterly rural in himself, his manners, his loves, his habits, his very appearance and dress, that I have to be on my guard against explaining the whole man, root and branch, person and work, by this sole criterion.'

How many more Kentish-born immortals have I left out? As I write this preface to the book after the main body dealing with outstanding historical figures, I realise afresh that it is the accumulation of folk of perhaps smaller talents and more private personalities who in the long run are the more expressive of the genius of place. A farmer here, a labourer's wife there, might be the final embodiment of Kent. I can think of some I have met, but I cannot pick out individuals because they are innumerable, and therefore inexpressible. They have made Kent as Kent has made them. They may not be articulate, in action or in voice, as some of our great ones, whose deeds and names are blazed across the history of the county; but like the bees, they have brought their pollen to the hive, this golden Kent, so rich in its store of honeyed achievement.

For me, the county has taken on a kind of mystical relationship, since I came from London half a life-time ago, to live here and recover my health. I once wrote a sonnet, which recorded the experience of coming to settle in the heart of the county, and the result was almost a religious gesture. Here it is, to conclude my Introduction both to this book and to the county, as I open the door to *Kent's Contribution*.

> At once I recognised him, for I saw
> Blood clotted in his palms, and on his shirt
> Above the ribs. His foot arched like a claw
> When it approached the ground; and in the dirt
> A spoor of blood stigmatised Camberwell.
> I traced the agony through Peckham Rye,
> Past parish church and Town Hall. I could tell
> That by the School of Art he paused, but why
> I could not understand. He may have hoped
> To find a healing symbol there. He failed.
> The trail of blood betrayed him as he groped
> Onward from London as the darkness paled
> Slowly before him, showing as he went
> His throne and resurrection over Kent.

The Fair Maid of Kent

EVERY student of history, at some time or other in the course of his reading, must be reduced to scepticism and despair as the story of mankind opens before him, weltering even during a period of apparent peace, raging in madness during times of storm, such as we are enduring in the twentieth century.

We look back on the fourteenth century as another such destructive era, with dynasties, nations and races at strife, destroying not only the material civilizations of the past eras, but tumbling philosophies, religions and social structures into a confusion out of which reformers and idealists, on the one hand, struggle to create a raft of regeneration from the debris, while on the other hand, adventurers enrich themselves temporarily on what they can loot from it.

Joan, immortalised as 'The Fair Maid of Kent', lived in the midst of that century, acquiring that charming name because of her birth as a daughter of Edmund, Earl of Kent, sixth son of King Edward the First. She was born in 1328, and died in 1385. Within that time, by reason of her royal status, and especially her second marriage to Edward, Prince of Wales as heir to Edward the Third, Joan was able to wield power behind the throne. Her husband also has a poetic name which ensures his immortality, for he was 'The Black Prince', who played so vigorous and ruthless a part in the Hundred Years' War between France and England, territories still intermingled and only vaguely nationalised, the one distinct from the other.

One of the causes of the tragedy of that century was this process of sorting out the two countries as separate kingdoms. The King of France held an enclave toward the north-east, with Paris as its capital. The English held Calais and maintained a foothold along the northern coast. They held practically the whole of central and south-western France between the Loire and the Gironde; lovely Aquitaine and the Dordogne, which the Black Prince, who had military genius, had acquired during the early stages of the War by hard fighting and ruthless plunder, the technique habitual in all warfare, no matter how benevolent the motives behind the contests may be. The Hundred Years' War was ferocious and destructive, especially in France where it was waged. It bled England dry economically. In both countries the horror was multiplied by the Black Death. From the beginning in 1337, when Joan was a child of nine, the tangle of dynastic claims by the English and French kings was complicated by the activities of the kings of Scotland and Burgundy, and the Emperor of what should be called the Most Unholy Roman Empire, all three seeking to profit from the general disturbance. Nor was the Vatican helpful. The spiritual authority of the Papacy during the two previous centuries, which almost made a Christian federation of Europe, was now diluted with temporal power-mongering. It became divided within itself, with rival Popes, the one in Rome and the other, as creature of the French power, at Avignon.

Here is not the place to try to disentangle the complexities of the Hundred Years' War, though foot-soldiers from Kent, and the other English counties, emerged as a new weapon of war, and thus produced from within their own status as serfs a consciousness of strength which began to break up the structure of the Feudal System, and instituted an elementary form of economic relation between master and man, employer and employed, that was to lead to the articulation of modern society, creating in the process a third estate, the mainly urban middle-class of merchants, bankers, industrialists, many of whose prototypes can be seen, as it were in embryo, in the characters on pilgrimage in Chaucer's *Canterbury Tales*, a poet's capital reporting on contemporary affairs. The period was that in which The Fair Maid of Kent flourished, maintaining her beauty and compassion in spite of her environment.

It was an environment of swift and continual change. Human existence was both vivid and violent in those days, and we of the equally violent twentieth century, differing from our parents and grandparents, have a fellow-feeling with those late-medieval folk who lived, conscious of fatality stalking behind them, 'the smiler with the knife'.

We do not know much of the early years of Joan's life. Her mother's name, Margaret Wake, suggests an origin in the fen country round Ely, where in 1070 the last of the Saxon thegns, Hereward the Wake, was belatedly subdued by William the Conqueror. The child's close association with her parents, however, was broken when she was two years old, for her father was beheaded in March 1330, probably as the result of some intrigue within the large Royal family. Edmund was the sixth son, and may have been trying to work his way nearer to the throne by methods prescribed in every mythology, from that of the Jews and the Greeks, to that of the Australian aboriginals.

Joan was probably younger than her sister Margaret, but even so, she was godmother, at that early age, to a brother John, who was born less than a month after his father's death. In October of that year, Queen Philippa adopted her. That was fortunate for Joan, whose development was observed by the Norman historian Froissart, famous for his *Chronicles*, written in so handsome a prose style that they stand as one of the strongest supports of French literary history. He saw Joan as 'in her time the most beautiful girl in the Kingdom of England, and the most loving.' It was he who called her 'cette jeune demoiselle de Kent', a vague description which nevertheless has made her immortal.

Queen Philippa, like so many women in that Age of Chivalry, demonstrated the increasing emphasis on the part played by the Virgin Mary in the Christian story, as it affected the status of motherhood, and the place of woman, throughout Christian society. The first signs of compassion and gentleness became apparent in human relationships, not only within family life, but in public, and on political occasions. The outstanding example of this is Queen Philippa's intervention during her husband's wanton and greedy war against France. Everybody knows the story of the Burghers of Calais. This incident followed soon after the opening of the second stage of the Hundred Years War, the lull between the parts having been due to England being so reduced, in blood and money, that Edward had to bring his forces home, if only to attend to troubles on his Scottish borders.

The Italian poet Petrarch, lyrical spokesman of the Age of Chivalry and the sanctification of womanhood, recorded what he saw in France at that time. 'I could not believe that this was the same France, which I had seen so rich and flourishing. Nothing presented itself to my eyes but a fearful solitude, an utter poverty, land uncultivated, houses in ruins. Even the neighbourhood of Paris showed everywhere marks of desolation and conflagration. The streets are deserted, the roads overgrown with weeds, the whole is a vast solitude'.

Froissart is more detailed, as a war correspondent. 'By the Englishmen was brent, exiled, robbed, wasted and pilled the good, plentiful country of Normandy. The soldiers made no account to the King nor to none of his officers of the gold and silver that they did get. They kept that to themselves'. The cacophonous recurrence of such scenes in all wars has been grimly demonstrated to us in the twentieth century, this time not in the name of chivalry, but of democracy.

After the battle of Cressy, where the Black Prince was allowed by his father to 'win his spurs', the English army laid siege to Calais. It lasted a year, and the valuable sea-port was starved into surrender. Edward was enraged by such obstinate endurance, and he agreed to spare a general slaughter of the citizens only if twelve of its aldermen were delivered to him for execution.

Then stood up the wealthiest burgess of the town, Master Eustache de St. Pierre by name, and spake thus before all: 'My masters, great grief and mishap it were for all to leave such a people as this is to die by famine and otherwise; and great charity and grace would he win from our Lord who could defend them from dying. For me, I have great hope in the Lord that if I can save this people by my death, I shall have pardon for my faults, and of my own will put myself barefoot in my shirt and with a halter round my neck in the mercy of King Edward'.

So the sacrificial victims came out of the town to confront the English. Edward, with his courtiers and generals, stood waiting. The burgomaster made an eloquent speech, pleading for the King's mercy. It reduced to tears not only the nearby citizens of Calais, who had been bold enough to follow their leaders out of the town, hoping perhaps that their silent plight might aid the orator: it also set the English knights weeping, and pleading with the King to show magnanimity.

But he was obdurate. 'Call the headsman!' he shouted. 'They of Calais have made so many of my men die, that they must die themselves!' And now came the moment when Queen Philippa intervened.

Then did the noble Queen of England a deed of noble lowliness, seeing she was great with child, and wept so tenderly for pity, that she could no longer stand upright; therefore she cast herself on her knees before her lord the King, and spake on this wise: 'Ah, gentle sire! from the day that I passed over sea in great peril, as you know, I have asked for nothing: now I pray and beseech you, with folded hands, for the love of our Lady's Son, to have mercy upon them.' The gentle King waited a while before speaking, and looked on the Queen as she knelt before him bitterly weeping. Then began his heart to soften a little, and he said, 'Lady, I would rather you had been otherwhere; you pray so tenderly, and I dare not refuse you; and though I do it against my will, nevertheless take them, I give them you'.

Thus Froissart, as quoted by the Victorian historian J. R. Green, in his *Short History of England* published in 1874, when we English mistakenly hoped that such scenes could never recur.

The quotation shows the character of Queen Philippa. We note how she pleaded in the name of Mary, the Mother of God. A sexual revolution is contained in that reference.

Joan, the Fair Maid of Kent, was a symbol of that revolution. She was an eager pupil of her godmother the Queen, and in later life played a similar role as intercessor against the male ascendency, but this time on behalf of her son, the young King Richard II and his officers, when they were at the mercy of the Kentish rebels.

But first let us see what were the problems caused by her outstanding beauty in girlhood, and the further dangers to which it was submitted because of her royal rank and her place at Court.

A young courtier, Sir Thomas Holland, fell in love with Joan, and the Queen again showed her unworldliness by permitting a contract of marriage. In those days a betrothal was a bond that included cohabitation. However, before the marriage could be solemnised, Holland's master, the second Earl of Salisbury, to whom he was steward of the household, contrived to have him sent away to the wars in France. The Earl, also infatuated by Joan's beauty and compassionate character, proffered his own contract.

Whether or not she was equally complacent toward this second approach we do not know. Holland appears to have believed in her fidelity towards him, for he came home and at once prepared a petition to the Pope Clement VI to restore his legal betrothal to Joan. The Pope referred the petition to the Cardinal Adhemar for investigation, and after both sides had presented their cases, judgment was given for Holland.

What part the girl played in the embarrassments that followed, we do not know. They must have been complex, but as Sir Thomas Holland so openly and eagerly claimed her after his return from the wars, we may assume that she had assured him of her fidelity, and that her relationship with his master the Earl of Salisbury had been one-sided, a formal approach by him. The Islip Register, in Lambeth Palace Library, does not record the first contract with Holland, and represents Joan as divorced from Salisbury for infidelity with Holland. John Selden, the great jurist and historian, writing nearly three hundred years later, rather irresponsibly identified Joan with the Countess of Salisbury, the dropping of whose garter while dancing was supposed to be the incident which caused the King to institute the *Order of the Garter*, with its very significant subscription, *Evil be to him who evil thinks*. This suggests that the wise King Edward III submitted to his wife's compassionate judgment, not only in public matters such as the treatment of the Burghers of Calais, but also in personal ones. He knew what the Queen thought of Joan, as her foster-child whom she had educated and reared in the religious ideas which were blowing like a cleansing wind through the English spiritual consciousness at that time. The easy cynicism of Court values may have suggested that a woman who drops her garter was of a disposition to drop much more, an insinuation which prompted the King to this now classical retort, and the proclamation thereby of his belief in Joan's gravity and responsible character. We have little evidence to be able to sort out the tangle of this problem, even if we still think it of importance to decide which of the two gentlemen deflowered the Fair Maid of Kent before she became Holland's wife, at the age of twenty-one.

Joan's elder brother Edmund, Earl of Kent, had died in 1333, the title going to the younger brother John, to whom Joan had been godmother since she was two years old. John died in 1352, and Joan thus became, in her own right, Countess of Kent and Lady Wake of Liddell. The King granted her a substantial pension. Holland, eight years later, assumed the right of his wife to the title of the Earldom of Kent, but died that same year, 1360.

Froissart takes up the story from that point, and states that Joan, within a few months, consented to a mutual love match with Edward, the Prince of Wales, but without the knowledge of the King. That was a dangerous situation, too near the Throne to be accepted lightly, or for long, clandestinely. The King had to know, though the short lapse of time since her widowhood and her infatuation for the Prince of Wales might suggest lightness of character. There was also the fact that the lovers were cousins.

However, the King again showed his absolute confidence in Joan by accepting the situation, while the Prince's court poet celebrated Joan as

> Une dame de grant pris
> Qe belle fuist, plesante et sage

and confirmed on behalf of his master that

> The prince her vowid unto a knight of his
> She said she would none by hymself I wis.

A Papal dispensation was obtained, and the royal cousins were married by the Archbishop of Canterbury, Simon Islip, at Lambeth Palace on 6 October 1361. Froissart says the couple, with the Royal Court, celebrated for five days. That shows no lack of enthusiasm in official quarters for the new 'set to partners'.

The following spring, in 1362, Joan and the Black Prince went to Aquitaine where they reigned as Viceroys for Edward III (yet another sign of his complete trust in Joan and her influence on his son). They remained there for nine years, during which the Prince, a soldier of military genius, again put into devastating use the new technique of ballistics, perfected in England with the use of the longbow, an infantry weapon which was used earlier, at the Battle of Poitiers in 1356, so effectually by the Prince with an army of 8,000 men, against the French King John's forces of over 60,000, the flower of France's chivalry.

This continued demonstration of the superiority of infantry as a weapon against the heavily armoured knights on horseback was to have an historical effect infinitely more far-reaching than was imagined at the time by the feudal king who first introduced it. It was to destroy the Feudal System, and by giving striking power to the rank and file, was to aid and abet the revolutionary, democratic ideas being infused into the Catholic Churches of north Europe by John Wyclif, and into the Parliamentary system of the English government.

During those blood-soaked nine years, while the Black Prince was concerned more with destroying the forces of the several princes of central France, than with administering and maintaining the rich province of Aquitaine, Joan appears to have exercised little restraining influence, as the Queen had after the fall of Calais at the end of the first half of the Hundred Years' War. She may have been more passive in disposition than the Queen, but it is also probable that she was closely concerned with family affairs. She had Holland's children, and two princes whom she bore to the Prince of Wales during the sojourn in Aquitaine. She had the grief of losing the elder, Edward, at the age of five. Richard, afterwards to be King of England, was born the year before the return to England in 1371. This was the domestic period of her life, one from which not even a princess, with adequate staff, can escape into the larger world of public affairs: larger, but not more important or, finally, permanently influential, since the child being father of the man, the nursery is the predication of Parliament.

So life went on for Joan in England for another five years. We do not know what her activities were, but she, with her foster-mother the Queen, would have been closely influenced by the changes taking place in religious consciousness. Those changes were first movements in the revolt against the decadence of the Roman Church, a degeneration into materialism from top to bottom of its structure, from the Papal Chair to the obscure priory, or the parish priest, wherever the Church carried its authority, by now too deliberately a material one in constant competition with the temporal kings and princes of Europe.

The death of the Black Prince in 1376, and the promotion of his and Joan's son Richard to the Principality of Wales, as heir apparent to the Throne of England and Aquitaine, revealed yet again the King's absolute trust in Joan, for until his death in 1377, the heir was left in the immediate care of his mother, and she was given the control of his household and income.

Her influence on the boy was perhaps too feminine and protective, for he proved to be too light-weight a character to be able to cope with the responsibility of ruling a kingdom thrown into confusion by the conjunction of major events; the renewal of the war with France, the economic and social consequences of The Black Death, and the feverish effect of the spreading of Wyclif's revolutionary teachings that challenged both Church and State. John of Gaunt emerged as the leader of the group of nobles who formed a loose and incoherent Regency to 'advise' the young King, who at first remained passive in their hands, while they worked such mischief, by power-mongering and intrigue in the realm, that the machinery of government evolved by the statesmanship of Edward III collapsed once more into anarchy, each great baron grabbing only for himself; a state of affairs which endured throughout the reign of Richard, and finally toppled him from the throne, already made insecure by the Peasants' Revolt in Kent.

Maybe Joan's gentleness of approach to affairs of State, in which the balancing of power is always the supreme task, was premature for those troubled times. Not even John of Gaunt, 'time-honoured Lancaster', the King's uncle, could restore the nation's flagging fortunes both at home and in France. The Church, rocking before the attack of Wyclif, the pioneer of The Reformation and the Protestant Faiths, was concerned only with its estates and the preservation of its wealth by such practices as the sale of pardons and other such panderings to the superstitions of the people, instead of to the spiritual man, at which Wyclif aimed.

This man had spent the early part of his life at Oxford, and was recognised amongst the schoolmen as one of the most impressive scholars in Europe. He was not appointed to the Mastership of Balliol College until he was middle-aged, and it was from that always formidable bastion of superior intellectuality that he directed his campaign, his own vernacular translation of the Bible in his hand. He aimed at cleansing the Church from the degradation into which its political preoccupations, its greedy power-mongering in the pursuit of temporal and material ascendency had dragged it. He saw the divine authority of the Papal Chair also degraded by the struggle of two Popes to sit in it. In England the people, as the historian Green wrote, 'scorned a "French Pope" and threatened his legates with stoning when they landed. The wit of Chaucer flouted the wallet of "pardons hot from Rome".'

Wyclif wrote and preached. He came out from the shelter of the academic cloisters, and stood at the ear of John of Gaunt, who saw in him a weapon with which to undermine the still powerful hold of the Papacy, through one 'spiritual' office or another, over the lives and loyalty of the people of England. Green's description of him is a vivid one.

It was only the struggle that lay before him which revealed in the dry and subtle schoolman the founder of our later English prose, a master of popular invective, of irony, of persuasion, a dexterous politician, an audacious partizan, the organiser of a religious order, the unsparing assailant of abuses, the boldest and most indefatigable of controversialists, the first Reformer who dared, when deserted and alone, to question and deny the creed of the christendom around him, to break through the tradition of the past, and with his last breath to assert the freedom of religious thought against the dogmas of the Papacy.

The Fair Maid of Kent, now a widow deeply embroiled in the conflict of the Church officers and the barons round the Throne, saw in this great

man's teachings a continuation of the instinctive compassion implanted
in her own character, and encouraged to become a way of life by Queen
Philippa. She saw in those teachings the religious truth, as her son's
'Good Parliament' saw in them an invigorating political truth, which
prompted what might be called an audacious 'white paper' attacking

the taxes levied by the Pope which amounted to five times those levied by the
King; that by reservation during the life of actual holders he disposed of the
same bishopric four or five times over, receiving each time the first fruits.
The brokers of the sinful City of Rome promote for money unlearned and
unworthy caitiffs to benefices of the value of a thousand marks, while the
poor and learned hardly obtain one of twenty. So decays sound learning.
They present aliens who neither see nor care to see their parishioners, despise
God's services, convey away the treasure of the Realm, and are worse than
Jews or Saracens. The Pope's revenue from England alone is larger than that
of any Prince in Christendom. God gave his sheep to be pastured, not to be
shaven and shorn.

It is a historical fact, and not cynical surmise, which suggests the conclusion that religious re-awakening always becomes acceptable when it
recognises economic advantage. Wyclif's proclamation of the iniquities of
the Catholic Church found instant approval throughout northern Europe,
in those States where the authority of the Vatican had never been easily
accepted. The decadence, and the attack on it from the North, was a
repetition of the decline of the Roman Empire. The difference was that
the Church survived because it still had a profound and timeless spiritual
basis, deeper than its voracious bureaucracy.

Even so, that spiritual basis also helped the critics, who accepted it as
their reason for revolt. So, with Wyclif's outcry, and his flinging open of
the teachings of the Bible through his translation into English, the Reformation began. The tremendous force of this direct approach to the sources of
the Jewish and Christian faiths found its instrument in the constitution
of the Lollards, whose example as a salvation army repudiating the Pope's
power of excommunication, spread across northern Europe as far as
Czecho-Slovakia (then called Bohemia), where it slumbered, latent, until
John Huss, and then Martin Luther in Germany, marshalled it to a worldwide campaign which the Church of Rome, to this day, looks upon as a
siege.

Wyclif's last words, that 'the Pope should surrender all temporal
authority to the civil power and advise his clergy to do the same', were

spoken only seven years after the beginning of the Peasant Revolt against the inequalities and injustice of that civil control. These evils had been exposed and emphasised by the economic consequences of the Black Death. More than half the serfs, or villeins, on whose bent backs and horny hands the Feudal System rested, had disappeared into the plague pits. Those who survived realised that their value as a labour force had gone up. The two forms of unrest, the religious and the economic, coalesced. A reactionary *Statute of Labourers* in 1350 for a time fixed the price of labour, and forbade the field workers to leave the parishes to which the Feudal System had tied them.

These parallel conditions, spiritual and physical, grew increasingly explosive for another twenty years. In Kent and East Anglia, where the new legal oppression pressed most heavily, rumblings of revolt came to a head in 1377 when a parish priest in Kent, named John Ball, with rabble-rousing eloquence, preached that 'things will never go well in England so long as goods be not in common, and so long as there be villeins and gentlemen. By what right are they whom we call Lords greater folk than we? On what grounds have they deserved it? Why do they hold us in serfage?' From his outcry, voicing the complaint of Cain against Abel, there evolved the deadly slogan, a bomb which to this day has not been effectually defused, 'When Adam delved and Eve span, who was then the gentleman?'

Edward the Third's death in 1377 removed an ageing but still firm hand from the helm of the ship of state. South-east England, from the Wash across to Somerset, rose in protest against a Poll Tax which had been imposed by the Regency government headed by the King's uncle, John of Gaunt. In Essex and Kent the uprising became organised in 1381 into a rough and ready militant shape. A mob in Essex, led by one Jack Straw, routed the royal commissioners and crossed the Thames into Kent. They found the people of Canterbury welcoming them with open gates. They plundered the Archbishop's palace and released the priest John Ball from the prison where the Ecclesiastical Court had immured him. Meanwhile the Kentish crowd, now combined with the Essex folk into a rustic and urban army of some hundred thousand folk, elected an ex-soldier, named Wat Tyler, home from France and unemployed (as most old soldiers were in those days) to be their leader. One rumour has it that he was enraged because a Poll Tax collector had entered his home and taken advantage of his daughter. But rumours, slogans and rough rhymes were legion, fanning the fire of revolution and carrying it westward to London.

There the full explosion involved the royal family. The rebel army camped on Blackheath, and from there raided Lambeth Palace and burned the prisons in Southwark. Apprentices and artizans within the City raised the drawbridge of London Bridge to let the insurgents cross the Thames. Joined by thousands of Londoners, they sacked John of Gaunt's palace of the Savoy, and burned Newgate and the Fleet prisons, thus gathering more recruits. Lawyers and churchmen were the favourite quarry, and many were murdered. This selective anger sought the top, and within a few days Archbishop Sudbury, the Chancellor, thus doubly an offender, with Sir Robert Hales the Treasurer and Chief Commissioner, were seized and beheaded on Tower Hill, in spite of the bravery of the young King, who had confronted the mob and tried to pacify it with sympathetic words.

For another day and night London was given over to slaughter and pillage. Flemish merchants, symbols of riches, suffered with the lawyers and the priests. John of Gaunt had fled to Scotland, but his followers and servants were singled out as sacrificial victims to the now intoxicated God of Equality.

The King, though only a boy of fourteen, suddenly asserted his royal authority and against the pleading of his officers of the Government, all of whom were temporarily paralysed by fear, rode out to Smithfield to confer again with the leaders of the rebels. Outside St Bartholomew's noble Romanesque Church, he met Wat Tyler. That worthy greeted him, shook him by the hand, and bade him be of good cheer. With this discarding of protocol, he then made a number of demands, which included the confiscation of ecclesiastical estates and the setting up of social equality.

The King hardly had time to reply, and his hesitation was misconstrued by Tyler, who began to threaten the royal person, whereupon the Mayor, Sir William Walworth, and John Standwick, one of the King's squires, drew their swords and killed Wat Tyler. This act of loyal folly would have been disastrous, as the crowd's angry reaction showed, had not the King regained confidence. He spurred his horse into the open, out of the protection of his followers, and into the range of the bows levelled against him. 'Sirs,' he cried, 'Will you shoot your King? I will be your chief and captain, you shall have from me all that you seek'.

This may have been bluff. It was more probably sincere; a demonstration of the temperament fostered by his upbringing in the atmosphere of

gentle optimism and sincere Christian compassion created by his grandmother and his mother, the Fair Maid of Kent. But another aspect of his
character, an impractical indecisiveness, a passivity, is also suggested as
we learn from the futilities of his reign, and the miserable and squalid
end of it. He meant well, but lacked the required strength to follow up
his good intentions and promises. Within a few days his magnanimous
gesture was betrayed. His flock retreated, pacified, but were immediately
set upon by the watchdogs. Over a hundred of the leaders were executed,
amongst them John Ball. The enfranchisement of villeins verbally granted
by the King was repudiated by Parliament, and King Richard betrayed
his promise by marching into Kent with an army of 40,000 men, where
he pursued the rebels through the forests of Anderida, plucking them one
by one out of that sylvan retreat and putting their leaders to death. He
then did the same in Essex, where, after two stubborn battles at Billericay,
the revolt was crushed. The Feudal System was resumed throughout the
Kingdom, but its foundations were shaken, leaving a weakness which
finally brought it down under the assault of the Wars of the Roses, and
the autocratic heel of the Tudor monarchs.

The King's essay into idealism was short-lived. Shakespeare, however,
saw more spirituality in him, and revealed it in bursts of rhetoric throughout the tragedy of his historical play, outcries of nobility from the mouth of
this weak-charactered creature of circumstance, who cried out to his
quarrelling kinsmen:

> Wrath-kindled gentlemen, be ruled by me,
> Let's purge this choler without letting blood:
> This we prescribe, though no physician;
> Deep malice makes too deep incision:
> Forget, forgive, conclude and be agreed. . .

but it was significant that his plea was ineffectual, and his gentleness
turned out to be nothing better than timidity, a characteristic later to bring
about his downfall. Musing in Pomfret Castle on the day of his murder,
he soliloquises

> I have been studying how I may compare
> This prison where I live unto the world:
> And for because the world is populous,
> And here is not a creature by myself,
> I cannot do it; yet I'll hammer it out.
> My brain I'll prove the female to my soul. . . .

That last line sums up the influence of his mother's upbringing. Had he not been an introspective, frustrated idealist, driven by the spirit of the age and his own rank to compulsory acts of violence and dreadful determinations repulsive to his innate sensibility, the outcome of Bolingbroke's revolt might have been to delay the reduction of the anarchic power of the barons. From such a small thing as the feminine, instinctive streak in this young king's nature, swifter urgencies were brought about in the evolution of our national Constitution. The paradox of life is that so often, passivity and gentleness can be the cause of bloodshed and disaster. It creates the story of human religions, and their reflections in human history.

Behind that equivocal quality in King Richard's character lay that of his mother, The Fair Maid of Kent. We can barely see her because of the regal glare. We sense her by whispers, by hand-touch, almost by an abstract presence. Yet she was positive in her intrusion into affairs of State, and her son accepted this maternal control. In 1378 he honoured her with the Order of the Garter, and in that same year she intervened to arrest the proceedings against Wyclif by the synod at Lambeth, prompted possibly by John of Gaunt, but certainly by her own progressive religious hopes for a cleansing of the Church of those detestable accretions which Wyclif had attacked. In Pope Clement's bull of 1377 she was emphatically cited, along with several of her knights who were all Lollards. Yet in her Will she affirmed her obedience to the Catholic Church.

At the time of the Peasants' Revolt, she was fifty-three years of age. Yet her beauty must have survived her corpulence, which is also recorded. Froissart wrote that while returning from Canterbury to London, she fell in with the Kentish rebels, 'but escaped with a few kisses'. She was all for kindness; and that is always an effectual persuasive *at the moment*. But we see what it did, as a policy, to her son's career. When for once he broke away from that golden tyranny, and condemned her son John Holland, his half-brother, for the murder of Ralph Stafford, the rigorous legalism of that act destroyed her spirit, and she died of an application of man's justice, her heart broken. The King was away in Scotland that day, 7 August 1385, but he ordered that her body should be wrapped in waxed swathings and kept in a lead coffin until his return. The interment, by her own request, was at the Friars Minor church in Stamford, *near the monument of her first husband, Holland*. This is the last instance of her emotional fidelity, and of the dominance in her crowded life of the spirit of personal love, that crowning authority of womanhood.

William Caxton

MANY people will be startled and incredulous if I suggest that William Caxton was the greatest, and historically the most influential native of Kent. But there would be much truth in the statement. He was a person who combined great business ability with an imaginative idealism. That combination always works toward a major achievement, because the first ability makes the most of the second. How often we see genius wasted because it is housed in a character that is muddle-minded. Caxton was not one of that kind. He was a business-man, a scholar and a visionary, and he organised those three potentials on a single basis. Added to this, he was born at the right time, with environment and circumstances harmonious to his temperament and interests. That is why he is an immortal, his name a household word even amongst the illiterates of the English-speaking world.

He was born in the very heart of Kent, the Weald. There is some dispute about the spot, due to the fact that his name was also spelt Cauxton and identified with a manor-house called Causton at Hadlow, near Tonbridge. But the general belief is that his birthplace was Tenterden, that proud little town of great beauty, with an unusually broad High Street, a noble church, and buildings expressive of the domestic architecture representative of our English way of life through many centuries. One cottage in the middle of the town is said to have the title-deeds from the twelfth century. There it stands today, leaning against one of its neighbours, as though weary of gazing across the road at the only twentieth-century horror in the town, a block of self-service shops that recently replaced a long garden bordering the pavement with a hedge of climbing roses.

Tenterden keeps its ancient town-hall, and it once had a little theatre down a side-street. During the festivities for Queen Elizabeth's coronation, I borrowed from Lord Kemsley his treasured collection of Caxtoniana, letters, deeds, specimens of printing, together with the cabinets that housed them, and staged an exhibition of the craft of printing and book-making in that town-hall. So convincing was the assumption that Tenterden was Caxton's native town that the brewers who owned one of the several inns along the high street re-named the house 'The Caxton Arms', and gave a memorial feast there, to the sound of most authoritative speeches. So let us assert that Tenterden was Caxton's birthplace.

We are not quite certain of the date of his birth. One biographer puts it at 1412. But the fact that he is recorded as being apprenticed to one Robert Large (a frequently found Kentish name) in 1438, which would be when he was about sixteen years of age, suggests that his birth year was more likely to be 1422.

His master was a rich silk mercer, so successful that in 1439 he became Lord Mayor of London. This suggests that an apprenticeship to a man of this affluence meant that Caxton's parents were also comfortably situated in the weaving trade, the principal industry of south-east England in the fifteenth century. When Large died in 1441, he left a small sum of money to his apprentice, which suggests that he had been appreciative of certain hopeful qualities in the youth. The executors of Large's will also thought so, for they sent Caxton to Bruges, the commercial centre of western Europe's woollen and weaving industry.

I remember noticing, while walking round the *Old Palace* in Florence, which was the Headquarters of the Medici family of bankers, that on the walls of the maproom the fifteenth-century relief map of England showed only four towns in Kent. One of them was Cranbrook! That was because Cranbrook was a major settlement of the Flemish weavers whom Edward III had shrewdly invited to come to England, so that instead of our export-ing raw wool, we could weave it into cloth at home and export the cloth to the Low Countries, thereby greatly increasing our national wealth. Unfortunately, the Black Death upsurged in its most violent outbreak at that time, wiping out half the population and upsetting the whole economy of Europe.

Caxton settled in Bruges and was soon heard of as a merchant on his own account. In 1463 he became acting governor of the company of Merchant Adventurers which was the equivalent of the Federation of British Industries of our time. The Mercers' Company played a large part in the Merchant Adventurers. Caxton was a liveryman of that Company. He had risen to the top of the industrial world of fifteenth-century England and the Low Countries. The Medici House, bankers to the wool trade (hence their interest in Cranbrook) must have thought well of him. That was why in 1464, when he was forty-two, he was appointed by King Edward IV, one of our most hard-headed monarchs, to negotiate with Philip, Duke of Burgundy, over the renewal of a treaty connected with the wool trade. He failed on this occasion, but later, in 1468, he succeeded with the new Duke, Charles the Bold, who had married the sister of our English King. Marriage, in those days, played as large a part in business combines as it did in politics and international relations. Caxton became commercial adviser to the Duke and his English Duchess.

Thus, when he returned to England, after some thirty years abroad, he was already closely associated with Edward IV, who admired not only his business ability but was interested in another activity of this remarkable man. Caxton had been a scholar from boyhood, and contrived to find time to translate medieval manuscripts. One of them was *The History of Troy*, by a French poet Raoul le Fevre. He presented his version to the Duchess of Burgundy, in whose rich library he had found the original manuscript. The key word is *manuscript*. This astute business-man realised how restrictive was the medieval necessity of copying one manuscript from another: that made only two copies; priceless in scarcity value, no doubt, but not a good business proposition in a world into which a new and mechanical process had just been introduced by a native of Mainz, working in Strasbourg.

His name was Johann Gutenberg, and he was born at the turn of the century, in 1398, also a son of affluent parents. The family got involved in complicated money matters, however, and moved to Strasbourg. Young Gutenberg pursued the legal squabbles and at one time had the Town Clerk of Mainz arrested. So he, like Caxton, was not lacking in enterprise and persistence. But he had only one interest in life. It was this novel idea of reproducing script by mechanical means of cutting out the letters of the alphabet on little wooden blocks, like engravings. We call it *printing*. What a simple beginning to something for which we can hardly find a name today! I can hear the roar of the vast machinery of the presses all round the world. It is like a demoniac laughter, increasing in volume year by year as one speedier process follows another, of literal reproduction.

Printing has always been an expensive job, however, and Gutenberg spent much of his energy in finding the money to further his purpose. But several people believed in him, and he contrived to borrow the necessary guilders to experiment in a big way at Strasbourg. He cut the type for printing a folio Latin Bible. Just as the first motor-cars followed the convention of horse carriages, so his print imitated the hand scribing of manuscript books. Gutenberg's Bible had 42 lines to the folio, and it built up to 1,282 printed pages. He pursued his mania with zeal, but without commercial success. His backers stepped in and removed the press to Mainz, but he followed, and went on printing book after book. It was obvious that the process had a future, and he always found backers. Toward the end of his career he was supported by the Cardinal Archbishop of his native town, and for the last three years of his busy and dedicated life he received a suit of livery, a salary and an allowance of corn and wine. He died in 1468, and was buried in the Franciscan Church in Mainz.

Caxton lived in the Low Countries during Gutenberg's revolutionary activities in the world of letters, and he caught the fever of excitement which was so rapidly spreading all over Europe. The invention did in that world what the internal combustion engine has done in that of transport. A man given to scholarship could not escape the infection. During his 33 years in Bruges as representative of the Merchant Adventurers, Caxton made his tertiary interest that of learning this new art of printing; business first, scholarship second, and now this exciting game which he saw as a means of promoting them both. He set up a press at Bruges, with another infatuate named Colard Mansion, and they produced their first book in 1476. It was called *The Recuyell of the Historyes of Troye*. That was the beginning, of we know not what! The book was Caxton's own translation, and it was thus the first printed book in English. The second was another of his own translations, *The Game and Playe of Chesse*. One can see the astute, potential publisher in this choice. Information, instruction, those are the subjects that sell.

He left the press in Bruges to carry on, and he came home to London where in September 1476, with King Edward IV's permission, he set up another press in the almonry beside Westminster Abbey, 'at the sign of the Red Pale', where he began by printing pamphlets, which were embryo newspapers, an elementary form of journal literature which was to last until news-sheets proper appeared, and even then the pamphlets were not to disappear completely.

Book after book came from 'the sign of the Red Pale', the first printed in England being Lord Rivers' translation of *The Sayings of the Philosophers*. Caxton revised the translation himself, for he was not neglecting his scholarship. We find him much concerned about the fluidity of the grammar of our language, and complaining of the arbitrary spelling not only region by region but through the whim of individuals.

Partly to try to stabilise a more easily recognisable convention, and partly through his devotion to the genius of Chaucer, whose verbal medium was already beginning to be authoritative, he printed *The Canterbury Tales*, *Troilus and Cressida* and *The House of Fame*. These were his best-sellers. He became not only our first printer but our first publisher working on a commercial basis. He followed these with another popular work, Malory's *Morte d'Arthur*, another specimen of what we may call *modern* English running crystal-clear at the source of the overwhelming stream of English literature.

He continued thus for the rest of his life, which came to an end, at least in the flesh, in 1491, in his seventieth year. To the end he fought his battle against what he generalised as 'idleness'. He combined three full-time careers in one, and by the power of his mind fused them into a monument of creative activity: business, scholarship, printing.

His translations were many, chief amongst them that of *The Golden Legend*, in 1483, toward the end of his life. The cost of printing it with some seventy woodcuts was helped out by the Earl of Arundel, his second faithful patron. As a compilation of the Lives of the Saints it survives as a major theological work, or more properly hagiographical.

In all, he printed 18,000 pages of type, hand-cut and hand-set; a monumental achievement. He trained three men who followed him as memorable printers, Wynkyn de Worde, Richard Pynson, and Robert Copland. From that beginning, one man's work, we have come to what we have come to; something indescribable and almost incomprehensible. And it still goes on, for 'of the making of books there is no end'. That was said in the time of Solomon, and probably by him. The form of books in those Old Testament days was cumbersome. Today the most advanced publicists say that our books are also clumsy and that this format for storing knowledge and the fruits of literary genius will soon be superseded by tiny casettes, the size of a cigarette-case, in one of which recordings for the aural reproduction of a hundred books may be stored. Thus Caxton's work will be done, after the passage of five hundred years and the expansion of his wooden printing press throughout the world. Will this man from Tenterden then be forgotten?

If so, the perpetuation of modern English, as an historically founded tongue, will be forgotten also. Caxton passed on Chaucer's language, that bell-like musical alloy, as a model for future writers and as an everyday medium of communication between one Englishman and another. Caxton as a translator and setter of a type-fount of printing with his own convention of spelling, also set the matrix into which Shakespeare poured his poetry, as do the others who still follow on.

Caxton soon found that he had to give all his business capacity to this new activity, and as far as we know he gave up his interest in the mercery trade. He had no rival in this business of making books, for though printing was being done in Venice and Rome, as well as in Mainz and Strasbourg, it was still being used there to augment scribing in the monasteries and universities. Caxton worked in the English community at large. He was the Northcliffe of his day, taking advantage of the first signs of literacy in the lay population, just as Northcliffe followed up the public demand created by the Education Act of 1870, which made reading and writing a compulsory accomplishment.

Poetry, until Caxton spread it about in print, had almost entirely an oral medium. He sought out these word-of-mouth verses and printed them. After producing his beloved Chaucer, he turned to other poets already widely known, such as Gower and Lydgate. He produced the works of our first English philosopher, Boethius, and some writings by Cicero. He translated a French version of Virgil's Aeneid and published it. Four thousand of the 18,000 printed pages that came from his hand press were his own translations. He describes his own labours charmingly:

Having no work in hand, I sitting in my study where as lay many divers pamphlets and books, happened that to my hand came a little book in French, which late was translated out of Latin by some noble clerk of France, which book is name *Eneydos*, and made in Latin by that noble poet and great clerk Vergyl, in which book I had great pleasure by reason of the fair and honest termes and wordes in French which I never saw to-fore-like, none so pleasant nor so well ordered, which book as me seemed should be much requisite for noble men to see, as well for the eloquence as for the histories; and when I had advised me to this said book I deliberated and concluded to translate it into English, and forthwith took a pen and ink and wrote a leaf or twain.

We see from that prose style how Chaucer's character as well as manner of writing had penetrated, almost as a *doppelganger*. Caxton needed this influence of a great creative genius, as a matrix for his own technique as a monitor of the English tongue, for now was the time of the more complete fusion of the several sources into our unique language, both colloquial and literary. Caxton consolidated Chaucer's pioneer work in making a medium out of the spoken tongue of the people, as Dante had done in Italy a hundred years earlier. The task was harder because the ingredients were more various and incongruous. The emulsion of the two separate languages, the Anglo-Saxon of the folk and the elaborate Romance tongue of the Norman ascendancy, kept separating out, with the thicker folk-tongue at the bottom.

Some honest and great clerks have been with me and desired me to write the most curious terms that I could find, while some gentlemen of late blamed me, saying that in my translations I have over many curious terms which could not be understood of common people, and desired me to use old and homely terms in my translations. Fain would I please every man. I took an old book and read therein, and certainly the English was so rude and broad I could not well understand it; more like to Dutch than to English.

The problem of differing dialects also puzzled him:

Common English that is spoken in one shire varieth from another so much, that in my days happened that certain merchants were in a ship in Thames, for to have sailed over the sea into Zealand, and for lack of wind they tarried at Foreland, and went on land for to refresh them. And one of them, named Sheffield, a mercer, came into a house and asked for meat, and especially he asked them for eggs. And the good wife answered that she could speak no French. And the merchant was angry, for he also could speak no French, but would have had eggs, but she understood him not. And then at last another said he would have *eyren*, then the good wife said she understood him well. Lo! what should a man in these days now write, eggs or eyren? Certainly it is hard to please everyman by cause of diversity and change of language.

J. R. Green, the most literary of our English historians, from whose oddly organised but enchanting *Short History of the English People* I have stolen the above quotations, reminds us that Caxton confessed his own mother-tongue to be that 'of Kent in the Weald, where I doubt not is spoken as broad and rude English as in any place of England' so that 'When all these things came to force me, I fell in despair of this work, and purposed never to have continued therein, and the quires laid apart, and in two years after laboured no more in this work'.

He was persuaded, however, by the Earl of Arundel, the Duchess of Somerset and many other aristocrats and Churchmen of high rank, to persevere with his translations and printing. Book collecting had now become fashionable, a snobbism brought over from France and Italy. An example of this beginning of the formation of country-house libraries, many of which even today have still not gone to America, is one made by a man named John Tiptoft, Earl of Worcester, who became a personal friend of Caxton and encouraged him when the physical and mental resources of the great printer were becoming drained by age. Caxton described Tiptoft as one 'which in his time flowered in virtue and cunning, to whom I know none like among the lords of the temporality in science and moral virtue'. This patron and aesthetic enthusiast was a true Renaissance character. Caxton exaggerated in speaking of 'his moral virtue', and as for his 'cunning', it so far excelled that this Earl of Worcester, as an executive of Edward IV's tycoon-like policies, was known widely as 'The Butcher'; which implies practices long held in abhorrence until they were revived in the twentieth century. Today, the wicked Earl's home, now reduced to the dimensions of a moated farmhouse called 'Tiptofts', stands on the wind-swept plateau between Thaxted and Saffron Walden, near a hamlet named Cole End. It has a slightly sinister appearance, as though shrugging off all human contacts; guilt-ridden perhaps. But that house must have contained some noble specimens of Caxton's work, and not a blood-stain to be seen on their immaculate pages.

Even after Edward IV's death, and his infamous brother Richard III had seized the throne, the royal interest in this new power, this greatest and most lasting of kingdoms which was created in the little kingdom of Kent, survived and was shrewdly ensured by King Richard's ukase against any lawmaking that should prevent 'any artificer or merchant stranger, of what nation or country he be, for bringing unto this realm or selling by retail or otherwise of any manner of books, written or imprinted'. Fervid book collectors may consider that this, in some small measure, mitigated what King Richard did to his nephews.

The birth of the printed book began to have instant effect upon the cultural structure of our social fabric. It may not have been apparent in the market and the street, or in the rustic scene. Credulous pilgrims still wended their way to Canterbury along the prehistoric Tin Road through Kent, as they had done a century earlier in the time of Chaucer. Superstition is ineradicable, even in a society ruled by technocrats and chemists.

But the crowd-consciousness which had been stirred to larger life by Wyclif's translation of the Bible, Langland's *Piers Plowman* and Chaucer's vast output of poetry and prose, was suddenly being nourished by the printed book and news-sheet co-incidentally with the establishment of more colleges in the primitive universities of Oxford and Cambridge. The Wars of the Roses ended at Bosworth in 1485, and the beginning of the Tudor autocracy gave the growing cultural life articulated by the printing press a more uniform tillage in which to flourish and multiply.

The change was instituted by this man from Tenterden in Kent, this member of the new middle class out of which our professions, our arts and sciences, our scholarship and general culture have mainly emerged, in spite of the animadversions against it by the aristocrats from above, and the proletariat from below. Now, in our new world in which all men are equal, the three classifications, in theory at least, all may contribute to the furtherance of knowledge, by the processes begun under Caxton's printing press. Unfortunately, the enlargement has not always been, as he expressly hoped 'by God's grace, according to my copy'.

Elizabeth Barton
A KENTISH ECCENTRIC

ECCENTRIC means flying from the centre. In general speech, we use the word as a metaphor, implying abnormal, unusual, and in consequence it plays a large part in our day-to-day vocabularies, for most of us to feel (rather than to think) that if a person does something which is beyond our ken, or has ideas and habits of which we do not approve, then that person is an 'eccentric'. The scope of such aberrations widens and narrows according to the religious, social and moral fashions which ebb and flow tidally, under influences which we still do not understand and are unable to control, in spite of the inquiries which science today is anxiously making into the mystery of crowd-psychology, watched even more anxiously by politicians and priests. Mob-emotion is still the manifest of an incalculable beast, functioning beneath the feet of individual men and women, damaging intelligence and character as earthquakes occasionally destroy our cities. In no period of human history has mankind been free from these eruptions, for we live mentally, as we live physically, upon a thin skin of sanity and stability.

There are certain rhythms, however, both in human and geological affairs, maintained by constant forces. One of those constants is superstition. It is a sub-conscious basis of human nature, like the fiery and magnetic forces within the envelope of Earth.

One of the oldest demonstrations of superstition is the dualism which has always existed between the priest and the king. Frazer's *Golden Bough* is a prolific case-book of that ever-lasting conflict, which has determined the course of human history worldwide. One of the excitements of being alive today is the watching of large-scale efforts to break this dualism with the instruments of economics, technology and science, and to establish unity in government, with politics and nationalities, prone to wars and other violence, banished and replaced by one mechanical, mass-produced overall control. At the thought of such an outcome to present-day trends, every individual knows that at once there surges up from the depths of his and her nature a protest against such an abhorrent possibility, despite its logical advantages. That protest is a proof that superstition is still a major ingredient in our life-force, this god-given and devilish power that still defies the bureaucracy of reason, with its sinister safety.

That bureaucratic control, however, is the signal of civilization, and hitherto it has been in the hands either of king or priest. Today, the leaders are finding for themselves a new nomenclature, and the twentieth century is not likely to decide that new naming. Only one thing is certain. It is the tendency for all leaders to have the same motive: the quest for power. The ding-dong battle has gone on since our human story began. The Old Testament is a record of the struggle of king versus priest. So is the history of Europe. For a while in the twelfth century it looked as though the priest had won, and that a unified European community could emerge. But the temporal ascendancy of the Popes produced the wrong sort of power, and the Holy Roman Empire (so-called, but as un-holy as the Church had become) emerged, with Ahab challenging Elisha once again.

Here in Kent, in the sixteenth century, we had an example of what can happen to individuals who get caught up in that external conflict between priest and king, which today we call power-politics. So often the intruders are innocent and simple souls, who go to their destruction hardly knowing what has hit them. They can also be singular in some faculty or other, as to be eccentric from the normal run of mankind. Elizabeth Barton was of this kind, and her story was so strange, and its consequences so far-reaching in violence, that it survives today almost as vividly as that of Joan of Arc. It is significant, but I am not sure of what, that both were illiterate peasant girls, caught up by spiritual illumination to a demonstration of power that has become legendary, with the ascription of miracle-working.

Elizabeth Barton lived in a part of Kent wholly remote and rural. All that is known of her early life is that she was a servant maid in a half-timbered house named Cobb's Hall. Her master was one Thomas Cobb, a bailiff to the Archbishop of Canterbury, whose estates included a major part of the county, studded with minor palaces where this Prince of the Church 'rested' during his frequent itineraries. One of them stood near Aldington Church. Thomas Cobb appears to have been a devout man, for he was one of a family which had given much money toward the rebuilding of the church, whose rector at the time of Elizabeth's *visitation* of the Holy Ghost was also a devout and serene local priest named Richard Master, whose modest life was for some years to be violently shaken up by publicity and no little danger.

Elizabeth Barton was illiterate, and she worked on the farm as well as in the house, but this occupation did not make her robust. She was a sickly creature, and at Easter, in the year 1525, she was attacked by a severe illness which lasted through the spring and summer of that year. It may not have been epilepsy, because she had continuous high temperatures, that carried her from time to time into trances and long periods of ecstacy in which she not only 'babbled o'green fields' but began to predict future events.

The first of these was immediately borne out. In the November of that year, one of the children of the house lay sick in a cradle in the same room as the ailing girl. One day she enquired after the child and was told that it was still alive. She replied that it would die, and her prediction was fulfilled that same night. A Catholic apologist named the Reverend J. R. McKee of the London Oratory, writing of her in 1925, in a little book published by Burns Oates and Washbourne, publishers to the Holy See, says that from that time, during her chronic illness with its recurring bouts of *ecstasia*, which is now called delirium, she

spoke of heaven, hell, purgatory, and the joys and sorrows that certain of the departed enjoyed or suffered there. She preached 'frankly' against corruption of manner and evil living, exhorted those who heard her to diligence in church-going, hearing Mass, confessing their sins, to prayer to Our Lady and the Saints; and all this so devoutly and discreetly, that her hearers were led to think that a higher power spoke through her. In one of these trances she declared that Our Blessed Lady had directed her to go to the chapel of Court-at-Street, and to make offering of a taper there, and that she would be cured of her sickness.

This hamlet of Court-at-Street was a typical little Kentish settlement, not large enough to be called a village. There are many of them scattered about the county, usually lost in the labyrinth of bye-lanes which cover the Garden of England, as Kent is still called, like a hair-net over the hair of a beautiful woman. There are invariably half a dozen ways of approaching these hamlets, as also the villages, most of the lanes with their criss-crossings invariably lacking a signpost. For over a quarter of a century I lived in one such hamlet, and never succeeded in being able to give directions to visitors from foreign parts such as Sussex and Surrey, while Londoners were incredulous of my geographical stupidity, until they finally found me, an hour late for luncheon. If the invitation was for dinner, after dark, I insisted that the visitors should come down by train and that I would fetch them from the nearest station, on the main line along the Weald. It took less expense of spirit than trying to explain by letter or telephone.

Court-at-Street lies eastward from my home, midway between the ancient Roman port (no longer a port) of Lympne and Aldington. Both these now sequestered villages lie along the ridge that was once the sea-coast cliff, when the tides came up as far as Smallhithe, near Tenterden. Smallhithe was industrious in boat-building. Probably the *White Ship*, carrying William, heir to King Henry the First, back from Normandy in 1120, was built at Smallhithe. The wrecking of that vessel was likely still to be remembered piously through local tradition and folklore during Elizabeth Barton's lifetime, for the disaster was caused by the impiety of the Prince and his noble companions aboard the ship, who were so inflamed with wine as they left France that they mocked the priests who assembled to give the customary blessing before their departure. Befuddled navigation caused the ship to strike a rock as soon as the harbour was passed, and all perished. Such events as this fed the credulity of the folk, and thereby added to the authority of the Church, giving it an armoury more powerful than the King's sword and sceptre. The law can be circumvented, or it could in those days; but spiritual fear cannot.

In our sceptical, matter-of-fact society today, we realise how this hair-trigger of superstition was cocked to everyone's hand; and I use the word not in a derogatory sense, but as I used it above, through its Latin root of standing near a thing, amazement, dread, religious awe, scruple, and even of witnessing. In that sense, it accepts a ghostly presence constantly at hand, day and night.

Such was the social and moral atmosphere of the community of mankind until modern times, and I doubt if even the worldwide revolution against it of the communist ideologies of mechanical behaviourism will permanently dispel it. It must survive so long as there remain some phenomena in the universe still uncomprehended.

Certainly the Reformation did nothing toward expelling superstition. Indeed, the revolt against the latitude and tolerance, which had increased to licence within the Catholic Church, making it as much a secular as a spiritual body, gave superstition back its primeval panic fragmentary variety. Sectarian religious doctrines sprang up in profusion, many of them poisonous with weeds, the most noxious being that of an increased belief in witchcraft and magic, both white and black.

In such an isolated community as that of the Kentish shore from which the sea was already beginning to retreat, leaving a saline marsh later to become the fertile pastureland of Romney Marsh, this confusion of the old Catholic faith with the percolations of the distorted fringes of the new theologies of the Reformers, with their cleansings and their contradictions, encouraged instant reaction to any untoward happenings and rumours of happenings such as the ravings of this sick girl in the kitchens of Cobb's Hall.

Her desire to be taken to the little chapel in Court-at-Street was at once granted by her pious master and mistress, and the apparent efficacy of the ceremony in the chapel carried the matter further to the rector of Aldington, to whose village church the chapel was attached as an easement in the hierarchy of the Church. These isolated chapels are scattered, now mostly in ruins or even only in historical rumour, about the English countryside. They may be survivals of the first excitements of the coming of the Christian faith with the marriage of Queen Bertha to King Ethelbert of Kent. Bertha was the daughter of the King of Paris, and a Christian. She brought with her the new faith and its priests, so that when later St. Augustine, sent unwillingly by Pope Gregory, arrived with his much more highly organised mission, the soil was already prepared for him to sow the seed.

In that district behind Romney Marsh, formerly coastal country, the recession of the sea caused considerable depopulation, especially during the fifteenth and sixteenth centuries. West Hythe, Hurst, Orgarswick, Blackmanstone, Eastbridge, Westenhanger offer examples of ancient communities, of Saxon origin, which decayed for this reason; and they were larger than Court-at-Street, with their own rectories. An Act in the reign of Edward VI tried to tidy up these survivals by abolishing over two thousand of these free chapels, because they were not subject to episcopal control. They had begun their existence, as they continued, as non-conformist, under some foundation by enthusiastic individuals long since forgotten.

Elizabeth Barton's apparent cure as a result of her visit to the Chapel in

Court-at-Street must have encouraged her to more confident predictions, so that local credulity, permanently at flash-point, rapidly caught fire. The pious Rector at nearby Aldington fanned the flames by proclaiming his absolute belief in her powers of divination. Further, her master and his wife accepted the fame which had now come upon their house. They made the girl a member of their own family, and fostered her gently, with the encouragement of the Rector.

This Richard Master was a parish priest of the wholly positive kind, from the point of view of the Church as a spiritual haven in a world of brutal materialism. At the time when he, with so many other people who had encouraged Elizabeth, was arraigned before the Star Chamber, an inventory was taken of his property, just as today the Inland Revenue Department dismembers the privacy of any citizen whom it suspects of evasive conduct. Thomas Cromwell, the most astute bureaucrat since King Henry II, had built up an efficient civil service with which to conduct the surgical operations on English society required by King Henry in order to transfer the wealth of the Church from Papal control, and to keep it within the country, at the disposal of his own Treasury.

The innocent and gentle Richard Master was recorded as possessing 'forty-two great books covered with boards, and thirty-three small books covered with leather and parchment'. That signified much scholarship, which in those days was likely to include the rudimentary medical lore that made him the only medical practitioner in the district. He attended Elizabeth during her attacks of hysteria, or high-temperatured divination, and wrote down her utterances.

With this evidence, he decided to consult Archbishop Warham at Canterbury, modestly feeling that the responsibility was too great for him to handle this potential saint alone.

He may have had misgivings, due to some unorthodox speculation in his scholastic studies, for his predecessor had been a much wider-ranging man, whose reputation was European; a pioneer. That man, a most unlikely incumbent of so rustic a living, was Erasmus: no less! He must have been a bird of passage, a resting eagle. But he knew his successor, Richard Master, and spoke of him as 'a young man, learned in divinity, and of good and sober life'.

It is certain, therefore, that Archbishop Warham would also know this greatly respected cleric in his own diocese. Warham was a friend of Erasmus, and may have been the recipient of this testimonial from the famous scholar, whose authority of character and knowledge is so vividly described by the historian J. R. Green.

Green's portrait of Erasmus explains why Warham and Thomas More valued this wandering scholar so reverently, though the encomium does not excuse him for mulcting the tiny parish of Aldington, and its Rector, of a pension of £20, a year (worth about £2,000 today). 'His enormous industry,' says Green,

the vast store of classical learning which he gradually accumulated, Erasmus shared with others of his day. In patristic reading he may have stood beneath Luther; in originality and profoundness of thought he was certainly inferior to More. His theology, though he made a far greater mark on the world by it than even by his scholarship, we have seen that he derived almost without change from Colet.   But his combination of vast learning with keen observation, of acuteness of remark with a lively fancy, of genial wit with a perfect good sense—his union of as sincere a piety and as profound a zeal for rational religion as Colet's with a dispassionate fairness towards older faiths, a large love of secular culture, and a genial freedom and play of mind—this union was his own, and it was through this that Erasmus embodies for the Teutonic peoples the quickening influence of the New Learning during the long scholer-life which began at Paris and ended amidst darkness and sorrow at Basle.

This was the man who remained a close friend of Archbishop Warham and maintained a correspondence with him, closing it at the Archbishop's death with an obituary that was an unofficial canonization. 'Had I found such a patron in my youth' wrote Erasmus, 'I too might have been counted among the fortunate ones'. The fact that after he had taught Greek for some years so brilliantly at Cambridge, the university left him 'to starve on sour beer', may explain why Warham offered him the sinecure of the parish of Aldington, neighbourly to Canterbury and the sustenance of the friendship between the two scholars, who together did so much toward the fructification of the New Learning in England.

However, that is a larger matter from which we have to focus down to this small, but typical side-issue, of the phenomenon of the career of the Holy Maid of Kent.

But these larger preoccupations of the Archbishop of Canterbury made him receive the Rector of Aldington's story of the inspired servant-maid with caution. It may have savoured to him of a reaction toward the mechanical credulities of the Middle Ages, all of which were now universally in question. He hedged, by appointing a commission to investigate the case. It consisted of three Benedictine monks of the cathedral priory of Christ Church, two friars of the convent of Franciscan Observants in Canterbury, his own official named Thomas Lawrence, and Richard Master.

The chairman of the commission was one of the monks, Dr Edward Bocking, Cellerer of the priory. He was a Doctor of Divinity of Oxford, member of an East Anglian family, and a man of judicial and administrative ability. Even so, through this spokesman, the commission reported favourably on the evidence of Elizabeth's sincerity, and the miraculous nature of her predictions. Further, Dr Bocking acceded to the girl's statement that it was the will of God that henceforth he should be 'her ghostly father', that is, her confessor, thus relieving poor Richard Master of the responsibility. This transference was later to save the Rector of Aldington from the fate that befell so many other credulous people implicated in the affair.

The enquiry of course publicised Elizabeth's powers of divination, and they were both distorted and magnified in the telling; bush telegraph has a tendency to be melodramatic. After the favourable report of the Commission, the girl 'at her next voyage to Our Lady of Court-at-Street, entered the Chapel with Ave Regina Caelorum in pricksong accompanied with these commissioners, many ladies, gentlemen, and gentlewomen of the best degree, and three thousand persons besides of the common sort of people'.

Prick-song is part-singing, or plainsong. England at that time was waking to a national faculty for making music, especially religious music, comparable to that of Rome and Venice. Not many years later, the genius of Thomas Tallis, resident musician at Waltham Abbey in Essex, was to become so famous that he rode the storms of the dissolution of the monasteries and had his compositions eagerly accepted in the new ritual of the English Church. He subsequently had some connection with Kent, for Queen Mary, in 1557, granted him a lease of the manor of Minster, in Thanet. After her death, Queen Elizabeth appointed him organist, jointly with his pupil William Byrd, at the Chapel Royal (though both retained the old Faith), and gave them a patent for the sole right to print music and music-paper in England. Such minor monopolies were general in Tudor times as rewards for services rendered to the Royal Person or to the State. The practice survived in the form of sinecure posts, such as Wordsworth's Collectorship of Stamps. It has its advantages where the recipient is engaged on creative or research work that is financially unremunerative.

Elizabeth Barton was so elated by her 'cure' that she claimed, under command direct from The Virgin Mary, to enter a convent, and that the shrine of Court-at-Street should be renovated and endowed. The fame of the little place was so great that an English student at Padua sent the sum of ten pounds, part of it to be spent on the erection of a decorative ceiling over the altar in the chapel.

Dr Bocking induced Archbishop Warham to establish Elizabeth in the convent of St. Sepulchre, near Canterbury, where she lived for nine years. Her reputation for holiness and supernatural powers of divination grew. The Victorian historian, J. A. Froude, says that 'her cell at Canterbury was the Delphic shrine of the Catholic oracle'. Bishop Fisher of Rochester, and Sir Thomas More (then Chancellor to Henry VIII) were approached and became interested. This suggests that Elizabeth was by now being used as a weapon in the political struggle raging in the outer world. Her quiet life in the convent, broken only by visits to other religious institutions, unfortunately coincided with the King's proposal to divorce his Spanish Queen and to marry the Kentish Anne Boleyn. The whole balance of power in Europe was disturbed by this spiritually and politically revolutionary proposal.

It is difficult to assess what caused this illiterate girl to be caught up in the consequent shudderings of so vast a machinery. But we may suspect that her confessor, to whom she had completely surrendered her mind, such as it was, and also her spirit, was a man of so devout a faith that he believed it his duty to use every available means of combatting the King's latest move toward the extension of the Reformation to the English realm. It had already spread over the northern principalities of the Holy Roman Empire, engulfing Martin Luther in a chaos of violent revolution from which his supporters, Erasmus and Melancthon, withdrew in despair. They were bookmen, philosophers, unlike the combative Luther in Germany and Calvin in France, the latter just having resigned his rectorship of Pont l'Eveque to become a militant Protestant. The Council of Trent was a declaration of war by the Pope, and the whole of central Europe went up in flames. The horror and misery throughout that vast area during the sixteenth century makes one of the darkest chapters in the bloody story of mankind.

A letter written by a Carthusian monk named Henry Man, procurator of the Charterhouse at Shene, to Dr Bocking, is indicative that the latter was politically-minded as well as devout, and that he saw in the girl's reputation a potential weapon to be used against the King's intentions, which must obviously lead to a break with Rome, and the submission of the Church in England to secular control by the Crown. He realised what dynamite lay in the devotional tone of that letter from the Carthusian monk, since it voiced the belief of an ever-growing mass of the population. The letter alludes to

the special elect virgin named Elizabeth Barton. . . . I also beseech you ofttimes to put that my good mother Elizabeth, in whom is my trust above all mortal creatures, in remembrance to offer me up in sacrifice to the most glorious Trinity, and to beg grace for me that may so mortify me that I may so set my desire, my delectation, my estuant affection, and my fervent love in God, that I may attain to such cognition and love of Him as may be had in this life.

Such passion as that was a powerful armoury against the bureaucracy by which the Crown, through its civil servant Cromwell, was drawing the enormous material wealth of the Church into the purse of the Treasury, a process that laid the foundations of modern nationalism. But the Crown at that time was a Tudor tyrant, hot-blooded and capable of extreme violence, a typical Renaissance figure.

Sir Thomas More, approached by Father Rich, Guardian of the Observant Convent of Richmond, refused to listen to the news that Elizabeth had already been granted an audience by the King, and had told him that if he married Anne Boleyn, he would not be King of England seven months afterwards. This was in April 1533, when Anne was proclaimed Queen. Seven months later Henry was excommunicated by Pope Clement VII. By the law of the Catholic Church this deprived the King of regal authority over his subjects. The dream-besotted girl also told Henry that his daughter Mary would reign in her own right before the Lady Elizabeth. That prophecy was more factually fulfilled.

Henry's first reaction was diplomatic. He offered to make her an abbess, and even when she refused the bribe, he played a discreet hand, evidently in the belief that she was an active and intelligent figure in the Papal Party, and a conscious representative of the public opposition to the marriage with Anne Boleyn and her enthronement.

By this time the butterfly was inextricably caught on the wheel. More saw this, for he was a shrewd lawyer as well as the visionary author of *Utopia*, that platonic prototype book for a separate field in world literature. He did not at first meet Elizabeth Barton, and when questioned by the King about her, was able to plead ignorance of treasonable statements by her. Archbishop Warham, however, persuaded Wolsey to see her, and she boldly told the Cardinal that as the Pope's legate it was his duty to oppose the King's will, or 'God would lay it sore to his charge'. God did so a year later, when Wolsey died on his way to London to be tried for treason.

When More at last saw Elizabeth, he again refused to judge her. He made notes during the interview, which put on record his belief in her visions. Later, after a 'confession' had been planted upon her and the several close directors who had used her, More played the part of Pilate. He had previously warned her not to dabble in affairs of State, but to confine her revelations 'to any such matters as may to the soul be profitable for you to show'. When she left him he gave her some money, and besought her to pray for him and his family. He was indeed 'the man for all seasons'.

This shows that the great man, later to be canonised by the Catholic Church, maintained an open mind about the girl's abnormal spiritual power. So also did the Ambassador of the Emperor Charles V, Chapuys, who spent three years in England, 1530 to 1533, in the vain effort to prevent the King from breaking from the Papacy and thereby strengthening the power of the dissident Protestant princes in the northern provinces of the Empire.

One Henry Gold, vicar of St Mary Aldermary in London, acted as interpreter when Elizabeth spoke with the Ambassador and convinced him of her divine authority. She was equally successful with another Papal emissary, Silvester Dario, who came from Lucca, whose city walls and sixteen churches survive today. The Italian was so overwhelmed by her that he is said to have fallen at her feet and kissed them reverently. He also sent Dr Bocking's testimony in writing to the Pope, an incident which adds to the probability that Dr Bocking was the impressario behind the girl's meteoric career, the sincerity of which was maintained by a large and devout public who believed her to be, as recorded in *Hall's Chronicles*, 'an excellent, virtuous, and an holy woman, and that all her words and deeds should appear to the world to proceed of a marvellous holiness, rebuking the common sins and vices of the world, as though she were taught and inspired of the Holy Spirit of God'.

Chapuys wrote to the Emperor, however, of the mercurial character of the English people at that time. 'This people', he wrote, 'is peculiarly credulous, and is easily moved to insurrection by prophecies, and in the present disposition is glad to hear any to the king's disadvantage'.

So Henry also believed, and as the fame of the Holy Maid of Kent rapidly spread over the country, he set the new machinery of Cromwell's making in action. All was done through the ceremonies of legality, but it was done steadily and ruthlessly.

Toward the end of 1533, the new and Anglican Archbishop Cranmer instructed the Prioress of St. Sepulchre's, Canterbury, to 'repair unto me at the manor of Otford'. The remains of that minor palace survive today, adjoining Otford Church. It was built by Thomas à Becket, who, emulating Moses, struck the ground with his episcopal crook, and produced a spring of water. The palace would be a convenient halt on the frequent journeys between Canterbury and Lambeth. There was another one at Charing. The Prioress was commanded to 'bring with you your nun which was some time at Court-at-Street'. The tone begins to take on that impersonal note of the civil service technique—ominous and sinister—which changes its users, privately humane individuals, into steel cogs on a complex of wheels.

At the same time, Dr Bocking and Richard Master, the original promoters of the girl's eight-year-long career, were arrested with several other people who had been indiscreet enough to write about her 'miracles'. One of them was the lord of the manor which included Court-at-Street, a gentleman of Kent named Edward Thwaites, who had broadcast a pamphlet on the subject. Cromwell, the astute politician, was now in a position to use the incident to promote the King's purpose. Chapuys reported back to the Emperor, 'Many think, and even believe, that those who now have the nun in their power will make her accuse many people unjustly, that they may thus have the occasion and the means of revenging themselves upon those who have supported the Queen'; by whom he meant Queen Katherine.

That everything should appear to be fair and above-board, a public show was staged on 23 November 1533. Elizabeth Barton, and the other people who had been arrested, were stood upon a scaffolding outside St Paul's Cathedral. What treatment they received during the weeks since September has not been revealed; but we in the twentieth century know much about the method. Elizabeth did not prophesy on that occasion. Instead, she read a confession of her 'guilt', and declared that she 'was the original of all this mischief, and by my falsehood I have deceived all these persons and many more'.

The prisoners were then returned to the Tower of London, that blood-soaked relic which still broods sullenly over the City and the Thames.

Those prisoners carried names of families, some of which survive today. For example, Dom John Dering, kinsman of the lord of the manor of Pluckley, had been arrested because he wrote a pamphlet, *De Duplici*

Spiritu, though he told Cranmer that he had burned it. A copy of it, however, was found in the possession of the parish priest of St Mary Alderbury in London. He too was apprehended and his papers confiscated. Cromwell's agent even arrested an old anchorite hidden away in the Dominican Friary in Canterbury, because he had been visited by Dr Bocking and Elizabeth Barton. Froude suggests that the monks were tortured, but Chapuy believed that the girl was treated as a great lady, so that her vanity and confidence might lead her to

accuse many people unjustly, that the King's agents may thus have the occasion and the means of revenging themselves upon those who have supported the Queen Katherine, and take from them large sums of money by way of a fine, which is the thing in this world the King likes the most.

Cromwell, with the help of Cranmer and Hugh Latimer, 'practised' upon the poor girl, and announced that 'it was found that all her inspiration and ecstasies were merely juggle and deceit, as she was instructed to do by certain friars and priests'. The process is reminiscent of that used in the trial of Joan of Arc. Pressure increased as the official machinery of State ground into action. Judges, bishops, selected individuals from the nobility, sat with the Privy Council for three days in November, and at the end of their conference the Chancellor made a speech whose subject was far removed from the sick little serving-maid from Cobb's Hall in the hidden recesses of Kent. He thanked God for 'permitting the damnable abuses and wicked deeds of the said nun, her adherents, and accomplices to be discovered and made manifest; which crimes and misdeeds he, for many good reasons, declined to specify'. After some fulsome flattery of the King, he concluded that 'no heed must be paid to the sentence of the Pope, His Holiness having been seduced principally by the damnable and diabolical instrumentality of the said nun and her accomplices'.

Thus Elizabeth Barton had become a figure notorious throughout Christendom, and a promoter of treason in the Kingdom of England. Though the heads of the legal party argued half-heartedly against the proof of treasonable conduct by the nun, who after all had spoken quite openly to the King himself, and had practised no deceit in her condemnation of his marriage to Anne Boleyn, there were many people both in and beyond the Court who turned their coats. Cries of 'To the stake!' were heard. The prisoners were returned to The Tower, while the proceedings against them were referred to the dreaded Star Chamber. Noblewomen who had taken up the nun during the years of her popularity now changed their tune. Lady Rutland wrote to Sir William Paston of 'the most abominable matters that ever I heard in my life'. The Marchioness of Exeter, prompted by Cromwell, recorded that she cannot excuse her own offences 'in listening to the seditious tales, blasphemies, and execrable and false prophesies set forth by the said most unworthy person and her adherents'.

The Imperial Ambassador Chapuy, however, informed the Emperor that

the King has hitherto failed in his attempt to make the judges declare guilty of high treason those who have had any dealings with the nun. I rather think that although some, perhaps the most learned and impartial amongst them, have declared that they would rather die than deal with the accused in that manner, should the King, as they say, come to dispute the case, he will have his own way, for no one in England dares contradict him in such matters, unless he chooses to be treated as a madman, or what is worse, as guilty of high treason.

As Chapuy predicted, the judges were over-ruled, and a bill of attainder was passed by the House of Lords in February 1534, to be given the royal assent in March. A month later Elizabeth Barton, the Benedictines Bocking and Dering, Risby a Franciscan, Henry Gold the vicar of Alderbury, were hanged at Tyburn. Elizabeth's body was buried at the Grey Friars, London, after being decapitated. Her head was displayed on London Bridge.

The only act of clemency shown was to the first ecclesiastic who had accepted the girl's visions as genuine, her parish priest Richard Master. He received a free pardon and was restored to his rectory, and his 'forty-two great books covered with boards, and thirty-three small books covered with leather and parchment'. No doubt his hand was inclined to tremble for some while, as he handled them. His attention to the black-letter print may have wandered, as he recalled from time to time how the victims had been allowed no defence, but 'attainted of high treason and condemned without any answer making of themselves'. Such a gentle soul must have felt as so many folk feel today when they learn of similar, world-wide abuse of justice both human and divine.

Anne Boleyn

MANY people in the twentieth century may think that to include crowned heads, 'royalties', among the immortals native to a small area such as Kent, is a gesture of out-of-date conventionality. Royalism is commonly believed to be politically dead, its surviving formalism and rituals no more effective than the scratching of a dog on the hearth-rug before circling round and tumbling to sleep.

Such scepticism is part of the general revolutionary concept in modern life of the so-called equalitarian structure of society, in all parts of the world, whether the communities subscribe to capitalist or communist theory and practice. But one can be just as sceptical of the principles to which most governments subscribe today, under the category of 'democracy'. That word denotes what Abraham Lincoln summed up as 'government of the people, by the people, for the people'. It is even practised, at least as a legal system, in communities which sincerely try to run a Welfare State, as in North America and Western Europe. But in spite of the vast improvement of economic conditions, and in education, of the vast masses of the people in those communities, there remains a total lack of equality, as between one individual and another. That totality is as absolute as ever it was, though today it may be disguised by the effects of 'equal opportunity', accessibility of leisure, commodities, and the rest of the techniques and luxuries which we all take for granted as normal ingredients in our twentieth-century way of life.

We still look out on nature, and we still contemplate ourselves, to realise, sooner or later in our experience, that this 'equality' of which we boast, and which we demand, is after all a device limited to the mechanics of our political life; limited even as a community structure. Even that machinery is run by a kind of élite, which by the demands of its vocation and activity becomes infected with the power-lust which leads to tyranny. And so government, and mankind's subscription to the authority of government, tend to come full circle. We openly *require* a leader.

Latent in that requirement is a mystical faith in a monarch (whose position is implied in that word). We may dilute him into committees, but that makes his authority only compromisory and frequently self-contradictory. We do not understand white papers and reports, until they are distilled into an instruction, an order, which we can obey. That obedience is a subscription to the symbolism of monarchy. We can call that crown what we like; king, president, or one of the many surrogates of that enthroned figure; the judge, the umpire, and all the lesser officials in a descending delegation of authority.

In the modern world that delegation is the order of the day, with each individual inclined to claim a share in its authority. This is what has given rise to the illusion that all men are equal, and that anarchy is a law of nature. We still do not know much about the laws of nature, although they permanently rule our conduct and our aspirations. If we interpret them through a knowledge of human history, we realise that they function on ever-receding principles, as in biological structures, at the endlessness of which a unified simplicity extends. We can call it the Eternal Paradox, or God. We do not remove it, nor destroy it.

For my present purpose, I am calling on it to justify my inclusion in this gallery of Kentish immortals two queens, whose fame survives by reason of their circumstances at birth, rather than by inherent qualities of personality, character, intellectual ability and moral distinction. This means that inequality amongst human beings, as in the rest of nature, is accepted as a fact, a reality. Political rebellion against this fact has gone on since the beginning of the story of man. Cain began it by murdering his brother. We may call him the first Romantic. We still acknowledge, even if not explicitly, that certain people, down the courses of time, by reason of their birthright, or birth-wrong, have worked so profoundly on human affairs as to have become immortal. Anne Boleyn was one such.

She was another typical Renaissance figure, in that stormy sixteenth century in which the everlasting conflict of priest versus king flared up with further complications under the rising winds of nationalism. The moral power of the Catholic Church had weakened from within, and the Protestant breakaway was already proving to be as equally corrupt and worldly. The New Learning was a heady wine, confused with the medieval scholasticism. The mixed drink confused saint and sinner alike. Never had language been so garbled in its nomenclatures. Never had the vocabulary of hypocrisy been so wildly expanded as men sought to justify the actions of greed, ambition, wild enthusiasms and lusts.

Yet in one respect nothing had changed, culturally and politically, since the beginning of recorded history of mankind. The absolute authority of individual governors still presided over the lives of the governed, right through every community from the prime lieutenants of those tyrants down to the most abject slaves. It is debatable whether or not, in such circumstances, an absolute monarch or an oligarchy of local chieftains was the lesser evil. The tendency of political evolution has been to work through the former, and then to reduce the power of that central tyrant by means of constitutionalism. That is how we work today, except in the recessive communist regimes.

The part played by women under regimes of centralised personal tyranny seems to have been that of the 'boudoir' technique. As civilization becomes more constitutional, women emerge into the open, substituting compassion for legalism, as we see both in the ameliorations and the permissiveness of our present-day way of life. But these are generalisations, and as such are untrue of individual cases. We cannot deduce a rule by comparing the conduct and influence of Ruth and Salome in the ancient world, and the Fair Maid of Kent and Anne Boleyn in the Renaissance world; those two worlds being much alike from a political point of view.

Here then, we are confronted with an endlessly debatable problem which complicates an otherwise pleasant task of portraying certain immortals of Kentish birth. These Tudors; how elusive they are as characters, everyone of them pronounced in several ways, as it were cancelling themselves out by their contrast of vices and virtues, all in excessive deployment at a period in European history when individual character was freed from all restraint because of the breakdown of medieval legalism through the Feudal System on the one hand, and the Catholic Church on the other.

Greenwich Palace, Henry VIII's favourite home, was at that time within the boundaries of the county of Kent. Both the princesses, Mary and Elizabeth, were born there. Their legitimacy and their bastardy were theories bandied about in the fury of public affairs during the reign of their father, a period of total upheaval as England realised itself to be a nation, self-determining against the temporal as well as the spiritual overlordship of the Papal claim throughout Europe.

The half-sisters, innocent symbols of such savagely opposed forces, were friendly enough together, the young Elizabeth freely deferring to her sister's seniority and legitimacy as claimant to the throne. But their careers were to be extended on such a vast scale, and so copiously recorded by historians, that it is impossible to reduce them to the scale of this small gallery of Kentish portraits. The same may be said of their father, that monstrous figure who dominates our national history as the impresario of its dramatic turn to modernity and the pioneer of its imperial domination.

But the personality of Anne Boleyn can be sufficiently reduced to the scope of our purpose. In spite of the explosive part she played in that vast drama, historians and biographers appear to have been shy of portraying her. Now there is little material available to fill the gap, and she must remain an elusive character, more catalyst than active in the world-shaking upheavals of the sixteenth century.

To think of her as an innocent country girl, daughter of a country gentleman rusticating in the heart of Kent, would be a mistake. But she was one of those personalities about whom there is no certainty. No two records, even about her physical appearance, agree. There is argument about the date of her birth. It is timed anywhere between 1500 and 1507. An early date is the more probable, because she is recorded as accompanying Mary Tudor to France in 1514 on the occasion of the marriage of the Princess to Louis XII, and remaining there after the little king's death to become one of the women in waiting to Queen Claude, wife of Francis I. So she was not likely to have been an infant of seven years of age to undertake such duties of Court procedure. Nor could she have been a creature only of provincial upbringing.

Her father, Sir Thomas Boleyn (or Bullen) was evidently a man of political ambition, not content to remain amongst his peers as one of the Kentish gentry, that unique body, almost a sodality, who were to play so shrewdly cohesive a part during the Civil War (see Chapter 12). Sir Thomas was active in the county, functioning from his estate, Hever Castle, which survives today as the headquarters of the Astor family. It is one of the beauty spots which abound in the western reaches of Kent below

Westerham. Sir Thomas was Sheriff of Kent in 1509 and 1518, and was
buried in Hever Church in 1538. His father, Sir Geoffrey Boleyn, had been
Lord Mayor of London in 1457, so that the family fortunes must have been
substantial when the estate of Hever was acquired.

Sir Thomas's appearance at the Royal Court of Greenwich was possibly
a consequence of his marriage to Elizabeth, the daughter of Thomas
Howard, Earl of Surrey, who defeated the Scots at Flodden Field in 1513.
The marriage was a step up toward the nobility, though Sir Thomas, as a
courtier, continued to live mainly at Hever, where his daughters Mary and
Anne spent their childhood. They continued to live there as they grew up
and went out into the world, for it was to Hever that the King came again
and again from Greenwich, until his infatuation so mastered him that he
openly indulged it and installed Anne at Court as one of the Queen's ladies.

Those lover's journeys were sometimes anticipated and shortened by a
rendezvous halfway at West Wickham Court, near Addington. Until well
into the twentieth century this part of Kent was an enchanted retreat, its
little church and lychgate isolated in a sylvan setting, and the nearby house
looking southward into the county, almost within sight of Hever. Today it
is a London suburb.

Anne's father may have supplied this meeting place in order to entangle
his master more surely. The manor had records back to the time of Edward
the Confessor. It was given by William of Normandy to his rapacious
brother, Bishop Odo. It had been in the hands of the Boleyns long before it
was put to amatory use. A story lingered in the neighbourhood that the
King had a system of signalling from the hill-top above the manor-house to
Hever. If so, it must have been over the tops of the dense forest oaks,
descendants of Druidical Anderida, which at that time still clothed the
Weald. One wonders, also, if the artificial secrecy of this love-play was
detected from nearby Addington, where the Archbishop of Canterbury had
a chapel-of-ease, with a residence. The legend is improbable, because the
King's interest in Anne was instantly adopted as an instrument of ingratia-
tion by her grandfather, Howard, who had by that time worked his way to
the Dukedom of Norfolk. Her father, Sir Thomas, saw much to his advantage in the liaison. It helped him to the Earldom of Wiltshire and Ormonde.

The early stages of the affair had a Theocritan touch, in the literary
mode of the Renaissance. The King was both poet and musician. Anne was
precociously educated, as were most gentlewomen. Her accomplishments,
wit and beauty were conspicuous even in the highly sophisticated Court

circle. The Catholic historian, Lingard, says of her that 'her French education gave her the superiority over her companions; she played and danced and sung with more grace than any other lady at Court; and the gaiety of her conversation, with the buoyancy of her disposition, attracted a crowd of admirers'. The poet and diplomat, Sir Thomas Wyatt, like her father, a Kentish squire, was one of those admirers. He probably knew her as a young girl, for there must have been some communication between Hever and his seat of Allington Castle, near Maidstone. He thought much of her beauty. 'It appeareth much more excellent by her favour, passing sweet and cheerful, and was enhanced by her whole presence of shape and fashion, representing both mildness and majesty, more than can be expressed'. He praised her skill in music and her singing voice. Another of her followers at Court said 'Beauty and sprightliness sat on her lips; in readiness of repartee, skill in the dance, and in playing on the lute, she was unsurpassed'.

This unanimity of praise may have been poured out during the few years of her ascendancy. There were later estimates, reflecting the lack of sympathy after her downfall, over which there appear to have been few regrets. She had never been popular with the people of England, and the merchant class hated her because of the threat to their trade with the Empire caused by the decisive part she played in forwarding the King's divorce from Queen Katherine, the Emperor's niece. An Italian diarist, probably an emissary of Charles V, described her as 'not one of the handsomest women in the world; she is of a middling stature, swarthy complexion, long neck, wide mouth, bosom not much raised, and in fact has nothing but the English king's great appetite, and her eyes which are black and beautiful, and take great effect'. One more word in her favour from Archbishop Cranmer, the first to hold this office in the newly established Church of England, outside the Papal pale. Cranmer sees her 'sitting in her hair, upon a horse litter, richly apparelled' at her coronation. But that can be construed as a diplomatic gesture from the new Primate. That poetic phrase, 'sitting in her hair', is a sample of the verbal genius with which Cranmer enriched the Scriptural literature of the Church of England.

The original policy of the Boleyn family, with the agreement of the girl's grandfather, Earl of Surrey (afterwards Duke of Norfolk), was to marry her to the Earl of Northumberland, principal among her many suitors. But the King, visiting Hever with Cardinal Wolsey during the period of the opening campaign for annulling the marriage with Queen Katherine, instantly showed an interest in Anne which put her relatives on the alert for even higher game. Henry openly confessed to Wolsey, his Chancellor, that 'he had been discoursing with a young lady who had the wit of an angel and was worthy of a crown'. The latter part of that suggestion disconcerted the Cardinal, who was about to be sent off to France, at his own suggestion, to negotiate a marriage with Renée, daughter of Louis XII. Throughout the matrimonial entanglements that were to follow, Wolsey played a political hand, seeking to maintain a balance of power between England, Scotland, France and the Empire. His detachment from the emotional human element was to bring him down. Anne's volatile nature revolted against his cold-blooded international machinations. Her feminine intuition made her realise that the Chancellor must be her enemy, and her reaction was reckless and instant. Queen Elizabeth's political genius was certainly not inherited from so self-indulgent a mother.

Anne may have 'had the wit of an angel', but she was no sooner openly established as the King's mistress than she began to exercise that 'power without responsibility' said to be the prerogative of the harlot. After the King's separation from Katherine in July 1531, Anne injudiciously accompanied the King on an official visit to France, where Francis I was now on the throne. Katherine, still legally Queen of England, was left at home, virtually a prisoner in banishment from the Court. This visit was another affront to the Emperor, overloading the nice balance which Wolsey was trying to maintain between France, and Spain, which was rapidly becoming a major constituent of the Empire.

The visits to and from Hever continued, and the lovers expressed their emotions through the literary medium fashionable throughout Renaissance Europe. The medium was to be maintained until the mid-twentieth century, when the use of the telephone became commonplace, and the art of language, both written and spoken, was degraded to the uses of the lowest common denomination. Few young lovers, in whatever walk of life, though today there is, culturally, only one walk of life, would write to each other as in the terms of this letter from Henry to Anne, and her reply to him.

My mistress and friend, my heart and I surrender ourselves into your hands, beseeching you to hold us commended to your favour, and that by absence your affection to us may not be lessened: for it were a great pity to increase our pain, of which absence produces enough and more than I could ever have thought could be felt, reminding us of a point in astronomy, which is this: the longer the days are, the more distant is the sun, and, nevertheless, the better; so it is with our love, for by absence we are kept at a distance from one another, and yet it retains its fervour, at least on my side; I hope the like on yours, assuring you that on my part the pain of absence is already too great for me; and when I think of the increase of that which I am forced to suffer, it would be almost intolerable but for the firm hope I have of your unchangeable affection for me: and to remind you of this sometimes, and, seeing that I cannot be personally present with you, I now send you the nearest thing I can to that, namely, my picture set in a bracelet, with the whole of the device, which you already know, wishing myself in their place, if it should please you. This is from the hand of your loyal servant and friend. H.R.

Anne's reply made less use of the colon, that subtle tool in the craft of punctuation which today is rarely used. But her literary skill is no less apparent:

For a present so beautiful that nothing could be more so (considering the whole of it), I thank you most cordially, not only on account of the fine diamond and the ship in which the solitary damsel is tossed about, but chiefly for the fine interpretation and the too humble submission which your goodness hath used toward me in this case, for I think it would be very difficult for me to find an occasion to deserve it, if I were not assisted by your great humanity and favour, which I have always sought to seek, and will seek to preserve by all the kindness in my power in which my hope has placed its unchangeable intention, which says *Aut illic, aut nullibi* [either there or nowhere]. The demonstrations of your affection are such, the beautiful mottoes of the letter so cordially expressed, that they oblige me for ever to honour, love and serve you sincerely, beseeching you to continue in the same firm and constant purpose, assuring you that, on my part, I will surpass it, rather than make it reciprocal, if loyalty of heart, and a desire to please you can accomplish it. I beg also, if at any time before this I have in any way offended you, that you would give me the same absolution that you ask, assuring you that henceforth my heart shall be dedicated to you alone. I wish my person was so too. God can do it if He pleases, to Whom I pray every day for that end, hoping that at length my prayers will be heard. I wish the time may be short, but I shall think it long till we see one another.   Written by the hand of that secretary who in heart, body and will is, your loyal and most assured servant. A.B.

Much can be read into Anne's somewhat sly reply. To what 'offence' was she referring? Was she already somewhat errant in her physical favours to the many Court gallants whom she attracted? Her mistress the Queen, a faithful, docile but dignified lady, who had to tolerate the liaison with the King, said to her one day 'My lady Anne, you have the good hap ever to stop at a King; but you are like others, you will have all or none'. That is a teasing accusation, somewhat oracular in its sense of foreboding and prophecy. It was to be quickly put to proof.

Anne was found to be pregnant. It was a fact more effective than epistolary courtship. It also speeded up the political and dynastic struggles already
intensified by the introduction of middle-class personalities into the field of
government. Both Wolsey and Thomas Cromwell were from this new stock;
pioneer intruders into the feudal world of the great landowners, the nobility
debilitated by the Wars of the Roses and thus unable to resist the power of
the central bureaucracy of the Tudor monarchy. Wolsey, like Becket four
hundred years earlier, had tried to divert that power, via his own pocket,
into the hands of the Church. Now Cromwell, the first really modern civil
servant, set up in the King's name an Exchequer on the lines of our present-
day Treasury. The seizure and dissolution of the monasteries was a process
that has a familiar ring to our ears today.

Anne's 'interesting condition' introduced a more urgent passion into the
trend of events. Although the Pope had not yet consented to the annulment
of the King's marriage to Katherine, and the declaration of Princess Mary's
bastardy, a secret ceremony of marriage between the lovers was held in
January 1533. At Easter the union was made public, and on 23 May the
marriage was declared valid and the King's first marriage nullified. A month
later Anne was crowned Queen, with full ceremony, in Westminster Abbey.

She now believed herself to be in an impregnable position, and she began
to conduct herself according to that grave illusion. The gift of histrionic
caprice, with its quick-change moods, that her daughter inherited and used
with a political expertise that baffled and dominated even her minister
Cecil and the professional ambassadors from France and the Empire,
appeared in Anne as instability of character and arrogance. She lacked the
forethought so necessary as a safeguard of her rank. Petty vindictiveness
made her add to the humiliations of Queen Katherine and the poor Princess
Mary, both serious and devout persons. She openly threatened their lives,
and asked the King for them to be brought to trial under the statute of
Succession passed in 1534, which made her own children the legitimate
heirs to the throne. One historian has said of this conduct that

in entering into schemes of self-agrandisement, which could only be achieved
by degrading Katherine and wounding to the heart a kind and indulgent
mistress and patroness, Anne Boleyn was guilty of crimes of a still deeper
dye than that of which she would have been in becoming the King's concu-
bine.

She also became active in more dangerous and deeper ploys. She hated
Wolsey, and he was still a powerful antagonist, with the international power

of the Vatican as his armoury. He was opposed to the royal divorce, and Anne accordingly entered the intrigue to bring him down. The cabal grew into a popular movement, for Wolsey's career had been one of self-agrandisement also. He had amassed great wealth, flagrantly displayed, as for example in the building of Hampton Court Palace, a morsel which toward the end of his flight from power he flung in vain to the wolves. The story of his downfall is one of the outstanding parables of history. His more subtle enemy, Thomas Cromwell, took his place, and for the next three years this ascendancy served Anne well, because she was a useful tool in Cromwell's policy of 'nationalisation' of the Church property, a sizeable proportion of the whole national wealth.

Even so, Anne failed to consolidate her position, as she might well have done, with the help of her father, her brother (now raised to the peerage as Lord Rochford), and her powerful uncle The Duke of Norfolk. But her behaviour became increasingly unrealistic. Adding to her frivolities at Court, she began to vent her jealousy on her husband, the King. This alarmed her uncle, whose warnings she rejected with such contempt that he turned against her, calling her 'a grande putaine'. She remained insensitive to the gathering storm. She was resolute against any who disputed the validity of her marriage and enthronement as Queen. The Holy Maid of Kent, that naive and innocent tool of what was now the Catholic faction, was executed with her manipulators. So too was the pious Bishop Fisher; Sir Thomas More, that 'man for all seasons', went to the block. Virtue and genius are poor currency in the political market.

Finally, toward the end of Anne's treacherous summer of triumph, Queen Katherine died, in January 1536. When Anne heard of this, she is said to have exclaimed 'Now I am indeed a Queen!' A courtier named Sir Richard Southwell brought the news, and found her washing her hands in a bowl of precious metal. She was so excited that she presented the bowl to this bearer of what she believed to be good tidings. The King ordered mourning to be worn on the day of Katherine's funeral, but Anne refused, and would not allow her ladies to do so.

Meanwhile, Anne had displeased the King by bearing a stillborn son. That was the beginning of the cooling-off process. Anne's behaviour became increasingly frenetic. She might have been playing a part in a drama by Sophocles. The day of the birth of the dead boy was that of Queen Katherine's funeral. Anne challenged this fateful sign by insisting that Princess Mary be given the humble post of nursemaid to the three-year old

Elizabeth, though she had previously stated that if the King were to give
her an opportunity by leaving England for awhile, she would have Mary
put to death.

Henry was no patient lover. He had already been attracted to one of
Anne's ladies, the gentle and lovely Jane Seymour. Shortly after the recent
critical events, Anne discovered the King one day in her rooms, sitting with
Jane on his knees. He forestalled a jealous outburst by turning on her savagely and accusing her of murdering his son! He stormed out of the room,
threatening vengeance.

He was as bad as his word. Anne tried in vain to persuade the King of
France to remonstrate with Henry, but she found that politics, and her own
clumsy conduct while in power, had caused her friends to drop away. Even
her own father and uncle had taken alarm, fearful for their own safety, titles
and properties acquired during the short course of Anne's ascendency.

There has been much dispute about the next stages in the tragedy. A
tremendous indictment of her faithlessness was concocted by the King and
his minister, but no circumstantial evidence was presented. On the 1st May,
a tournament was held at Greenwich, at which Anne took her regal place,
although unbeknown to her that dreadful threat of vengeance was already
taking 'legal' shape. Four young men, Norris, Brereton, Weston and Anne's
Court musician named Smeaton, had already been selected for arrest on the
charge of carnal relations with their mistress. Her own brother, Lord
Rochford, was also marked down, on the charge of incest.

Rochford and Norris took part in a tilting match at the Tournament.
Anne and the King sat together. The historian Lingard describes what next
happened.

It is said that, in one of the intervals between the courses, the Queen through
accident or design, dropped her handkerchief from the balcony; that Norris,
at whose feet it fell, took it up and wiped his face with it; and that Henry
instantly changed colour, started from his seat and retired. This tale was
probably invented to explain what followed: but the match was suddenly
interrupted; and the King rode back to Whitehall with only six persons in
his train, one of whom was Norris, hitherto an acknowledged favourite both
with him and the Queen. On the way Henry rode with Norris apart and
earnestly solicited him to deserve pardon by the confession of his guilt. He
refused, strongly maintaining his innocence and, on his arrival at Westminster, was committed to the Tower.

The young musician was already there, and submitted to torture, likewise
without a confession.

The next day Anne was sent to the Tower of London, on a charge of adultery with the four men, and incest with her brother. The trial lasted until the 15th before a Court of 26 peers presided over by Anne's uncle, the Duke of Norfolk. Her father had been excused attendance at her trial, but he had declared at the trial of the other victims that he believed his daughter to be guilty.

Throughout the trial Anne behaved with dignity, and insisted on her innocence. Sir William Kingston, the Lieutenant of the Tower, recorded her despair and grief, but never a confession of guilt. He said that she told him 'I am as clear from the company of man, as for sin, as I am clear from you'. She wrote a long, poignant letter to the King, headed 'from the Ladie in the Tower' and beginning, 'Sir, Your grace's displeasure and my imprisonment are things strange unto me, that what to write, or what to excuse, I am altogether ignorant'. She mentioned Cromwell as 'mine ancient confessed enemy', now the bearer of the summons. She reminded her husband that

you have chosen me from a low estate to be your queen and companion, far beyond my desert or my desire; if then you found me worthy of such honour, good your grace, let not any light fancy, or bad council of my enemies, withdraw your princely favour from me. Neither let that stain—that unworthy stain—of a disloyal heart towards your good Grace ever cast so foul a blot on me, and on the infant princess, your daughter.

She hinted at the vagary of the King's affection toward Jane Seymour as a cause of his

already being determined of me, and that not only my death but an infamous slander, must bring you the joying of your desired happiness, then I desire God that He will pardon your great sin herein, and likewise my enemies, the instruments thereof; and that He will not call you to a strict account for your unprincely and cruel usage of me at His general judgment-seat, where both you and myself must shortly appear; and in Whose judgment I doubt not (whatsoever the world may think of me), mine innocence shall be openly known and sufficiently cleared.

The last plea from 'my doleful prison in the Tower' is for 'the poor gentlemen, who, as I understand, are likewise in strict imprisonment for my sake'.

It is said that Smeaton, under torture, admitted something incriminating, as also did Norris. Anne, at her trial, was given no opportunity to refute this so-called evidence. Crispin, Lord Milherve, present in court, recorded that 'she presented herself at the bar with the true dignity of a Queen, and curtsied to her judges, looking round upon them all without any signs of fear'. He believed the indictment was one of 'base and lying charges brought forward by that most wicked Monarch, who regarded neither the life nor the honour of any man or woman—no, nor of his own children—when it was his wish to be rid of them.' The poet Sir Thomas Wyatt, lifelong a faithful admirer of Anne Boleyn, said 'As for the evidence, as I could never hear of any, small I believe it was'. Such as it was, came from dubious sources, servants and other folk whom she had offended by her treatment of them in the past; those trivial offences due to casual manners or insensibility. One such was Lady Boleyn, wife of Anne's uncle Sir Edward. Another was a Mrs Cosyns, wife of the Master of Horse to Anne.

Lord Rochford defended himself so bravely and with so powerful an eloquence, that the Court was temporarily cowed, and this in spite of the fact that his wife, another family enemy of Anne, gave evidence against him, saying 'that she had found him leaning on Anne's bed'. But he was condemned, since 'Henry willed it, and that was enough'. This sister-in-law was found afterwards to be an infamous person, involved in the intrigues of Catherine Howard, an entanglement for which she too lost her head.

It is probable that Anne was a tough character, a quality which her daughter partly inherited from her. She certainly lacked wisdom and forethought, and thus made enemies both at Court and in the country. The people hated her, and there was none to mourn her after her violent death. Yet she spoke for herself with great courage at the trial, and at one turn it was thought that she would be acquitted. 'But alas!' said a commentator,

it was neither wisdom, wit, truth, innocence, eloquence, nor all the powers and virtues which could draw an acquittal from the court of slaves bound by selfish terror to the yoke of the most blood-thirsty despot who ever disgraced a throne.

When the verdict was given, her uncle passed sentence, that she was to be burnt or beheaded as the King might decide. Anne heard this without fear. She clasped her hands, looked upwards as though in supplication to a more powerful authority than that of her judges, and cried 'O, Father! O, Creator! Thou, the Way, the Life and the Truth, knowest whether I have deserved this death!"

After a pause, she lowered her attention to the Court, and spoke to the judges:

My lords, I will not say that your sentence is unjust, nor presume that my reasons can prevail against your convictions. I am willing to believe that you have sufficient reasons for what you have done; but they must be other than those which have been produced in this Court, for I am clear of all the offences which you there laid to my charge. I have ever been a faithful wife to the King; though I do not say I have always shown him that humility, which his goodness to me, and that honour to which he raised me, merited. I confess I have had jealous fancies and suspicions of him, which I had not discretion and wisdom enough to conceal at times; but God knows, and is my witness, that I have never sinned against him any other way. Think not that I say this in hope to prolong my life. God hath taught me how to die, and He will strengthen my faith. Think not that I am so bewildered in my mind as not to lay the honour of my chastity to heart now in mine extremity, when I have maintained it all my life long, as much as ever Queen did. I know these last words will avail me nothing, but for the justification of my honour and chastity. As for my brother and those others who are unjustly condemned, I would willingly suffer many deaths to deliver them; but since I see it so pleaseth the King, I shall willingly accompany them to death, with this assurance that I shall lead an endless life with them in peace.

That is a direct enough statement, made by a person already removed, emotionally, beyond the illusions of hope or fear. It is an oath, also, taken in the name of a God who, at that day and age, was a real and concrete authority, president over the society, the everyday life, in which the Christian world existed. Even where they did not obey, they believed. Even where a few individuals here and there among the revolutionary intellectuals of the Renaissance pretended to atheism, it was a passionate protest, a kind of devil-worship, which in its essence was a kind of negative subscription to the general faith. Anne, therefore, could not have deliberately lied in the face of her God, an all-surrounding God, at this moment of impending confrontation with Him.

The speech has that ring of nobility which always hovers as an overtone to a simple statement of truth. The Lord Mayor of London, who was present, said that 'he could not observe anything in the proceedings against her, but that they were resolved to make an occasion to get rid of her.' He watched her rise, bow to the judges, and leave the Court, and it was her serenity as she walked out that determined his belief.

The King signed her death warrant that same day. Next morning Archbishop Cranmer had her brought from the Tower to Lambeth Palace, and induced her to sign a statement that her marriage with Henry was null and void. This was a curious postscript to the judgment of adultery, for that could obtain only if she had been guilty, as the King's wife. Cranmer was a sensitive but somewhat craven man. He was no Thomas More. Can he be blamed, since Parliament was also subservient to the King's ruthlessness, and confirmed Cranmer's pusillanimous contradiction?

Anne returned to the Tower for one more day. She spent it in prayer, and conversation with the Lieutenant of the Tower and his wife. She asked the latter to go to Princess Mary to ask forgiveness for the humiliations put upon her by Anne's pride of power.

The King had commanded the execution to take place on the green, within the precincts of the Tower, where the ravens, birds of ill omen, may still be seen as custodians of evil historical memory. In order to prolong her suspense, he would not state the hour of execution, and it was delayed until the hour of noon. Just before the hour, the Lieutenant of the Tower, whom she called 'Mr Kingston', came to her, and assured her that 'the pain will be very little, it was so subtle'. He told her that a swordsman from Calais had been brought over; a nice concession to relieve her of the crudeness of the use of the axe. She put her hands around her throat, and said, laughing, 'And I have a little neck'.

She wore a robe of black damask, and was attended by her four maids. An onlooker recorded that she had 'a fresh colour in her cheeks, and a bright splendour of the eyes, which astonished all who beheld her. Never had the Queen looked so beautiful before. Her composure was equal to her beauty'. She took off her hat and collar and put a small linen cap on her head. Then she made another little speech, which may have been her own words or something officially commanded upon her by the bureaucrat Cromwell, a stickler for formality:

Masters, I here humbly submit me to the law, as the law hath judged me; and, as for my offences (I here accuse no man) God knoweth them. I remit them to God, beseeching Him to have mercy on my soul; and I beseech Jesus save my sovereign and master the King, the most goodliest, noblest and greatest prince that is, and make him long to reign over you.

Such an oblation as that must surely have come already from another world, where not even truth, as we humans know it, has any significance. Consciousness, up to the last second of its habitation in the body, remains a mystery whose values are consistently immaterial between the cradle and the grave. Thus all 'famous last words' tend to be oracular, and beyond rational understanding.

After her speech, Anne gave to Mary Wyatt, the poet's sister and her friend, her book of devotions. Then she laid her head on the block.

She died at the age of 36, after a life tumultuous with intrigue, against the background of rural Kent, of Hever half hidden in the Wealden forest which even today has an atmosphere of brooding recollection. Like most women of the period, she had been a tool in the social system based on family ascendancies. But these women were individual souls, with minds of their own. Anne's daughter was to give powerful proof of this.

The body was covered in a shroud by Anne's maids, and placed in a chest brought from the armoury. There was no coffin. She was buried in the chapel of the Tower, alongside her brother.

Next day, King Henry married Jane Seymour.

The Wyatts

FOR THE past 400 years there has been much controversy about the character and gifts of the two Thomas Wyatts, father and son. One thing is certain about them. They were both bold, out-spoken men, and consequently got themselves into more trouble than they need have done. They were thus typical of the Kentish gentry, whose independence of spirit, combined with shrewd self-interest, has been discussed in other parts of this book, as a prominent factor in the history of the county. The way of life in the disturbed sixteenth century, lurid with the lightning of the Renaissance, and thunderous with the social and economic repercussions of the Reformation, make it difficult for later commentators to single out individuals for praise or blame according to modern standards of right and wrong.

The difficulty applies to aesthetic as well as moral manners, and judgments on the quality of the elder Wyatt's poetry have varied accordingly. The idiosyncrasies of rhythm and measure in his verse have puzzled many critics, most of them looking upon him as a rough rhymer still subject to the poetic lull in our literary history which lingered for a century after the genius of Chaucer had set the English language in a new and permanent mould. After him, a rustic darkness fell. The only star to lighten it was the Scottish diplomat William Dunbar, who lived on until 1520, when Wyatt was a boy of seventeen. They may even have met, for Dunbar came to London, in the service of the King of Scotland, and young Wyatt was likely to have been around the Court, as apprentice to the Diplomatic Service of Henry VIII. Dunbar's technique in verse-making shows the influence of his professional visits to France. His verse was made with sophistication and a sense of verbal music which restored to English poetry qualities lost since Chaucer died in 1400 A.D.

Wyatt was to follow Dunbar abroad, on similar errands in France and Italy. He may have known what to look for there, upon the suggestion of Dunbar's poetry, if not from personal conversation with him in London.

Historians, however, condemn conjecture, especially if they claim that their branch of the art of letters is a science; and this dubious supposition, which has done so much harm to the reputation of the great historians who wrote before this theory inhibited the general reader of history, has been applied to some of the latterday practitioners of literary criticism, with equally intimidating effect.

So before trying to assess the quality of Thomas Wyatt's contribution to English poetry, I must give a brief account of his life during that hazardous period of the Tudor autocracy. But danger always begets gaiety, as a sort of anti-body in the blood and brain, as we learned during the air-raids of the second world war. G. M. Trevelyan, in his Social History of England, wrote that 'the gay Court owed its character to the young, athletic Henry, one of the best archers in his own kingdom, not yet grown an obese and angry tyrant, but himself the glass of fashion and the mould of form. Leaving policy to his still trusted Wolsey, he spent in delights and pageants and masques the treasure which his careful father had laid up for the nation's need. Not to have been at Court was indeed, in Touchstone's words, to be damned. There the gentlemen of England learnt not only the intrigues of love and politics, but music and poetry, and a taste for scholarship and the arts, seeds which they took back to their rural homes to plant there. The culture, art and scholarship of the Italian Courts of the Renaissance had great influence on the courtiers and nobles of England, from the time of the Wars of the Roses until the reign of Elizabeth. The medieval distinction between the learned clerk and the barbarous fighting baron was coming to an end, blending in the ideal of the all-accomplished "gentleman" '.

Trevelyan follows this with a reference to Sir Thomas Wyatt as 'a kind and faithful public servant in a hard-hearted and faithless Court'. That is a true description of all governments throughout Europe. None of them was to be distinguished from oriental despotisms. True justice, indeed, was still no more than a theological idea, always suspended from practice in the world of everyday life, even by the Church which claimed to promote it. The Angevin King Henry II began to evolve a concept of Common Law, but it was frustrated by Becket. Both of them were victims of the perpetual tidal ebb and flow of the conflict between King and priest, a systole and diastole that moves the whole human race, from the small, primitive tribes in central Africa, to the vast movements of present-day ideological confrontations. The Old Testament of the Bible is largely a war record of this conflict. The unique contribution of England is that through our painful growth of Parliamentary government, we have evolved a principle of Common Law, which even today creaks and groans in the process of advancing the revolutionary idea of the chief figure in the New Testament, that every individual should have sanctuary within the law and his own conscience. The concept is still in its infancy, still tossed half-drowned in the derisive tides of the power-lusts of the opposed claimants to authority.

Sir Thomas Wyatt, as Trevelyan infers, was one of the few here and there who support that struggling infant. Born at Allington Castle, near Maidstone on the river Medway, in 1503, Wyatt entered the theatre of European life just as the great drama of the Renaissance and the Reformation in religious thought and dogma was at its crisis. The printing press was doing, throughout Europe, what the television set is doing worldwide today. The extension of awareness, of solid knowledge, of speculation, and consequently of questioning and of revolt, moved like a forest fire through the surface growth of human culture. Literacy, for the first time in the habits of civilised mankind, burst through its confinement to the priestly élite, and the laboriously decorative hand-written manuscript. The book was born; another aspect of consciousness, bringing God nearer, and more widely, to Man's image. Here is not the place to discuss what man has made of it, as he has made of all other prospectuses of Divinity.

Six years after Wyatt's birth, Henry VIII succeeded to the throne of England, with the wealth and central authority which his father had built up during the prostration of the great land-owning barons after the Wars of the Roses, conducted while the mercantile class was steadily growing. The King was still a young man when Wyatt came to Court. Henry VII had favoured Wyatt's father Sir Henry, who had been imprisoned and tortured by Richard III, as a humble follower of the Lancastrian party, in the last phase of the Wars which ended at Bosworth. Henry VII knighted Wyatt and appointed him to his civil service, which was to be once again an organised administrative machine, nevermore to be wholly abandoned to the caprice of the Court, because of the recruitment of such men as Wyatt, of true administrative and executive ability.

Wyatt was of Yorkshire origin, but under the royal favour came south and bought Allington Castle in 1493 or thereabouts. By the time his son Thomas was ten, he was firmly established in Kent, amongst the gentry who were still a fairly cohesive body of small landowners, able to protect themselves as a county in spite of Kent being a corridor of power between the Court in England and its connections and interests on the Continent; a condition that caused constant traffic of sophisticated people to and fro, with a certain amount of settling. But this was a hazard for conservation which had existed since before the Roman occupation.

Thomas was a bright boy, inheriting his father's diplomatic temperament. He was twelve years old when he was admitted to St John's College, Cambridge. He took his Arts degree in 1518, and consolidated this as a Master of Arts in 1522. His marriage was also precocious, at least by our standards. It was a county marriage, no doubt promoted by his father to strengthen the family roots in Kent. The girl was Elizabeth Brooke, daughter of Lord Cobham. It was no love match, and later Wyatt accused his wife of infidelity and lived apart from her. The King set no good example in the matter of marital fidelity, and Wyatt had been subject to the contamination of Court life since 1516, when he was appointed 'server extraordinary' to the King. He was already acquainted with Anne Boleyn, and continued to celebrate her in verse. Meanwhile, the wife whom he had married in 1520 at the age of seventeen, bore him two children, a son Thomas and a daughter Elizabeth. We know little of the girl, but the son was later to play a tragic part in the continuous struggle between Church and State.

It may be that the subsequent infidelity of Thomas's wife was her form of protest against his attention to Anne Boleyn: for there can be little doubt that his relation with this attractive Kentish neighbour was what he openly confessed it to have been, at a critical and dangerous moment in his career, when he was likely to be cited as one of the several lovers of Anne Boleyn who had cuckolded the King; a treasonable act.

From the appointment to the King's service at the age of thirteen, as 'server extraordinary', he was gradually promoted. In 1524 he became keeper of the King's jewels; a responsible post for a young man of twenty-one. Two years later he was sent with the royal plenipotentiary to congratulate the King of France on his safe return from the campaign in Spain. In

1527 he went with Sir John Russell, afterwards the first Earl of Russell, to represent the King at the Vatican. His chief sent him from Rome to Venice, on a diplomatic communication with that very subtle Republic.

He did the job satisfactorily, but was captured by some Spanish soldiers on his way back to Rome. They demanded a large ransom, but he managed to escape without paying it. After that posting, he was given the job of High Marshall of Calais, which he held for two years. So from one responsible position to another, he continued in the King's service, and in close touch with the Royal Person, without interruption of favour until the disastrous year of 1536.

Much history had been woven during those few years while Wyatt's career as diplomat, and his vocation as a pioneering poet, matured without setback. The whole structure of England's economy had been changed by the break with Rome and the seizure of the property of the Church. That vast fraction of the national wealth was now Crown-owned, and Henry used much of it to pay some of his debts. It thus went to the new middle-class, mercantile section of the community, some of whose members were able to buy their way into the landed gentry and even into the nobility. Priories and abbeys became country seats, and most of the material of the holy buildings was pillaged, either by these new landlords or by the country folk.

International relations were thrown into a condition of utmost turmoil by Henry's repudiation of his marriage with Katherine of Spain. The diplomatic storms were to welter for the rest of the century, English interests being drawn into the perpetual conflict between Spain, France, the Empire and the Papacy. Henry's extreme action led to equally extreme reactions, with the fulcrum of the European balance of power constantly shifting.

In all this, Wyatt the young diplomat played a part which must have been skilful, or it would not have endured so long. However, he was arrested and sent to the Tower of London in 1536, the year of Anne Boleyn's doom. It is still uncertain whether or not this was because he had been cited as one of the lovers of Anne. Historians are still divided about the so-called evidence of guilt amongst the poor creatures whom Henry murdered, along with his second Queen, during that blood-soaked year.

In the papers of the Camden Society there is a statement by a Catholic writer that Wyatt approached the King at the time the marriage with Anne Boleyn was being forwarded, and warned him that Anne was no virgin because some years earlier she and Wyatt had been lovers. Henry's reactions were always unpredictable (a Tudor characteristic); but was it likely that he would have maintained Wyatt in favour after this disclosure, and still gone on with the marriage with Anne? Libertines are inclined to prefer unblemished blossoms. We know, however, that Wyatt was released after a month in the Tower. He was the only one pardoned, and some historians believe that his arrest had nothing to do with the arraignment of Anne and her reputed lovers, but that it was connected with the political rivalries which flared up almost hour by hour in the inflammable atmosphere of the tyrant's Court.

In 1537 Wyatt was knighted by Henry and sent as Ambassador to the Emperor Charles V, with the impossible task of soothing the Imperial fury over Henry's treatment of Queen Katherine and the declaration that her daughter Mary was illegitimate. Cromwell, the new-type civil servant, sent two officials, one of them the turn-coat priest Bonner who was later to be Bishop of London during Queen Mary's revival of the religious practice of the burning of heretics. In that office, Bonner presided at these horrors.

He took a dislike to Wyatt; the instinctive hatred of the intriguer for the person of open character. He wrote home to Cromwell, saying that Wyatt was betraying the King's orders, and treating the two officers with disdain. The latter accusation was probably true. But Cromwell trusted Wyatt, and though the mission failed, as it was likely to do, he ignored Bonner's furtive accusations. He even sorted out Wyatt's personal financial affairs, being a good business man, which Wyatt apparently was not. He was more concerned with poetic measures than with monetary ones. Wyatt was recalled, but sent a year later on another mission to the Emperor, then on his way to the Netherlands.

After Cromwell's death in 1540 (the reward of working for King Henry), another trumped-up charge was made against Wyatt and once again he was arrested and sent to the Tower, accused of treasonable correspondence with Cardinal Pole. He was tried, and conducted his own defence with great eloquence. The Queen, Catherine Howard, also a maid of Kent and relative of the Culpepper family, pleaded for Wyatt, and he was released on condition that he took back his wife. This appears to be a most arbitrary use of the machinery of justice. It shows how the law worked in those days. Fifteen years had passed since man and wife parted.

They were not rejoined for long. A year later Wyatt was sent to Falmouth to receive ambassadors sent over by the Emperor Charles. He caught a fever there during a heat-wave, and died at Sherborne on his way home. He was only thirty-nine. His had been a crowded life, the literary part of it bringing him immortality.

Much has been written about Wyatt's character and poetic achievement. The best and most detailed edition of his verse is that by Kenneth Muir, of Leeds University, published in 1949. It is an admirable piece of scholarship and sensitive technical criticism. Sensitiveness, from a musical point of view, is essential to the adequate appreciation of Wyatt's poetry, for he brought to the making of verse a quality which Chaucer introduced into our English poetry. It was colloquial speech rhythm sublimated into that arresting dramatic ecstacy, which I would call the highest *condition* verse can attain. Some folk rhymes touch it, rising unexpectedly out of doggerel. After Chaucer, most writers of verse, over the next century and a half, seldom soared in their imitations of his seemingly easy sublimity.

Wyatt was the fore-runner of the second dawn-chorus of the ' full-throated ease ' which was to follow during the latter part of the sixteenth century and to continue through the seventeenth, never entirely to disappear, even during the enclosures of the literary formalism accepted by poets in the eighteenth century.

What it was Wyatt brought back to verse-making is not easy to define. It may be called a suddenness of attack, with a phrase like a sword-thrust lunging upward out of adequate but forgettable verse. It has the effect of speech, of words heard on the pulse of passion, either physical or spiritual emotion. Its force broke into English prosody like rain upon parched earth bringing new growth. We see the almost instant response in the writings of the Elizabethans later in the same century; especially in the poetry of John Donne, who caught the device of this close, buttonholing speech rhythm, so that the verse, fully to be grasped in its urgent authority, has to be spoken, as well as read on the printed page.

The verse used for plays was revolutionised. During the lull after Chaucer, even plays written by sophisticated scholars, such as *Ralph Roister Doister*, by Nicholas Udall, the Headmaster of Eton, were rough stuff, tedious in their long metres, crude in their phrasing. But Wyatt gave the example which Christopher Marlowe took up, and Shakespeare perfected.

It is misleading to say that this elusive quality was an expression of personal character. It could not have been so in the poetry of Marlowe, for instance. He was a graceless young egoist, whose conceit and debauchery brought him to an early and violent end. Yet I see in Wyatt's poetry a direct reflection of candour of mind and spirit. This element in his nature responded to what was sunny and lyrical in the poetry of France and Italy, the fine flower of the Renaissance. As George Puttenham wrote of him in 1589, among the many encomiums long after his death, 'he was the leader of the company of courtly makers who, having travailed in Italie and there tasted the sweet and stately measures and stile of the Italian Poesie, as novices newly crept out of the schooles of Dante, Ariose and Petrache, greatly pollished our rude and homely maner of vulger Poesie, from that it had been before'.

So it was in a sophisticated and newly ornamental verse that he framed this feature revived from the genius of Chaucer; this sudden personal note, this kind of caesura breaking the flow of metrical oratory, a device so powerful that it became set apart from its context, with a little pause of silence before its utterance, and another after, which when the verse is spoken, should be faithfully observed.

He was the first English poet to bring the sonnet into our prosody. He wrote thirty-one, of which ten were translations of sonnets by Petrarch. They do not reveal his genius, and are less melodious than those of his follower, the Earl of Surrey, who passed on the marvellous form to Spenser, Sidney, Drayton, Daniel, Shakespeare and most of the rest of the practitioners of verse in our English pantheon. The structure and the rhyme-schemes of the contrasting Italian and English forms of the sonnet I have described elsewhere in this book (see *The Sidneys of Penshurst*).

Wyatt's originality, his combination of virtue and passion in these moments of incandescent poetic light, appears in his lyrics, and in his experiments in *terza rima*, the Dantesque form which he also introduced into English verse.

Like Robert Browning, Wyatt is a poet whose work defies classification. It is so varied, especially in technical quality and form: sometimes cramped and staggering along like a wounded soldier trying to keep in step; sometimes deliberately breaking away from the discipline of the march, and hurrying along with an agility created by his passion and eagerness. We can never quite place him, in either the ranks of convention, or his inspired *pas de seul*. Kenneth Muir, in his Introduction to the collected poems which he has edited with close devotion, sums up this difficulty of assessing the poems:

His rugged versification, in his greater lyrics at least, conveys the force and subtlety of his emotion, while preserving the illusion of a man talking to men. His imagery is often well-worn and derivative and his fondness for conceits aroused the scorn of Warton (who wrote about him in *The History of English Poetry* in 1778). But he breathed new life into the conventions he imported and his greatest poems possess an extraordinary intensity which revivifies the imagery and makes the reader accept the imaginative truth of the conceits.

E. K. Chambers, perhaps, reveals the unique quality which I have been trying to isolate. He says, after some sharp criticism and the dubious statement that Wyatt 'is at the end rather than the beginning of a tradition', that 'He makes little use of visual imagery. His range of metaphor is restricted and rather conventional. For the most part he is content with the plainest of words, and relies for his effect upon his rhythmical accomplishment. This economy of speech gives him at times a singular plangency. *In appeal or reproach every line tells like a hammer-stroke.*' That line which I have italicised holds the secret of Wyatt's survival as a poet with a claim to majority. It comes so abruptly, summoning our attention. A sonnet, the form which though he introduced it, did not display him at his best, begins

> 'The long love, that in my thought doth harbour
> And in mine heart doth keep his residence. . . . . .

That opening phrase, 'the long love', so brief, so commonplace, so blunt, yet is radiant with poetic light; and we do not know why. It is like Browning's 'blue spurt of a lighted match', a deceptively matter-of-fact touch in a passionate nocturne, which yet adds magic and a speciality to the scene. The same device is used twice in the second stanza of the following poem, which is the most famous in all Wyatt's work, and may be celebrated as one of the great love poems in the language.

> They flee from me that sometime did me seek,
> With naked foot stalking in my chamber.
> I have seen them gentle, tame and meek
> That now are wild and do not remember
> That sometime they put themself in danger
> To take bread at my hand; and now they range
> Busily seeking with a continual change.
>
> Thanked by fortune, it hath been otherwise
> Twenty times better; but once in special,
> In thin array after a pleasant guise,
> When her loose gown from her shoulders did fall,
> And she caught me in her arms long and small;

> Therewithall sweetly did me kiss,
> And softly said, *dear heart, how like you this* ?

> It was no dream: I lay broad waking,
> But all is turned through my gentleness
> Into a strange fashion of forsaking;
> And I have leave to go of her goodness,
> And she also to use new fangleness.
> But since that I so kindly am served,
> I would fain know what she hath deserved.

Testimony to the man himself is always favourable. The French critic Legouis says of him 'His nature was frank and manly, like the proud portrait which Holbein made of him'. Trevelyan calls him 'a kind and faithful public-servant in a hard-hearted and faithless Court'. He was just as happy in the privacy of his country estate:

> This maketh me at home to hunt and hawk
> And in foul weather at my book to sit.
> In frost and snow then with my bow to stalk
> No man doth mark where I so ride or go;
> In lusty lees my liberty I take. . . .
> Here I am in Kent and Christendome,
> Among the muses where I read and rhyme.

Wyatt wrote in this vein to his son and namesake, the second Thomas, urging him to piety, patience and courtesy toward all men. There must have been something in this son's make-up that disturbed the anxious father, and what subsequently happened to this impetuous young man justifies that anxiety.

The younger Wyatt was over 21 at the time of his father's death, and already notorious for an unstable temper. This may have been the cause of the parental sermonisings from time to time, which did no good. Trying to induce a leopard to change its spots only enrages it. Young Thomas gave way to dissipation at an early age, and seduced the daughter of Sir Edward Darrell of Littlecote, the result being an illegitimate son. In 1537 he married another girl, the daughter of Sir William Hawte of Bishopsbourne, by whom he had ten children. His local reputation therefore cannot have been high. Besides playing around among his neighbours' womenfolk, he led a wild and disorderly life, quarrelsome and self-opinionated. He was a trouble-maker, and saw himself as a righter of wrongs, so long as he could be the leader. An opportunity arose in due course, which was to give him a sinister place in our history.

On his father's death in 1542 he inherited Allington Castle and nearby Boxley Abbey. The sedate life of a country gentleman was too tame for him, and a year later he went abroad to the Low Countries to take part in the perpetual warfare against the Spanish domination there. For seven years he came and went, begetting his family during the vacations from camp life. What happened to his estates meanwhile is a matter of conjecture. Maybe his wife, as well as coping with the demands of the nursery, contrived to administer the farms, woodlands and the needs and demands of the tenants, combining two whole-time jobs, as so many women have done, and still do, who have large families and wayward husbands.

In 1554, Queen Mary's proposal to marry Phillip II of Spain, the dour, fanatical son of the great Emperor Charles V, caused her English subjects to overlook her good qualities and to concentrate on her foreignness. She had never had contact with the English way of life, its steady drift toward political independence and the beginnings of a democratic constitution. She combined the Tudor tyrannical temperament with the Spanish submission to the practices of the Inquisition. She was determined to avenge the degradation of her mother and to restore the authority of the Catholic Church. In the five years of her reign she burned three hundred Protestants at the stake. Even so, the mystique of royalty remained to subdue the indignation of the people, though throughout the country dangerous murmurings of protest arose.

Kent, perhaps by reason of its prosperity and greater vitality, was always foremost in times of ferment. Rumours of conspiracy were rife in the county, but they remained quiescent until an individual came forward to bring them to a head. That individual was Thomas Wyatt the younger.

He had seen something of the methods of the Inquisition when he accompanied his father on a mission to Spain. He had fought against Spain in the Netherlands for seven years. Now he saw that power being exerted in his own country. The Queen's proposed marriage to King Phillip of Spain would make England an appendage of the Empire. On January 22nd Wyatt summoned a meeting at Allington Castle of all the gentlemen of the county who expressed discontent with this dreaded proposal. In four days he organised a revolt, marched on Rochester, occupied it and issued a general proclamation to the people of Kent. Some of the gentry and a host of the folk collected in Rochester. He had little time to organise them as a military force, and the Sheriff of the County, Sir Robert Southwell, with the aid of Lord Abergavenny, a large landowner on the county border, contrived to bring sufficient loyalists and militia to check the uprising.

But public anger and fear of the Spanish marriage quickly spread in Kent. Furthermore, the majority of its wide acreage, which had been Church property, was parcelled out piecemeal, and the gentry and yeomen who now held those profitable farmsteads feared for their title-deeds. In addition, a genuine religious creed, as dogmatic as that of the Catholics, fed both conscience and obstinacy in what was now the Protestant ascendency. The two loyal leaders found that their hastily assembled force was talked over by the rebels in Rochester.

They called on the Queen for help, and she despatched a regiment of the London trained bands under the Duke of Norfolk into Kent. But these troops also deserted to the rebels, thus giving the revolt so much force that the Queen for once became aware of the character of her own people. She sent her officers to parley with Wyatt. The foolish braggart, instead of taking realistic advantage of this opening, insisted that the tower of London should be given up to him, and that the Queen should submit to his control. He had not the sense to see that with tact he might have brought the whole power of London, the key to the Kingdom, to his side.

Instead, his melodramatic gesture made the hard-headed London merchants and bankers realise that they were dealing with a fool. They persuaded the lively and shrewd citizens of Cockaigne likewise. When Wyatt with his still untrained followers reached the south bank of the Thames on 3 February, he found London Bridge occupied against him, and the guns of the Tower trained for firing on the rebel crowd across the water.

That was a damping discovery and delay. His strategy now was a bad second best. He marched those of his followers still willing to accompany him, up river on the south side as far as Kingston, crossed the river and doubled back to London, where he reached Ludgate, after losing some of his men along the route. It was a long walk, and time and fatigue are great reducers of enthusiasm. However, he attacked Ludgate, which at that time *was* a gate. But there was no spirit in the attack. The Kentish folk, as in their former excursion outside the bounds of the county under the leadership of Wat Tyler, lacked confidence when away from home. The Londoners were resolved not to admit these strangers to the City, for general disorder and plunder. They fought with vigour and Wyatt was forced to surrender.

He was arrested and brought to trial on 15 March. There could be no question of a legal defence. He was not immediately executed, however, for the authorities hoped that by tricking him with the false promise of a pardon they might induce him to incriminate more important people, and principally the Princess Elizabeth, whose name had been used during the insurrection as a battle cry.

But Wyatt here showed himself as his father's son. He was no craven. He refused to betray anybody, and when making his obsequy on the scaffold, on 11 April, he firmly stated that the Princess Elizabeth had no knowledge of or part in the uprising. Mary, who liked her half-sister, accepted this. Elizabeth's life was saved, and a future stateswoman preserved for England's greater glory.

Wyatt's estates at Allington Castle were confiscated, but part of them was restored later to his son Sir George Wyatt, the father of a Sir Francis who became Governor of Virginia during the first half of the seventeenth century.

The most evocative description of this noble estate appears in a book on Kent by Marcus Crouch, Deputy Librarian of the county, also a gracious and scholarly writer. He has just explored Maidstone, and leaves it by the road to Chatham, that

runs past barracks and county offices to the outskirts of the town. Here, where there is a rather over-done thatched inn, a lane goes left to Aylesford. A hundred yards or so down this there is a very narrow lane on the left which goes to the river. This is Allington, the lowest lock on the river (the Medway). It is an attractive scene here. The river is lined on its western bank with poplars, and the lock buildings are in Kentish rag. . . . Grey towers can be seen through the trees on the other bank. They belong to Allington Castle, the ancient home of the Wyatts. Seen from the water this is not far short of being the romantic castle of the imagination. The buildings, substantially but discreetly restored in the present century, belong to the reign of Edward I. They were built, or rather reconstructed from a manor-house, by Sir Stephen de Penchester, whose tomb is in Penshurst Church. In early Tudor times the Wyatt family added to the amenities of the castle and made it into an agreeable house.   It was the home of Sir Thomas Wyatt, who trod a delicate course through the lethal mazes of Henry VIII's Court and who enriched the life of the Court with his songs and sonnets.

That phrase 'who trod a delicate course through the lethal mazes of Henry VIII's Court' has the magic of absolute truth in it. It is a jewel in a fine passage of evocative writing, which adds to the poetic substantiality of the story of Sir Thomas Wyatt, diplomat and unique poet, and of his son, non-diplomat and ineffective rebel.

The Sackville Family

THE SACKVILLE family offers a dominant example of the gradual penetration of Norman blood into the Saxon landowning folk who had already formed a concise aristocracy with their own kings in Kent, before the coming of William the Conqueror. One of his followers was a man of Danish origin, whose forbear had trekked southward two centuries earlier and settled in a place south-east of Dieppe, on the way to Rouen. The village was called Sauqueville, and the settler's family took this name. But the family did not lose its instinct for migration which is common to all humanity, or at least sufficient members of it to keep mankind ever on the move, ever expanding like an incoming tide.

The Saqueville who came to England with Duke William of Normandy was rewarded with various parcels of the land expropriated from the Saxon communes. He was given land in Essex, Hertfordshire, and more lavishly in Sussex, just over the Kentish border at Withyam, which included an estate called Buckhurst. The future history of the family, which continues even today, was to evolve round this base, and the first barony given to the family carried the name of Buckhurst.

The family prospered because its members passed on certain character-istics of prudence and honesty which were pronounced or diminished by individuals generation after generation, but never wholly lost. One Robert de Sackville went with Richard I on the Third Crusade, and it was he who did some land-grabbing in Normandy that got him into trouble with the abbot of Mont St. Michel. His son also appears to have inherited a grudge against the already consistent avarice of the clerics who had so quickly introduced temporal and political interests into the Christian Church. This Nigel de Sackville took some part in Thomas à Becket's conflict with King Henry II. When, in the final act of that struggle, Becket came back to England, Nigel seems to have had dealings with the four conspiring knights who were following Becket, determined to administer the rough justice of violence, a method which their master, Henry II, was trying to replace by a rudimentary system of legal justice. The King's efforts were frustrated by the murder of Becket, which furthered the abominable practice of one law for the priest and another for the layman. The evolution of English Common Law, our greatest contribution to Western Civilisation, was delayed for centuries by that brutal act in Canterbury Cathedral on 29 December 1170.

It appears that this Nigel de Sackville was a priest who had usurped the rectorship of Harrow without authority, and had accordingly been excommunicated by the Archbishop in 1169. Becket stayed for some days at Harrow on his way back to Canterbury from Woodstock, where he had gone in a vain attempt to see the King's eldest son. It was a false move in the elaborate game of intrigue. When Becket set off from Harrow, this Nigel de Sackville maimed one of the baggage horses carrying the Archbishop's provisions.

In the great comminatory sermon preached by Becket in Canterbury Cathedral on the eve of his murder, he repeated the words of excommunication of several of his enemies, and included Nigel de Sackville. 'May they be cursed' he said, 'by Jesus Christ. May the memory of those who sow discord between me and my Lord the King be blotted out of the memory of the Saints!' And as he thus ended his Christmas Day sermon, he threw the lighted candle from the pulpit to the ground, to signify the snuffing out of his enemies. The story shows to what a petty condition the functioning of the Church had fallen into. The scene that followed four days later restored something of the vast scope of the struggle, the range and endurance of mankind's lust for power.

The Sackville family prospered, serving the Crown, no matter on whose head it weighed. Sons and daughters, generation after generation, were profitably married, or grafted into flourishing branches of the Church. The Norman ascendency in England quickly created a close community of land-owning aristocracy, sufficiently loyal to the Crown to maintain this superstructure on the ground-base of the Feudal System. Estate was married to estate, fortune to fortune, while the Church steadily acquired a major portion of the national wealth. The old Anglo-Saxon communal tenure of land almost disappeared beneath this centralised holding of it by the Crown, and its passing to the Feudal lords. Some of the pre-Conquest families contrived, by submission, to work their way into the system. Man does not live by greed alone. Individual relationships of love and friendship, mental and spiritual devotion, resulted in inter-marriage not wholly determined by territorial or commercial considerations.

The Sackvilles profited by this trait in human nature, for in general they bred likeable sons and daughters, with only rarely a wastrel or a scoundrel. Their genes persisted in handing down the gift of charm, as well as considerable intellectual ability. Thus generation after generation of them found their way to the Court and royal service. It happened to be the principal road to promotion. So the Sackvilles gathered more and more estates, linking them up with territorial marriages and purchases. Buckhurst in Sussex remained their headquarters from 1200 to 1603 A.D. Not until that latter date did the family come into the orbit of our interest in this book about Kentish-born immortals. The two members who vastly enhanced the power and wealth of the family, father and son, were born outside our county.

Sir Richard Sackville first carried the family out of the country gentry class into the higher reaches of national fame and power. He was the son of a Sir John who had enlarged and lavishly decorated the family home at Buckhurst, and made a closer connection with Kent by marrying Margaret Boleyn, an aunt of Anne Boleyn. One of his daughters married Robert Roberts of Glassenbury, a noble estate at Goudhurst. The first Roberts to settle there was a Scottish wool merchant, who came to Goudhurst, a busy village in the weaving trade, in the reign of Henry III. The Roberts family are still in residence at Glassenbury, and the latter part of their pedigree is inscribed on the wall of the south aisle in Cranbrook Church, 'the cathedral of the Weald'.

From the point of view of worldly success and dynastic prosperity, Sir Richard Sackville was the greatest member of the family. He began with a good endowment, for by the time of his birth in 1507, the Sackvilles were kinsmen of the Earls of Surrey (The Fitzalans) and the Dukes of Norfolk. But they were realistic in an age of chivalry, for one of Sir John's sons became 'a draper of London', thus opening the flood-gates for younger sons of feudal landowners to join the creators of middle-class industrial wealth which was later to sweep most of the aristocracy down the river of time.

Sir Richard's wife was the daughter of a London knight named Bruges, a Lord Mayor, and therefore likely to have been a man of business, this ever increasing activity which was proving the pen to be mightier than the feudal sword. Richard became a lawyer, and was appointed Lent Reader at Gray's Inn. With this intellectual discipline as his armour, he entered the fight for wealth and power. He became Treasurer of the Exchequer to Queen Elizabeth. During one of the periodic visitations of plague in 1565, we find him at Windsor, with the Queen, Sir William Cecil, and Roger Ascham, that great humanist, tutor to the Queen during her youthful years, and a noted scholar. At dinner with that assembly, Ascham made a revolutionary statement which was to survive. He said that 'young children were sooner allured by love than driven by beating to attain good learning'. It has taken us 400 years to put that precept into practice; and even now we are over-doing it by substituting an indifferent permissiveness for that exacting element of love, which requires a disciplinary responsibility.

Ascham has also left on record the effect of his dictum on Sir Richard Sackville, who drew him aside next morning in the Queen's privy chamber and took him by the hand, saying

'Mr Ascham, I would not for a good deal of money, have been this day absent from dinner, where, though I said nothing, yet I gave a good care, as any one did there. Mr Secretary said very wisely and most truly, that many young wits be driven to hate learning, before they know what learning is. I can be good witness to this myself, for a fond Schoolmaster before I was fully fourteen years old, drove me so, with fear of beating, from all love of learning, as now I feel it my greatest grief. But I will make this, my mishap, some occasion of good hap to little Robert Sackville, my sons' son, for whose bringing up I would gladly use specially your good advice'. We had then further talk together of bringing up children.

The boy Robert was educated by Roger Ascham as a result of this talk, and the great humanist's theory of education was justified by his pupil's subsequent career, for this eldest son of Sir Thomas Sackville became a brilliant scholar in Latin and Greek, and what passed for science in those days. His life of public service maintained the family reputation, status and great wealth. Unfortunately, his own son and heir, another Richard, turned out to be a black sheep; a gambler, lecher, and idle participant in all the pleasures of King James the First's dubious Court. He brought the family estates into such embarrassment that they never fully recovered the affluence brought to them by his great-grandfather and grandfather, the latter being one of the two members of the Sackville family whom I wish to include amongst the immortals of *Kent's Contribution.*

It was Sir Richard Sackville, however, who made it possible for his famous son to begin life at the top of the tree. Sir Richard was a man of benevolent but shrewd character. He steered a hazardous course through the stormy political seas disturbed by Henry's withdrawal from the Catholic comity of Europe, and again by Queen Mary's temporary return to it. The whole structure of our English society and constitution was changed during those wild decades, which enabled every kind of adventurer and charlatan to find fame and fortune, and many honest men and women to be destroyed. The state of public affairs was similar to the welter of our twentieth century. Sir Richard quietly, steadily, and honourably, protected his family and advanced its authority and possessions.

Thus his son came to a great inheritance. Though he was born in 1537 just over the Kentish border, at Buckhurst, in Withyham parish, I include Sir Thomas Sackville in this book because he had so much to do with our county, and was the first member of the family to associate it permanently with Kent, when Queen Elizabeth presented him with Knole in 1566. He was not able, however, to take up residence there until 1603, as the great house had been sub-let by the Earl of Leicester to another party. So Sir Thomas Sackville (as he is always known to posterity) lived in Kent for only five years, until his death in 1608. His descendents have been, and are still, native to the county.

Nepotism was not considered to be disgraceful in Tudor and Stuart times. I suppose it has never been so, though in democratic society it has no good name, and is indeed elevated to a place amongst the deadly sins. Death duties, on the scale of those imposed today, are a direct assault upon family favour, on which nepotism is based, but the emotion behind its practice is a primary animal instinct which has not yet been eliminated even by communist rule. Parents all the world over like to do something toward the advancement of their children, and even more removed relatives. The results of such natural favouritism are often deplorable. But the practice can be commended as saving a lot of drudgery and spadework, thus enabling a brilliant man, by inheritance and family influence, to conserve his energies for work commensurate with his abilities. By that argument, nepotism may be looked upon as comparable to the process of selective breeding, in animals and plants. But human nature does not conform in the same way as dogs, horses and roses. It is liable to vagary, sometimes called original sin, or psychological aberration.

That is why it shocks one to learn that Thomas Sackville, at the age of nine, was made incumbent of the church at Lullington, in Sussex, while he was attending the grammar school there. He derived a small income thereby.

When he was 16, he went up to Oxford, and lived in Hertford College for awhile, but left there to go to St John's College, Cambridge, taking with him the reputation of being a poet. He wrote in both English and Latin, and was much praised by contemporary writers, though whether this was sincere or to find favour, we do not know. For little of his writing has survived, and it is surprising that literary historians include his name with those of Wyatt and the Earl of Surrey as a pioneer in the introduction of the sonnet form into English Poetry. John Heywood, a playwright who was one of the first men of the theatre to break away from moral instruction and to write for the entertainment of his audience, wrote in 1560 that 'There Sackville's sonnets sweetly saused, featly fyned be', an archaic allusion which suggests an almost culinary praise.

The writing of sonnets was a social requirement, expected of every educated person, by the time Thomas emerged into Court life. With him, however, writing was more than a fashionable hobby. He followed his father in being a character of sober persistence, with a strong moral and religious purpose at the base of all his activities. But this did not cause him to withdraw into a scholarly solitude. He entered Parliament at the age of twenty.

A year later, in 1558, Queen Elizabeth came to the throne. The young Sackville was her kinsman, and he was quickly brought to her notice. She was a shrewd judge of character, except for being blinded by her womanly love for Robert Dudley, Earl of Leicester, whose faults outweighed his abilities.

The Queen was devoted to her cousin Sir Richard, and she extended this affection to his son Thomas. She offered him and his wife an apartment in Sheen Palace in Surrey. He had married in 1555 at the age of eighteen, Cecily Baker, daughter of Sir John Baker, of Sissinghurst Castle, a large mansion built by him in Kent. This gives me a second excuse for including Sir Thomas amongst the Kentish worthies. Baker had been Recorder of London, Attorney General, Chancellor of the Exchequer to Henry VIII,

Secretary to the Privy Council and Speaker of the House of Commons. He had remained a Papist, and Queen Mary accordingly kept him in his various offices during her reign, and he had a dubious reputation as a persecutor of the Protestants, and of enriching himself by fines from them, during those few years of Papist re-ascendency. If that was so, it is surprising that Elizabeth also favoured him, and even visited him in his mansion at Sissinghurst.

The marriage of Thomas and Cecily Baker, at so early an age, was likely to be the usual dynastic arrangement, linking lands and fortunes. But at the end, when Thomas's death separated them, his Will referred to her with endearments that could only be an assurance of true love and a happy harmonious marriage; it lasted for 51 years. She survived him by seven years, and was buried beside him in the family tomb at Withyham, in 1615. She appears to have been a woman of serene and discreet character, supporting him behind the scenes. She gave him four sons and three daughters, and helped an illegitimate son born through an early indiscretion of Sir Thomas.

Though no worthwhile sonnets by Thomas Sackville have survived, the quality of his poetic gift may be judged by a long poem called an 'induction', to a yet longer work with a heavily moral tendency, imitative of Lydgate, whose 'Fall of Princes' he admired. Thomas was also a devoté of Dante, whose genius towered over the whole of civilised Europe throughout the Renaissance, a medieval panache sheltering it from its own consuming illumination. As in Dante's *Inferno*, the narrator makes a guided tour of Hell.

Having written the 'Induction' Sackville was caught up in service to the Crown, mostly as ambassador in the Courts of Europe, and he had no time to pursue the work to be called *A Mirror for Magistrates*. He handed it to two men of letters, Richard Baldwin and George Ferrers, who completed it, in the seven-line stanza he had employed in *The Induction*. It was the stanza used by Chaucer in *The Clerk's Tale* and *Troilus and Cressida*.

King James of Scotland also used it in his *King's Quair*, and it thus became known as *rhyme royal*.

The *Mirror for Magistrates* was a heavily moral concept, as its sub-title proclaimed: 'Wherein may be seen by example of others, with how grievous plagues vices are punished, and how frail and unstable worldly prosperity is found even of those whom fortune seemeth most highly to favour'. The poem was in two volumes, and made tedious reading, for the lieutenants

who wrote the body of the work lacked the poetic imagination of Sackville.
The first volume was published (or rather, printed, for in those days sales
promotion had not been applied to books) in 1559 and the second in 1563,
the year before the birth of Shakespeare and Marlowe. Six more editions
appeared during the remainder of the sixteenth century, one more in 1610
and the last in 1815.

The *Induction* begins with a bit of stage-setting, with astrological props
to illustrate the passing of summer and the dreadful coming on of winter,

> The cruel season, bidding me withhold
> Myself within, for I was gotten out
> Into the fields whereas I walkt about.

But something drives him out into the winter night, and he meets 'a piteous
sighte' in great trouble, for

> Forth on her eyes the Cristall tears out burst,
> And sighing sore her hands she wrung and fold,
> Tear all her hair that ruth was to behold.

So begins the conducted tour of the regions of despair and remorse. The
imagery is hard and vivid, and the versification urgent, giving an effect of
the poet being driven on by horror. The gloom and pessimism of the poem
recall the medieval world which Dante forcefully portrayed. There is
nothing of the eager light of the Renaissance in Sackville's conjuring. Three
stanzas describing an incarnation of the evil of famine give an intimation of
the mood of the whole poem. They justify the outburst of praise which
greeted the young poet, who was still in his twenties when *The Mirror for
Magistrates* appeared.

> But of the doleful sight that then we see,
> We turned our look and on the other side
> A grisly shape of Famine might we see,
> With greedy looks, and gaping mouth that cried,
> And roared for meat as she should there have died,
> Her body thin and bare as any bone,
> Whereto was left nought but the case alone.
>
> And that alas was gnawed on every where,
> All full of holes, that I ne might refrain
> From tears to see how she her arms could tear
> And with her teeth gnash on the bones in vain:
> When all for nought she fain would so sustain
> Her starving corpse, that rather seemed a shade,
> Than any substance of a creature made.

> Great was her force whom stone wall could not stay,
> Her tearing nails snatching at all she saw:
> With gaping jaws that by no means ymay
> Be satisfied by hunger of her maw,
> But eats herself as that she hath no law:
> Gnawing alas her carcase all in vain,
> Where you may count each sinew, bone and vein.

So it goes on for 79 stanzas of sustained objective narration, engraved as sharply as Durer's *Melancolia*. It appeared during a lull in English poetic creativity which had lasted since Chaucer's death. Another twenty years were to pass before Edmund Spenser and Philip Sidney heralded a new outburst of music, unexampled in volume and beauty. So Sackville's *Induction*, glowing on *The Mirror for Magistrates* like a ruby on a piece of sacking, was greeted, 'like a star, when only one is shining in the sky'.

That was not his only contribution to English literature. He had collaborated with two fellow lawyers in the first essay. He next worked with a third, Thomas Norton, in the writing of a verse-play, a lugubrious tragedy called *Gorboduc*. Norton wrote the first three acts and Sackville the last two. It deals, like the opening chapters of the Old Testament, with fratricide. The two brothers, Ferrex and Porrex, are the sons of Gorboduc, King of Britain, who like Lear divided his realm during his lifetime between his children. Porrex, the younger, killed the elder, who was his mother's favourite. A revolution followed, headed by the nobility, and the murderer and his rebel followers were killed. This provoked a civil war, in which the kingdom was reduced to desolation.

The authors made what might be called a court case of the theme, for Norton was a powerful legalist and politician. Only a year after the play was acted at the Christmas revels of the Inner Temple in 1561-1562, and repeated before the Queen at Whitehall, Norton as Chairman of the Committee of the House of Commons drew up a petition 'for Limitation of the Succession' for presentation to Elizabeth. Its purpose was an obvious bid for greater Parliamentary power. Nor was Sackville, still a young man, lacking in political experience. He loads the play with theories of statesmanship. The critic George Saintsbury rightly compared him to Seneca, the stately Roman tragedian on whose plays Racine modelled his classical and marmoreal masterpieces. The last two lines of Gorboduc sum up Thomas Sackville's philosophy of life:

> For right will always live, and rise at length,
> But wrong can never take deep root to last.

Turning from literature to diplomacy and politics (which in the Tudor autocracy meant plunging ever deeper into Court life), Sackville never deviated from that principle. His honesty and diplomatic skill, inherited from his father, served him in good stead, for the Queen trusted him implicitly, and he had few enemies, in spite of his increasing power and wealth. He was created Baron Buckhurst in 1567, and Earl of Dorset in 1603. His wealth was so great that the Queen sent him, with twenty knights, to represent her at the wedding of Charles IX of France to Elizabeth of Austria, daughter of the resplendent Emperor Maximilian. The French Ambassador in England, recommending the plenipotentiate, described Sackville as 'a very unassuming gentleman, and as well disposed as anyone at this Court'. Servants of Elizabeth worked for her at their own expense. Sackville's undertaking in France was carried out with so much entertainment and splendour that it rivalled the proceedings and ceremonies of The Field of the Cloth of Gold. During the revelries, Sackville negotiated with the Queen Mother of France (Catherine de Medici) on the project of the marriage of Elizabeth and the Duke of Anjou, the King's brother, a ploy which Elizabeth maintained as a political tool for as long as it suited her policy in international affairs.

Sackville was one of the judges at the trial of the Duke of Norfolk, who had been embroiled in one of the Catholic plots to replace the Queen by Mary of Scotland. The Duke was executed in 1572. Fourteen years later, Sackville's eldest son married the Duke's only daughter.

Again, Sackville was chosen as a commissioner for the trial of Mary Stuart, when Elizabeth's efforts to protect her dangerous cousin (and the sanctity of royalty) were defeated by Parliament, and the demands of foreign policy. After her condemnation, the Queen sent him, because of his great gentleness, to announce the verdict to Mary, and if possible, to comfort her. He was so successful that Mary accepted her fate with equanimity, and was so charmed by Sackville's approach, that she gave him a set of five wooden carvings of the Stations of the Cross. I believe they are still to be seen at Knole.

Sent on an embassy to Holland, to replace Leicester, who had badly blundered there by starving the English troops and also plundering the Dutch merchants, Sackville straightened out these malpractices, only to return home to find that Leicester had lied to the Queen about him. This led to his retirement from Court. He subjected himself to so strict a 'house arrest' that he refused even to see his wife and children. Fortunately for him, and the nation, the Earl of Leicester died in September 1588, and the Queen recovered her political sanity.

Sackville was at once restored to favour and to his many offices. He bore no grudge, and his letter of acceptance was a model of humility. It began 'Most gracious Sovereign, although the burden of my sorrows so heavily oppressing my poor heart, in respect of my restraint from your Majesty's presence, hath oft times moved me . . .' and so it goes on, from one prostration to another, in spite of the fact that his mission in Holland had been performed, as the historian Motley said in his book on the Dutch Republic,

with sagacity, without passion, with unaffected sincerity, he had unravelled the complicated web of Netherland politics, and, with clear vision, had penetrated the designs of the mighty enemy whom England and Holland had to encounter in mortal combat. He had pointed out the errors of the Earl's administration—he had fearlessly, earnestly, but respectfully deplored the misplaced parsimony of the Queen. . . . For deeds such as these the able and high-minded ambassador, the accomplished statesman and poet, was forbidden to approach his sovereign's presence, and was ignominiously imprisoned in his own house until the death of Leicester; disgraced for the conscientious discharge of the most important functions that had yet been confided to him.

That incident in Sackville's otherwise unimpeded career reveals the moral quality of the man, especially his modesty and selflessness.

After the Queen reinstated him in office, he returned to the Netherlands and compounded a treaty which saved England an expenditure of what would be the present-day equivalent of some twenty million pounds a year. He was awarded the Order of the Garter and made Chief Butler of England and Wales, with an appropriate income.

He was still unable to take possession of Knole, and being anxious to come and live in Kent, he tried to rent Otford Park, but Sir Robert Sidney of Penshurst forestalled him by promising it to Lord Cobham. Negotiations went on for so long that Sackville's need for a home in Kent was satisfied in 1603 by Knole being released for him to take possession there. It is significant that he had brought no pressure to bear, by means of the fact that he was Lord High Treasurer of England, during the legal dealings over the Otford property. His post, which had been that of the great Lord Burghley, was the most powerful under the Crown. He held it until the death of Elizabeth, and James I immediately confirmed him in it, with a patent for life.

One of the last major judgments he made under the Queen's authority, before her death in 1603, was to condemn the rash Earl of Essex to death, as a result of that young man's disastrous campaign in Ireland, and subsequent angry effort to raise a rebellion at home; an irresponsible act due solely to wounded vanity.

For the rest of his life, Sackville, Earl of Dorset, continued in his high office of Lord Treasurer. He gave himself to large issues of foreign policy and Parliamentary development. No matter was too small for his careful attention. For example, he set up a commission to examine the dangers of the use of tobacco being extended from medicinal purposes to a general indulgence by the public as 'a gluttonous exercise'. The result was that in 1604 the tax of twopence on a pound of tobacco was increased by 6s. 8d.! On his own initiative, without consulting Parliament, he imposed a duty on currants imported from the Middle East. The merchants appealed to Parliament, and the matter went to the Court of Exchequer. The four judges unanimously upheld the Lord Treasurer's action, and the Commons accepted the decision meekly. But Sackville was not dictatorial. Less than a year before his death, he wrote a letter to Henry, the eldest son of the King, imploring,

that it pleaseth your Highness so graciously and so many ways to manifest your special favour and respect towards me your poor servant. And would to God that the humble and infinite desire of my heart to do such acceptable service to your Highness (as so great a merit proceeding from so renowned and so rare a prince towards so simple a servant doth require) might be visibly seen and made known unto your Highness such as it is in truth and in deed. . . .

The long letter in this vein of humility (according to modern fashion, it would be called servility) was sincerely intended as homage to a future king: but it was superfluous, for Henry died before his father. Had he become King, says G. M. Trevelyan, 'he might possibly have become a Protestant Henry V on the Continent during the Thirty Years' War, and totally changed the course of political development in England by adopting policies pleasing to Parliament and so keeping it in voluntary subordination to the Crown', just as Sackville did over that smaller matter of the duty on the insidious drug, tobacco.

The poet-statesman died at work. On 19 April 1608 he was attending a meeting of the Privy Council before the King, and reading aloud a paper for discussion, when he suddenly fell forward, dead. He died of overwork, which caused a blood vessel in the brain to burst. He had been ailing for two years, but had refused to rest. His final rest was in the family tomb in the Sackville Chapel at Withyham.

With characteristic thoroughness, he left a Will that filled 165 foolscap pages. It dealt with every acre of his vast and scattered properties, and all his furniture and other possessions, dealing them out to members of his family, his servants, his friends and neighbours, so that there could be no confusion after his departure to the Catholic heaven in which he had believed, without this simple faith interfering with his career and his careful accumulation of wealth, the worldly goods for which so many people perjure their souls and destroy the harmonious relationship of their descendants.

It can be said of him that he was one of the most *complete* men, in the philosophic meaning of that word, to be associated with Kent. Though born just over the border of the county, he was a true man of Kent. For power of intellect and spirit, he stands with William Harvey, the great doctor.

Adding to his father's achievement, Thomas Sackville established his family as one of the most powerful of the aristocratic ascendency which was to govern Britain until the coming of the social revolution which began with the cancerous growth of industrialism in the nineteenth century, and burst into open oligarchy after the first world war of the twentieth century.

In general, family characteristics survived as a stable element, with the outstanding exception of the unfortunate third Earl of Dorset. The inter-dynastic marriages persisted, linking the kinship of the Sackvilles with more and more of the nobility throughout the Kingdom. The standard of states-manship was maintained so effectively that the seventh Earl was promoted to a dukedom of Dorset. His name was Lionel Cranfield Sackville, who began his career at Court (which meant in Government circles) while play-ing as an infant with a toy cart in the corridor of Kensington Palace, where William and Mary had chosen to live because the country air of the district eased the King's asthma. The child, hearing that the Queen was impatiently awaiting the King's habitual attendance at her daily tea-party, burst into the King's room, along with the cart, and ordered him to come at once. They arrived at the tea table with the King pushing the infant Sackville in the cart.

The boy succeeded to the title at the age of eighteen in 1705. A year later he began his diplomatic career as a junior on a commission to Hanover, to secure the succession to the Crown of Britain of the Elector who was to become George I. Dorset's promotions went through a familiar procedure. He was made Lord Warden of the Cinque Ports. He was sent to Hanover to notify the Elector of the death of Queen Anne, and to prepare the welcome of the new King to England. He was befriended by the Prince of Wales, who paid a visit to Knole in 1716, which cost a lot of money. The wine bill alone for that one night was £66., worth about £1,300 today. Sackville was created Duke of Dorset in 1720. The title lasted through five generations. It lapsed upon the celibacy of the fifth Duke of Dorset, Charles Sackville-Germain, a cousin of the fourth Duke. The last Duke, who died in 1843, had never possessed nor lived at Knole, so he had no connection with Kent. He was a man of 'irregular habits', but as he was a friend of both George IV and William IV, he must have been of a tolerant and flexible disposition.

The history of the Sackville family subsequently became entangled with lawsuits, owing perhaps to the ever-increasing skein of marriages within the ranks of the English nobility. A daughter of the third Duke of Dorset married the fifth Earl de la Warr, whose family name was West; he assumed the name of Sackville as well. Their descendants fell out over the succession to the barony of Sackville and possession of Knole. The reader would find it tedious to follow these family disputes. The first Baron Sackville (his title being a creation by Queen Victoria to fill the gap left by the last Duke) also had a notorious quarrel with the public of Sevenoaks, over the use of a right-of-way through the park at Knole. He shut it, because the privilege was abused by people who trespassed off the footpath, defied the keepers and frightened the deer. The rowdies besieged the great house and swore they would hang Lord Sackville, and a guard of 80 police had to be brought along.

After this touch of drama, the family history was lightened by one of romance. Lionel Sackville-West, the second Baron Sackville, was the fifth son of the Earl de la Warr and his wife, Lady Elizabeth Sackville. One can see how complicated the relationships had become. He was born in 1827 and educated privately. He spent his whole adult life in the diplomatic service. In the course of this distinguished career, he was posted to Madrid in 1864 as Secretary of Legation, and frequently he acted as *Chargé d'Affaires*. He also 'acted' as husband to a Spanish dancer of European fame and humble birth, who bore him several children. Her name was Josefa Ortega, and she was known professionally as Pepita. Her father, dead when she came into Lionel Sackville-West's life, had been a barber in Malaga, married to a powerful peasant woman named Catalina. The eldest of

Pepita's four illegitimate children by Sackville-West was Victoria Josefa. Her beauty and personality captured the heart of her father's nephew, also named Lionel Sackville-West, who came out to Spain as a junior in the diplomatic service. They married, and had a daughter named Victoria Sackville-West whose life and writings are likely to make her, along with her great ancestor Thomas Sackville, the poet and statesman, the most famous of this long line of English aristocrats. She has written a book called *Pepita* which tells with frankness the romantic story of her grand-parents and parents. It is written with an ingenuous dignity, in a prose disciplined by the practice of poetry.

The story, like so many other family tales of the Victorian age, disproves the frequently accepted theory that English society in the nineteenth century was prudish and puritanical. Here is Victoria Sackville-West's account: 'My grandfather had been Minister at Washington for seven peaceful years, from 1881 to 1888, before events suddenly rushed at him and changed the course of his destiny. My grandfather, as I have indicated, was by nature a peace-loving and indeed a lazy man who liked to have everything arranged for him and did not want to be bothered. Considering the very unconventional private life he had led, running parallel to the most conventional of professions, he had succeeded with remarkable skill in achieving his desire. He had managed to keep Pepita as his mistress and Queen Victoria as his employer concurrently for nearly twenty years. Then, when he had lost Pepita, he had managed to get his illegitimate daughter sent out to look after him, and not only allowed himself and his Legation to be run by her but observed with detached amusement the whole fastidious society of Washington accepting this irregular situation.' It was not this matter of domestic irregularity which broke his career in the diplomatic service. His mistake was in writing a letter to a con man who before a Presidential election wrote pretending to ask his advice about voting, the man posing as an Englishman naturalised as an American.

The reply to this decoy appears to be completely innocuous; but to a layman untrained in diplomatic diction, the American Government's reaction to the British *Chargé d'Affaire*'s polite response is quite incomprehensible, except that for some unknown reason the White House may have wanted to get rid of Lionel Sackville-West, whose methods of protocol could have been too languid and amateur, in the English *grand manner*. The reason could not have been that the illegitimacy of his official hostess was a cause, for she had run the social affairs of the Embassy with an astonishing expertise, and her personality had seemingly triumphed in American high society. Her daughter's description of her explains why:

She was lovely, ingenuous, and irresistably charming. I hope I shall not be accused of prejudice if I say that my mother was a truly beautiful woman. No photograph or portrait ever showed her as she was, for no photograph or portrait could indicate the changes of her expression or the extraordinary sweetness of her smile. If ever the phrase 'turn one's heart to water' meant anything, it meant when my mother looked at you and smiled. I, of course, remember her only in her middle years and her old age, for she was already thirty when I was born, but those who knew her as a girl and a young woman unanimously tell me that seldom have they known such charm allied to such beauty. One of them added, 'It really wasn't fair. She did exactly what she liked with everybody.' That dark hair, those dark blue eyes, that marvellously curving mouth, those lovely hands and expressive gestures, that broken English, that mixture of innocence and imperiousness—Washington was at her feet, and Mrs Russell Selfridge, who still refused to receive her, found herself in a minority of one.

In her later life, the imperiousness was to take command and to become eccentricity, with results that make the later chapter of Vita Sackville-West's book all the more enchanting to read, but they must have been embarrassing to her family, for 'innocent though she was, she had a will of her own and no hesitation about exercising it.'

The result of the Diplomatic *faux-pas* was that the White House demanded the withdrawal of the British representative, which distressed Lord Salisbury, our Prime Minister at that time. Fortunately, Lionel's brother died a month after the incident, and the younger man succeeded to to the barony. This enabled him to offer his resignation without appearing to have been kicked out by the American Government. His brilliant daughter supervised the public auction of the furniture and effects of the Legation. Her daughter wrote 'Two thousand five hundred cards of admission had to supplemented by a further five hundred before the sale had even begun. The reserve prices which had been fixed by my mother—who was not Catalina's (the Spanish peasant) grand-daughter for nothing—were in most cases far exceeded.' I should think, too, that the inheritance of shrewdness from those two ancestors who had both been Chancellors of the Exchequer, played a part in that enterprise.

Father and daughter came home to Knole, but not immediately, for some months were spent in France while the late Baron's will was sorted out, at great expense in legal fees, because he had left his personal estate to be equally divided between the Queen's four maids-of-honour, his intention being to disguise to which one he had been attached. Complicated love affairs, tangled with results deriving from the *droit de seigneur*, are commonplace amongst the aristocracy everywhere in the world; and not only amongst the aristocracy, but where great riches and property are involved, the consequences are more exaggeratedly apparent.

Once such consequence, on a vast scale, hit the Sackville-West family. One of Pepita's four children was a son, who since 1896 had been claiming that his mother's relationship with Lord Sackville had been legalised by marriage. The case dragged on until 1910, and it cost the family some forty thousand pounds. A page, alleged to contain the evidence of the marriage and also alleged to have been torn out of the register, was involved; a perfect ingredient of a stage melodrama. The story is told vividly in *Pepita*, and it ends with a description of the triumphant return home to Knole, after the verdict in favour of the Sackville family. The case had roused as much public interest and excitement as the Tichborne case some twenty years earlier, over a claim by a man named Orton to be the son and heir of Sir Roger Tichborne, recently deceased. Orton had even persuaded the widow to recognise him as her son.

Vita Sackville-West describes how her parents abandoned their car at the foot of Tubb's Hill and

transferred ourselves into the victoria, that chic little victoria which my father had once given to my mother as a Christmas present, with its smart little pair of cobs, driven by our incomparable coachman Bond, who wore his top-hat at an angle a Regency dandy might envy and who had a figure that any Savile Row tailor might have been proud to dress. Where were the *chulos* of Madrid in their automobile caps, trying to bribe Don Ricardo Doreemocea in the taverns; trying to get him to tear leaves out of marriage registers ? . . . I wished Pepita could have been in the victoria with us to share the fun. She was very vivid to me just then, for her photographs had been in all the papers. She would, I felt, have enjoyed it. I enjoyed it myself. Never, before or since, have I felt so much like royalty. . . . For once in one's life it is quite an amusing experience, on arriving at the top of the hill to have the horses taken out of the traces, and to be pulled by the local fire-brigade through the main streets of Sevenoaks and then right through the park up to Knole, with cheering crowds all the way and carefully coached children presenting bouquets at intervals. And then, finally, being pulled right through the first courtyard at Knole, when normally one had always drawn up outside.

And she cleverly brings this local glory down to earth by ending her chapter with a description of the ugly, stinking oil lamp, so dear as a symbol of home, by whose light they sat down to dinner that night at Knole, the great country palace with its 365 rooms and its 52 staircases, the mighty relic of a way of life which had given its last flicker with that touch of feudal homage, and that smoky lamp's flame.

The girl was 18 years of age at that time in 1910. We know what a handsome addition she must have made to the picture of that carriage drawn by the pair of cobs, for only a year earlier the fashionable portrait painter de Laszlo had portrayed her. The picture hangs now in the library of her last home, Sissinghurst Castle, where she died on 2 June 1962.

What, however, is her claim to appear among some immortals native to Kent? My answer might be disputed by some latterday literary critics in the second half of the twentieth century, for I recall that one of these so-called 'modernists', when reviewing a volume of Sir Harold Nicolson's Diaries in one of the Sunday newspapers, expressed wonder at Sir Harold's admiration of his wife's poetry (the critic called it 'verse', with an inferred expletive) while being so fastidious and sophisticated in his literary taste. I read that review with dismay, for I recalled that this short-sighted and prejudiced critic had written novels which had given me much pleasure. So I will not name him, though when I read that review, and the irrelevant sneer at Vita Sackville-West's poetry, I sympathised with Robert Browning, who was alleged to have gone and stamped on the grave of Edward Fitzgerald, because that crusty bachelor had disparaged the poetry of Elizabeth Barrett Browning.

Victoria Sackville-West remained throughout her life, with complete unselfconsciousness, an old-world aristocrat. She had a territorial passion for land and visible money; an emotion which aristocrats shared with their peasants. This proud inheritance of a static way of life was augmented by the strain of Spanish peasant blood which also added to her personal beauty, giving a shadowy bloom to her features, and a slow grace to her movements and her speech. The resultant quality of grandeur distinguished her from her contemporaries, even her social equals, most of whom today do their best to abase themselves to the tastes and practices of democracy. She remained in a cordial isolation which would have been at Knole, had she been a male to inherit that magnificent show-piece. But she had to remain in Kent, and most of her married life was spent there, with almost unwilling excursions out of England, and out of the beloved county in which she was so deeply rooted.

She took little active part in promoting her husband's career. As diplomat and politician he had to try and make his way in those fields alone, and he failed. Yet her devotion to him was made apparent by the letters written to him and published in the three volumes of his Diaries, edited by his son. Even in those candid books she remains aloof, static, a feudal monument, monolithic in the modern world. Yet with this, she emitted a generous warmth, like the good earth at evening after a hot summer day. She smouldered with benevolence: a deep love of the things of nature, the relics of past English history, because her ancestors had acted in its major parts and she had entered the last chapter of that phase of the drama. She had many friends; but the friends came to her, to sit with her in her tall rose-red brick tower at Sissinghurst Castle, or walk with her in the famous garden which she had clothed with abundance over the design on which her husband had planned it. In a curious way, as it were by correspondence rather than by domestic contact, the unique couple made a harmonious marriage; and after death, both have left a memorial of it, not only in their literary achievement, which is considerable, but in the legend of their personalities, and the enigma of their happy union.

One of her most celebrated friends, Virginia Woolf, tried to portray her in a fictional fantasy called 'Orlando'. It is a study in sexual ambiguity, nervously beautiful in its mystical inflexions. But the aloofness which it conveys is more the unjustified and contemptible aloofness of the so-called Bloomsbury set than the massive, earthy seclusion in which Vita Sackville-West was enclosed by the nature of her birth, and her strange up-bringing. She had no literary sense of superiority. She wrote her books as she cultivated her garden, moved by a quiet but constant appetite for both activities, which were in essence, the same activity.

She had many interests, but they were all subordinated to her preoccupation with the history of her famous family, which she symbolised in the house where she was born. Her marriage to Harold Nicolson in 1913 took her abroad to Persia, where he was posted for some years in the diplomatic service, following in his father's footsteps. While there, she wrote the most local of her books, the bucolic poem, *The Land*. It is likely to survive as her most characteristic and memorable work.

Her first published books, however, were novels, whose themes varied between romance and symbolical realism. Poetic sensibility warmed her prose in these early works, and the fusion was made complete in her book *Knole and the Sackvilles*. The poet, the historian, and the storyteller were unified. This book, which appeared in 1922, when she was thirty, was the seed-bed of a novel called *The Edwardians* written eight years later. It was followed immediately, as though in contrition for the exposure of Edwardian smart-set spiritual shabbiness in the earlier novel, by *All Passion Spent*, in which social and political responsibility are portrayed, to suggest a counter-balance of the pseudo-Restoration atmosphere of the Edwardian Court and rich upper-class society in the decade before the first world war.

The Land, published in 1926, found immediate recognition and was awarded the Hawthornden Prize. When Vita Sackville-West's *Collected Poems, Volume One* appeared in 1934, I discussed *The Land* at the end of a review in *The New Statesman*, and suggested its Virgilian affinities, qualities already brought into English poetry by Cowper and Thomas Gray, whose diction with its eighteenth-century formality so patently influenced Vita's style, and set the nostalgic tone of all her verse. I said, 'She can offer us a line such as

> The sower with his gesture like a gift.

and

> Exalted, deathly, silent and alone.

All these examples are most characteristic of this poet. Their technique (notice the lovely use of the labial in the last) is an emanation of the very spirit of the person who creates it; betraying her cultural origins and also the hand-touch, lips, eyes, and hair-perfume of her spirit. As in Gray, the aloofness, the convention, only attract attention to the shyness they are intended to disguise. The failure becomes one of the excellences of the poet's style; savouring the poetic dish with a touch of intrigue, of duplicity more innocent than naivety can ever be. Such the circumstances, such the character, which make *The Land* one of the most complete and beautiful bucolics written in English. It is so satisfying a poem that one tends to neglect her other work, and to reread it again and again, just as one lingers before a landscape dear by association and present beauty; lingers, perhaps, when one should be gone, to fight one's way in the word of today and to-morrow.'

The criticism implied in my last words, written in 1934, was that nostalgia for the feudal way of life, into which she had been born, might finally enclose her within a mannersim alien to the taste of the younger generations in the twentieth century. But she published little more verse, other than a sequel to *The Land*, a tamer piece called *The Garden*. She turned to biography and wrote *Saint Joan of Arc* in 1936 and *Pepita* a year later. Meanwhile, she had found another and larger public in her writings about gardening, a steady discourse in the press around her work in making the famous garden at Sissinghurst Castle in Kent. These articles, collected into book-form have a permanent public. While giving practical advice, they exhale the scent of poetry; the colours of her garden, the hue of her personality. That last is difficult to describe. Perhaps a postscript to a letter written by Rudyard Kipling about Vita Sackville-West's mother, might also be applied to the daughter. He said

On mature reflection, *the* most wonderful person I have ever met. And to think of that indomitable flame burning through all the dark years in those five acres of Knole buildings! And like all organisers of the highest type with no traces of pressure and apparently time in which to do personally kind things to the merest stranger. It's outside all my experiences and of a type to which I know no duplicate.

The interest in biography matured with *The Eagle and the Dove*, in which Saint Teresa of Avila, that powerful and organising intellectual mystic, is compared with the naive, child-like Saint Teresa of Lisieux. As a counterpart to her life of St Joan of Arc she wrote *Daughter of France*, a life of La Grande Demoiselle. Her interest was always drawn to women who broke out of the bondage of femininity, which had so affected her own life by depriving her of the possession of Knole, the great house whose history, and whose wealth of contents, were a major obsession in her life. It was this lifelong preoccupation which brought her back to Kent and anchored her there. She made Sissinghurst a symbol of the greater domain, and lived there for the later part of her life, from 1930 until her death in 1962, only reluctantly going out into the world and the surge of the twentieth century.

The power of her personality did not wither, for kindness nourished it, and gave it the means of expressing itself in her garden, where she welcomed visitors, both friends and strangers, with an autumnal geniality that remained regal even when her body was humiliated by cancer. She wrote her own epitaph in a poem called *Testament*, which may be quoted also as a memorial to a great family, which rose like a Kentish oak in the landscape of English history, and has remained there for four hundred years:

> And, like the ashes I was wont to save
> Preciously from the hearth beneath my fire,
> Lighten the soil with mine. Not, not the grave!
> I loved the soil I fought, and this is my desire.

The Sidneys of Penshurst

IN ANOTHER book, I have discussed the dominance of the gentry, rather than the nobility, in Kent, especially during the difficult years of the Civil War. I inferred that this structure of the administrative machinery of the country made Kent different from the rest of the English shires; a difference which began with the resistance to Duke William of Normandy in 1066, when the imposition of the Feudal System was rejected, and the rule of land tenure known as Gavelkind was retained. A man named Hawke wrote some verses in 1778 explaining this ancient fold-custom of Gavelkind. Here they are.

> Custom in Kent encouraging the brave,
> Distinguished well the brother from the slave,
> And to each son an equal portion gave.
> With just regard, since the same amorous fire
> Caused the last birth, that did the first inspire.
> The generous youth, pleased with such equal laws,
> Fought for their honour, and their Country's cause,
> With such resistence that the French Brigade
> Which conquered Harold, durst not Kent invade;
> But solemn peace with oaken squadrons made,
> Granted those laws for which the patriot strove,
> And kissed the Gospel to the moving grove.

But perhaps I have made too much of this, for a critic may rightly point out that as time passed, the influence and authority of the Crown were bound to intrude, because of the proximity of Kent to the capital, London, and to the fact that the county was always a corridor to France and subject to a constant social osmosis. Kent has also been enviously rich in natural resources; mineral, sylvan, coastal and scenic. From prehistoric times, adventurers coming into Kent were frequently inclined to settle here rather than to explore further. Why not, with such persuasive natural attraction of downland, wealden woods, fertile soils, and wealth of iron ore in the subsoil?

So too, powerful figures in the central government, and newly rich commercial characters—wool merchants, lawyers, and other astute members of the gradually increasing middle-class urbanites—have come to Kent as acquisitive men come after a woman possessed of both beauty and wealth. Thus the long-settled minor gentry of the county have tended to acquire more sophisticated, cosmopolitan and often more cultured neighbours, many of them recipients of royal bounty, lands seized from the Church at the dissolution of the monasteries in the sixteenth century. Great houses arose, among the small manors, and they expanded architecturally as their families grew more powerful and richer in national rather than county expansions.

Cobham Hall, in north Kent near Gravesend, is a typical example. Here is a magnificent palace which began as a Kentish manor house about the year 1300 A.D. as 'a messuage with garden worth 6s. 8d. per annum.' It was the home of a John de Cobham, one of the local gentry who was little more than a freehold farmer. But half a century later there was a Lord Cobham, who must have flourished, maybe by activities extra to the cultivation of his small estate. And the house grew accordingly. This family's name was Brooke. The Brookes of Cobham remained rooted there, as firm as the gigantic oaks, one of which may still be seen near the mansion. But when the Stuarts came south, something went wrong with the fortunes and speculations, both political and financial, of the house of Brooke. A Henry, Lord Cobham and his brother George were attainted on a charge of treason, with Henry losing his estate and George his head. Thus the Crown stepped in, a grim forerunner of the Inland Revenue Department. King James a few years later gave the property to his cousin Lodowick Stuart, the Duke of Lennox and also Earl of Darnley. This family held the estate until very recently, since the second world war, when the mansion became a girls' school.

The Duke of Lennox was not content to inhabit it as it had been lived in by the long-rooted gentry, the Brookes. He pulled down the centre and commissioned the leading architect of the day, Inigo Jones, to build a magnificent substitute and façade between the two wings. All that is left of the original Brooke family in Kent, or at least of its former substantiality, is a brass in Cobham Church, which says

> Dame Jone de Cobeham gist ici
> Dieu de sa Alme eyt merci
> Ki ke pur alme priera
> Quarante jours de pardoun auera.

Cobham is but one of several manors which grew out of their local setting into national, and sometimes even international fame and grandeur. I think of Knole, the great congeries of medieval and Tudor brickwork, with its 365 rooms and 52 staircases, home of the Sackville family for the last 400 years. But I have discussed some members of that family elsewhere in these pages.

Of the courtiers, diplomats, politicians, who have trod the stage of history and acquired power and wealth, subsequently to display it in Kent, the Sidney family is one of the most outstanding. They have been neighbours of the Sackvilles, settling in the county round about the same time, when the further waves of the Renaissance reached our island, and the Reformation whipped them up into storms that shook the foundations of our social structure.

Penshurst, the seat of the Sidneys, was never a manor home of one of those Anglo-Saxon families who defied William the Conqueror. It was built in the mid-fourteenth century by one Sir John de Pulteney, a middle-class merchant from London, who no doubt made his fortune in the woollen industry, then the main source of our national wealth, thanks to King Edward the Third's shrewd idea of manufacturing the wool into cloth instead of exporting all of it raw to the Low Countries. Flemish weavers were invited here to set up looms. They came and stayed, bringing not only the skill but their wealth and their much greater culture with them. Kent and East Anglia profited thereby. Their weaving houses, and many of the rebuilt churches in Kent, Cranbrook for example, survive as witnesses of this great advance in our island civilization.

Penshurst is a noble building, more austere and dignified than Knole. Pulteney was licensed by King Edward III to embattle it with walls of chalk and stone. It has been added to since, even as late as during the nineteenth century, but its simplicity is unimpaired. Ben Jonson, one of the many poets invited to Penshurst during its early years in the hands of the Sidneys, aptly described the house:

> Thou art not, Penshurst, built to envious show,
> Of touch, or marble; nor canst boast a row
> Of polished pillars, or a roof of gold;
> Thou hast no lantern, whereof tales are told;
> Of stairs, or courts; but stand'st an ancient pile,
> And, these grudged at, are reverenced the while.

The first we hear of the Sidney family is that a Sir William Sidney was a courtier in the entourage of King Henry VIII. He had a brilliant son named Henry, whose administrative ability won him the onerous distinction of being sent out to Ireland as Lord Deputy. In all such posts, 'deputy' means the man on the spot who does the work, while his official chief takes the credit. However, Sir Henry had also been brought up at Court as the companion of Prince Edward, who afterwards maintained his foster-brotherhood. There must have been a permanent strain of charm as well as ability in the Sidney blood. Edward, while King for so short a time, made several grants of land to Sir Henry. Amongst them was the manor of Penshurst. Sir Henry further consolidated his position by marrying his sister Frances to his Chief in Ireland, the Earl of Sussex, a reluctant Governor of that wild island. By a combination of military skill and political persuasiveness, Sir Henry patched up a semblance of peacefulness in Ireland. He was then appointed President of the Welsh Marches, and for some years he lived in Ludlow Castle. Fresh troubles in Ireland during the reign of Queen Elizabeth caused Sidney to be sent back there as Lord Governor, where once again he gradually restored order, not without severity.

In 1571, however, he left Ireland, disgruntled by the Queen's lack of appreciation of his loyal work and statesmanship; but four years later, and for the third time, he returned, the Queen having restored his confidence by a flash of her political genius in his direction.

In the course of these official activities, he married, in 1551, Mary, the daughter of John Dudley, Duke of Northumberland, by whom he had a large family of three sons and four daughters. His eldest son was the immortal Sir Philip Sidney, and his second was Robert, later to become the Earl of Leicester. His daughter Mary married Henry Herbert, Earl of Pembroke, thus uniting two families destined to literary fame. A century later, a younger son of the family, the Reverend George Herbert, was to write some of the most beautiful religious poetry in the English language.

Thus we have the nucleus of the Sidney family which during Sir Henry's active career made its headquarters at Penshurst. It has remained there to this day, for the present owner, Lord de Lisle, is also a Philip Sidney, a gallant soldier who won the Victoria Cross in the last world war, and has since been Governor General of Australia. He refers to Penshurst Place as 'my house'. Such simplicity signifies deep roots, which the bull-dozers of modernity have not yet disturbed.

For some years, the present writer lived within a few miles of Penshurst, before moving further into Kent. They were impressionable years of young manhood, when environment puts an indelible mark upon one's personality. Decades later, Penshurst haunts me still; a serene benevolence, 'a green thought in a green shade'. This quiet rural authority of place has gone down the ages and is as potent as ever. Poet after poet has gravitated there, Ben Jonson among them. So did his contemporary Michael Drayton, who des-cribed its sylvan setting in his long and, alas, rather tedious topographical poem *Polyalbion*, written in hexameters, always a somnolent metre in English.

At all times of the year, I would find myself lingering in the park, some-times re-visiting the house to brood and day-dream over the pictures and furniture, much of which was given by Queen Elizabeth to her favourite the Earl of Leicester. One summer afternoon I sat on a fallen oak in the park looking toward the front of the house. I had been reading a biography of Sir Philip Sidney written by a Kentish man, C. Henry Warren, a native of Mereworth, only a few miles away. Halfway out of my day-dream, I took my notebook from my jacket pocket, and wrote the following lines, while ephemerids flickered around the pages, and several cows drew doubtfully near, their bovine curiosity aroused by so static a figure.

Sidney's Love
Is it not sad to think
Of Penelope Devereux,
Child-love, as it were,
Of a man whose word and act
Will never be forgotten
Till time itself shall sink
With fable and with fact,
Finally confused and rotten
In the sedimentary floor
Of earth bereaved and bare
Even of its cloak of air,
And mankind is no more?

He met her, we are told,
When she was twelve years old,
A tousled little thing
With hair a fiery red;
But a voice which even then,
Were she induced to sing,
Would make men drop their swords
And clinking cups to listen;
Such is man's thrall to words,
Especially when they fasten
Their magic to the sound
Of a human throat endowed
By some freak will of the gods
With music never found
In the rest, the speaking clods
Who fill Court, Theatre, Church,
Nor know that what they touch
With verbiage, they smirch.

Also he heard her laughter,
Through the halls of Kenilworth
It suddenly would break
Bounds, piercing decorum through
With innocence and mirth,
That happiness which hovers
On the brink of knowledge, when
Still undeclared as lovers,
Hesitant girls and men
Shun love, for love's own sake;
To succumb the moment after.

'Biting my truant pen,'
Sir Philip Sidney wrote
'Beating my breast for spite'
—This in a perfect sonnet—
He stared at that singing throat,
And knew that if he won it
He were blinded from too much light.

As for the child, she felt
The magnet in his eye.
The spirit in her knelt.
Her soul was prepared to die,
If soul *can* die, to give
That recognition scope
To cling, and clinging, live,
And living, feed on hope.

> Neither dared speak, the Queen
> And a shallow-hearted brother,
> —But not too shallow to hate—
> All-powerful at that time,
> Were watching. And once seen
> By that sovereign, golden eye,
> Who knows what the crime
> And punishment had been?
> Sir Philip, foreseeing fate,
> Let pass the cup to another.

With that interlude, too intimate in tone perhaps, I have hinted at a love affair which never ripened, not so much because of the Queen's pretended monopoly in such matters, but because the lovely girl did not in fact respond, and later married elsewhere, first and unhappily to Lord Rich, and secondly to her true sweetheart, Charles Blount. But Philip's attraction was never forgotten, and later he consolidated it by his famous sonnet sequence *Astrophel and Stella*, though he was then married to the daughter of the Ambassador in Paris, Sir Francis Walsingham, under whom he worked. This Sir Francis was also the founder of the powerful Secret Service which served Elizabeth so well in her elaborate foreign manipulations.

Penshurst Place must have been a remote Arcadia when Philip Sidney was born there on the 29 or 30 November 1544. It has that magic about it even today, now that most great country houses, and their estates, have been deprived of their privacy by the demands of an ever-proliferating democracy. But from the point of view of general justice, there are compensations today. Our modern social conscience, for instance, would not tolerate what Philip's father did in the boy's tenth year. He appointed him lay rector of a place called Whitford, in distant Flintshire, and put in a deputy to fulfil the duties of the post. Philip drew the revenue of the benefice for the rest of his life. No doubt this sort of thing goes on today, in one sphere and another, but it is frowned on, even if it serves a good purpose, such as supplying a sinecure to a man of genius whose creative ability is not financially remunerative, so that he needs rentier support. The community, through the State, makes grants on the grand scale to millions of students today; and not all of them are potential Sir Philip Sidneys.

In the same year that he received this 'grant', Philip was entered at Shrewsbury School, in October, on the same day as another boy named Fulke Greville, with whom he formed a lasting friendship, and ensured a faithful biographer. What might be called tributary literature, which was

Greville's contribution, broke through again in this family some three hundred years later, when Charles Cavendish Fulke Greville, whose family by that time had been granted the Earldom of Warwick, bequeathed a diary, or journal, to posterity, which has added much detail to the history of the governing stratum of Regency and early Victorian England.

The schoolboy friendship with Greville was symptomatic of the enriched relationships which filled Sidney's life. With one exception, there is no record of anybody having disliked him, or been unenchanted by his personality, his rare gifts as poet, diplomat, soldier, courtier (though a reluctant one), and a man of spiritual sensibility. His name still stands as a symbol of heroic conduct in that Age of Chivalry of which he was a lingering survival, prior to the coming of the more flagrantly commercial society which has survived until today, as we see it in its decadence, dangerously brittle because of the technological weapons it wields.

In 1568, when he was fourteen, Sidney was sent to Christ Church, Oxford, while Greville entered Pembroke College. Two new friends were drawn into this magnetic orbit; Richard Hakluyt and William Camden, both writers whose work has survived the attrition of time. Hakluyt wrote the account of the Elizabethan voyagers, at that time in the forefront of public excitement. Camden was one of the first of our antiquarians.

Sidney was possessed of a passion for learning, but he combined this with a lively activity in archery and wall tennis (an importation from France). He became a stylist in Latin and French. This all-round ability was later referred to by Greville, who wrote 'Though I knew him from a child, yet I never knew him other than a man: with such staidness of mind, lovely and familiar gravity as carried grace and reverence above greater years.'

Even so, Sidney did not graduate at Oxford, for when he was seventeen, plague broke out at the university and his college closed down. His father, and the Earl of Leicester (whose heir he was) decided to send him abroad to enlarge his education. The Queen's permission had to be granted, for the Tudors were absolute monarchs, 'little fathers' in the manner of the Tzars of Russia. He went first to Paris, where Sir Francis Walsingham, the Queen's Ambassador, introduced him to the King and Court. The magic worked again. His charm and abilities caused the King of France to give him an honorary post. At that time France was roughly divided into two halves, Catholic and Protestant. The marriage of the King's sister Margaret of Valois to Henry of Navarre was intended to unite the factions. Philip assisted at the ceremony as one of the young King's attendants. Henry also had fallen under the spell. He was later to become the great Henry IV, but not too great to treat Philip 'like an equal in nature and fit for friendship with a king.'

No sooner was the marriage completed, than the French King Charles' mother, Catherine of Medici, contrived the massacre of the Huguenots, thousands of whom had flocked to Paris for the Protestant wedding. The whole of France went mad, and 50,000 people were murdered. Catherine was congratulated by Pope Gregory XIII, who had a commemorative medal struck.

Walsingham, a cautious English realist, Machiavellian in his political technique, despatched young Sidney to Germany, as he was responsible for the young man's safety.

This continued sojourn abroad was not solely to enlarge Sidney's education. Before he left England, he had spent some time at Court, and his father, thinking of his future career in politics, an activity at that time controlled by family affiliations, had got the boy betrothed to Anne, the daughter of Sir William Cecil, the Queen's most powerful minister. But for some reason unknown to history, the match was broken off and the girl married Edward de Vere, the Earl of Oxford. This man was a quarrelsome bully, a typical Renaissance villain, and it was he who, some time later, was to be the cause of Sidney's temporary sequestration from Elizabeth's Court, a setback which proved to be a blessing, since it caused him to withdraw to the home of his sister Mary, Countess of Pembroke, at Wilton, where he had sufficient leisure to be able to write, with her assistance, what may be called the first novel in the English language, the meandering romance called *Arcadia*.

With a tutor named Dr Watson, who later became Bishop of Winchester, Sidney left Paris and stayed for some months in Lorraine, whence he moved on to the great free city of Frankfurt-on-Main. Until the second world war this city maintained its medieval gothic character, with its narrow streets, its rich merchants' mansions, its *Rathaus* (the crown of Germanic architectural genius), and the birthplace of Goethe, whose father was the Burgomaster, a position comparable to that of the Doge of Venice. Post-war restoration has done its worst in Frankfort, with concrete blocks of offices laid across the historical alleys. Cologne, on the other hand, which suffered even worse, has been restored with a touch of gaiety and good taste. What dreadful authority municipal councils can have, especially when they are composed by a majority of cheese-paring philistines, ignorant of the significance of past history, and impermeable to aesthetic influence.

In Frankfurt Sidney lodged in the house of a famous printer, Andrew Mechel, and there met Hubert Languet, a humanist who supported the Protestant cause, as had Erasmus and Melancthon earlier in the century, giving philosophic support to Luther's more rumbustious campaign which was to split Middle Europe and give rise to the Thirty Years' War. The acquaintance with Languet ripened quickly into friendship, and the two men went together to Vienna. They parted in the autumn, when Sidney left for Italy, but both undertook to write to each other. Letter writing in those days, when books were still scarce, was the main vehicle of the art of literature. Languet, a Burgundian, had been a wandering scholar, studying at one European university after another, discoursing and debating learnedly on the arts of government, what today we call 'P.P.E.'

The survival of the friendship for the rest of Sidney's life added greatly to his cultural wisdom, which, but for his early death on the battlefield, would certainly have blossomed into statesmanship that might have made the transition from the Tudor to the Stuart dynasties less violently disturbing to the social structure of our English constitution. He might, for example, have been sent back to Ireland to further, and improve upon, his father's constructive work, whose lack of completion still makes havoc there today. Languet said of him 'The day on which I beheld him shone propitious upon me.'

This nonpareil was still only nineteen, in 1573, when he came to Italy and settled in Venice. While he stayed there he sat for his portrait to Paolo Veronese, who was working in the monastery of St Sebastian, where his uncle was prior. Veronese was praised as comparable to the two contemporary giants of Venetian art, Titian and Tintoretto. He was forty-five, at the height of his exuberant genius for capturing visual effects, when he portrayed Sidney, a work commissioned by Languet.

During these travels, Sidney had sent home what we would now call despatches in the diplomatic bag. They were addressed to Lord Burghley, at that time the *eminence grise* of international politics, with the help of Sir Francis Walsingham and his efficiently organised secret service. Walsingham saw in these despatches a tendency to sympathy with the Catholic cause and he persuaded the Queen to command the young diplomat to return home. Sidney contrived, however, to put in some study at Padua, at that time one of the largest and most famous universities in the Western

World. He worked there at music, philosophy and science with such absorbed enthusiasm that his friend and mentor Languet begged him to ease off somewhat. He replied 'I am never so little troubled with melancholy as when my mind is employed about something particularly difficult.' This reference to melancholy, a frequent sickness of the adolescent mind, may have led to the preoccupation with religious matters, which Walsingham viewed as an inclination to turn to the Catholic faith.

Sidney was not yet 21 when he returned to England in 1575. He was expected to join the Queen's governing staff at Court. He attached himself to the party of his uncle the Earl of Leicester, a dangerous man because in this favourite, whom the Queen is assumed to have loved, vanity and self-interest predominated over intellect and wisdom. He was no match for the astute Cecil, Lord Burghley.

Soon after Sidney's return, in May, the Court set out on one of the Royal Progresses, in which the monarch was entertained at the expense of those nobles whose estates happened to fall within the scope of the itineraries. These glorious progresses have dwindled away. They are now represented by the Assizes which perambulate the country during the legal term-times, administering justice in a less personal manner, but still in the name of the Sovereign.

The Summer Progress in 1575 had for its last sojourn a visit to Kenilworth Castle, followed by a less official stay at Chartley Castle, the seat of a rising young favourite, the Earl of Essex. There Sidney met the child of twelve, Penelope Devereux, the Earl's sister. The impression made on him is the subject of my poem, the verbal daydream recorded while I sat on a fallen oak in the park in front of Penshurst Place, in the early nineteen-twenties. So human emotions, roused nobody knows how or whence, survive the terms of our physical lives, and continue to reverberate in the consciousness of other individuals, year after year, century after century. Thus the grief of Achilles for Patroclus, the passion of Cleopatra for Antony, still surge down the ages, through the accoustical magic of poetry and history, sisters in the art of perpetuating our human agonies and triumphs, our mischiefs and achievements.

This hopeless love, probably no more actual than that of Petrarch for Laura, released the pent-up genius which already distinguished Philip Sidney. The most popular outlet for such powers in the sixteenth century, not only in England but throughout Europe, was through literature. Every educated person had something to say in verse, or an ornamental prose hardly to be distinguished from verse. Enough of the vast output has survived to make us look back on the sixteenth century as the Golden Age of English letters. Much of it, nevertheless, is otiose and clumsy, especially the prose. But the first Bible to be printed in English, a translation by Miles Coverdale with the assistance of Tindale, and possibly some cribbing from Wyclif's translation, had been available in every church, at Cromwell's command, since 1539. Its imagery and rhythms formed a ground-base to the elaborate verbal additions to our national literature which were being imported from the French and Italian by the young gentlemen, wandering scholars and diplomats, whose education was not complete without the Grand Tour. So many of them were men of Kentish birth, sons of families whose wealth was steadily increasing by the secularisation of Church property, and the expansion of farming and iron-founding which made Kent at that time the richest county in the kingdom.

Sidney was a prime example of these importers of the culture of the Renaissance. He signalled his return to England with an essay on *An Apology for Poetry*, intended to restore this art of verse to the authoritative position in our cultural life from which it had degenerated since Chaucer established it there more than a century earlier. His purpose was similar to that of Wordsworth and Shelley in their defensive prose essays on the art of poetry when the waves of industrial materialism again threatened to engulf the arts and to destroy their spiritual ascendency.

The most direct effect of his oblation to Penelope Devereux, the little blonde beauty who did not return his affection, was the composition of his sonnet sequence, *Astrophel and Stella*, which he wrote in the mood of literary despair when her family married her to Lord Rich, whose qualities were exemplified by his name. To write a sonnet sequence was in the convention, since Wyatt and Sackville had brought home this concise prosodic form from Italy earlier in the century. It is said to have been first formulated by a monk named Fra Guittone in the hill-town Arezzo, above the lovely lake of Trasimeno, a town already famous in Roman history because it first made the red Samian pottery which during the Empire was used wherever the Legions settled.

The rhyme scheme of the 14 lines of the Petrachan sonnet was changed in our English adaptation, mainly by the influence of Edmund Spenser. He altered the whole structure of the form, from its octave and sextet, to a cluster of three quatrains clenched by a powerful rhyming couplet. The result is less sensitive, less reflective and philosophic, and more impulsive and dramatic. Both forms have survived, and are still used today, though I remember that T. S. Eliot once said to me, in the years before he became so well known, that he found it no longer possible to read sonnets, or to write them. But the form is still able to rise to the Great Occasion, in the hands of even a moderately inspired master of verse. I doubt, however, if a long sonnet sequence today would find a publisher, except at the author's expense.

Of Sidney's contribution, the sonnet universally known is the following:

> My true love hath my heart, and I have his;
> By just exchange, one for the other given.
> I hold his dear, and mine he cannot miss:
> There never was a better bargain driven.
>
> His heart in me, keeps me and him in one;
> My heart in him, his thoughts and senses guides:
> He loves my heart, for once it was his own;
> I cherish his, because in me it bides.
>
> His heart his wound received from my sight;
> My heart was wounded, with his wounded heart,
> For as from me, on him his hurt did light,
> So still me thought in me his hurt did smart:
>
> Both equal hurt, in this change sought our bliss.
> My true love hath my heart, and I have his.

That is a pretty fancy, characteristic of the mode which began a millenium and a half earlier in Sicily with the poetry of Theocritus; a sophistication of rustic simplicity which developed into the Italian and French elaborations reflecting the Age of Chivalry, a secular offshoot of Mariolatry, or maybe even the primaeval worship of woman as the spring of life, figured in the sea-born Aphrodite who landed at Paphos in Cyprus, a marvellous symbol of the biological fact of the evolution of living creatures from the salt ocean.

Also Theocritan is Sidney's poetry about nature, and the embodiment of it in his native Penshurst. His expression of his love still can be empathetically understood today, because the scene which he celebrates is very little changed, even by the intrusion of the motor-car and the revelries of the tourist trade. Can we not at once recognise the following evocation?

> O sweet woods, the delight of solitariness,
> O how much I do like your solitariness!

Where man's mind hath a freed consideration
Of goodness to receive lovely direction;
Where senses do behold the order of heavenly host,
And wise thought to behold what the Creator is.
Contemplation here holdeth his only seat,
Bounded with no limits, borne with a wing of hope,
Climbs even unto the stars; Nature is under it.
Nought disturbs thy quiet, all to thy service yields;
Each sight draws on a thought (thought, mother of science);
Sweet birds do grant harmony unto thee;
Fair trees' shade is enough fortification,
Nor danger to thyself if be not in thyself.

Those last lines are the index of a great man, rich in moral intuition and intellectual power, truly 'bounded with no limits'. The recognition of his genius was instant, wherever he went, at home and abroad. History has recorded only one occasion where devotion and respect were not offered him. I have referred to it above, but it was so exceptional that it should be told in more detail.

Sidney was playing wall tennis one day with a friend, during attendance at Greenwich Palace, when Edward de Vere, the Earl of Oxford, an arrogant and quarrelsome character, walked on to the court, interrupted the game and demanded that Sidney should give way for him to play. The demand was made so offensively that Sidney declined, whereupon Lord Oxford lost his temper and called Sidney a 'young puppy'. This was in the hearing of some French gentlemen in the train of the Duke of Anjou, the brother of the King of France, over here to conduct marriage negotiations with Queen Elizabeth (a prolonged ploy which the Queen was conducting solely for political reasons). It may have been that Lord Oxford was deliberately rude to Sidney because he was of the party at Court who favoured the match with Anjou, while Sidney followed his uncle the Earl of Leicester, who wanted no such tip-over in the delicate matter of the European Balance of Power. Whatever the cause, Sidney challenged Lord Oxford, an action forbidden within the Royal Precincts. The quarrel was reported to the Queen, who commanded Sidney to withdraw his challenge, and to realise the difference in degree between a gentleman and a nobleman. She said that to neglect this would 'teach the peasant to insult both'; a remark that throws an unromantic light on the relationships between the classes in those glorious days of the Golden Age of Chivalry. The 'folk', both rustic and urban, were beginning to feel their power, and indeed had never lost an opportunity of demonstrating it, especially in Kent, as for instance, when in the reign of Richard II the Archbishop of Canterbury was murdered by the mob that surged up from the county to the Tower of London.

The duel was cancelled, and Sidney sent away to cool off, not seriously in disgrace, for the Queen was as appreciative of his personality as were most of her subjects who came into contact with him. He went down to Wilton, the noble house near Salisbury, the seat of his brother-in-law the Earl of Pembroke, where his beloved sister Mary maintained a centre of culture so wide and so various that it might be compared with the several Italian Ducal Courts whose university cities made Tuscany and Umbria the centre of Western civilization during those fiery centuries when the Christian culture of the Catholic Church was letting its glory pass to the secular genius of the scholars of the Renaissance, who were sustained by the great banking and mercantile families of the free cities of Italy and northern Europe, and international organizations such as the English Merchant Adventurers and the German Hanseatic League.

In our modern way of life with its swift transport and other means of quick communication, we cannot appreciate what a power geographical sequestration could be in a country still sparsely populated. A country house in Tudor England even ten miles from the capital was almost completely cut off in winter, when roads were miry tracks that discouraged all wheeled traffic. The isolation had its advantages. Much of the intensive scholarship fostered in the great houses was due to it. So was the exquisite handicraft. We still enjoy the results of so static a culture, in which the disproportionate wealth of the aristocrats had to be spent on their homes and their personal adornment, in clothes and jewellery. The Queen's vast wardrobe contained some two thousand costumes, whose elaborate and expensive ornamentation must have cost years of skilled labour in the making. The nobility and the gentry, and after them, the increasingly rich merchants and lawyers followed suit. The puritan reaction had not yet begun to dominate the fashions, reducing even the costume of the nobility to an expensive sobriety.

A scrutiny of the portraits of the Elizabethan period, and especially the miniatures of that master, Nicholas Hilliard (c. 1537–1619), shows the incredible extravagance and fantasy of the costume. A glance at the eyes of his sitters also reveals the desperate fear of life in those hazardous days of anarchy, superstition and permanent epidemics. We need to remember also that those garments cost small fortunes, and were worn lifelong, over bodies that were rarely washed. That may be one reason why even our almost legendary knight, Sir Philip Sidney, was said to be facially disfigured by chronic acne.

Sidney retired to Wilton in 1579. He was then 25, but already a proved diplomat. Maybe the Queen somewhat feared his political ability, and wished to play *pianissimo* with him for awhile. He had already met Don John of Austria, the winner of the battle of Lepanto, and exerted his charm in that contact. He had been busy in the Low Countries, trying to promote a league of Protestant States. At Prague he tried to persuade the Emperor of the Holy Roman Empire to head this League in a campaign against Spain and Rome. Failing there, he similarly approached William of Orange, who was so impressed by him that Elizabeth, fearing too precise an entanglement, recalled him to Court, where he at once became active in defending his father against intrigues promoted by the Earl of Ormonde, over Irish affairs. He wrote a detailed minute to the Queen, on the state of things in that troublesome Island whose people then, as now, wanted only to be left to their own devices, no matter how devious as amongst themselves.

While thus engaged, as well as watching events in the Netherlands, he was not neglecting his interest in the arts, especially that of literature. He kept up a constant practice in the art of verse, at that time a wide-spread mania. He also contrived to meet the leading men of letters. In 1578 he made the acquaintance of Edmund Spenser, a London-born civil servant who also wrote a long dissertation on 'The State of Ireland', from the bureaucratic point of view. Spenser dedicated his early poem to Sidney. It was called the *Shepherdes Calender*, and was marked by an addiction to the use of words already archaic, thus reviving branches of our English vocabulary that would otherwise have died with the Anglo-Saxon customs they articulated.

Our contemporary Kentish poet Edmund Blunden followed this practice in his early poetry, with such good effect that the poet Laureate, Robert Bridges, wrote a pamphlet on the value of so fecund a verbal use of the historical imagination. I almost regret that Spenser was not born in Kent, so that I could find an excuse for discussing his genius, and the part it played in forwarding the musical potentialities of the English tongue, exploring every use of the adjective, and creating one of the most valuable verse forms, known as 'the Spenserian Stanza', an adaptation of the Italian *ottava rima*, which he used in his vast allegorical poem *The Faerie Queene*, the latter part of which was lost in manuscript when he hastily fled from

Ireland, after his home was burned by the native Irish, and crossed the Irish
Sea during a violent storm. The Spenserian Stanza has been used by many
poets since.

In 1578, Sidney wrote a masque, *The Lady of the May*, for performance
at Wanstead in Essex, in the grounds of the house of his uncle the Earl of
Leicester, where the Queen was entertained, in an effort to counteract her
displeasure at his marriage to the Countess of Essex, a powerful widow.
The musical ploy failed, and Sidney's retreat to Wilton in 1579 was partly
consequential to his uncle's temporary obscuration. He was also in disgrace
on his own account, for he wrote another over-enthusiastic minute (a weakness of poets when they dabble in diplomacy) setting forth arguments
against the marriage of the Queen to the Duke of Anjou. Her subtle vanity
made her resent this, and his dismissal from Court was partly a reminder
not to teach grandmother how to suck eggs.

Life at Wilton, however, was temporarily idyllic. With his amiable
brother-in-law, and his adored sister, he settled into a bucolic life that
seemed timeless and *legato*. His reaction to it took the form of a prose
romance, endless, sprawling, episodic with intermissions of lyricism. It
might be called one of the first novels in the English language. His passion
for Penelope Devereux, sublimated by her marriage with Lord Rich (as of
Beauty to a genuine Beast) may have stimulated him, as he said, to 'look in
thy heart and write'.

In his earlier essay, *An Apology for Poetry*, he defended the literary
forms of the classical tradition, which dominated French and Italian writing.
But poets' theories do not always coincide with their practice, which has
always a more personal genesis. A contradictory influence of the rich flood
of the Renaissance was that it tumbled and tossed the rules which it had
brought in from the dispersal of the libraries of Byzantium and Alexandria
after the great Arabic culture had taken over the Middle East. The consequent fragmentation of the vast Classical treasury resulted in many vagaries
of thought and experiment in a Europe where the aesthetic as well as the
theological authority of the Catholic Church had been questioned, and in
some parts rejected, by the Reformation, leaving the people hungry for a
new culture.

We see these uncertainties and paradoxes represented in Sidney's prose
fantasia *Arcadia*. He let himself go in this strange work. The French critic
Legouis has called it an arabesque. There is no more fitting word for it. He
mingled with his own fancies and miscellanies of knowledge, and was lost

in the crowd. The pastorals of Theocritus, the chivalries of the *Romance of the Rose*, are called into a story, if so inconsequential a fugue can be called a story, in which the only dominant is a love theme touched with the melancholy that reflected the uncertainties of an age in which monarchical tyranny was becoming more capricious than ever: a mood of despairing submission that was to tincture the arts for centuries to come, under the guise of Romanticism, which became its only means of expostulation against the surrounding uncertainties of individual human fate. *Arcadia* subconsciously voices that protest.

This country invented by the exiled poet is ruled by a King Basileus who brings up his daughters as shepherdesses. All is rustic innocence and happiness. But the outside world (and it is obvious what Sidney meant by that) intrudes in the persons of two princes in disguise, Musidorus and Pyrocles. There follow the most incredible and bewildering complications, in the form of the fashionable trick of one sex posing as its opposite, with consequent absurd love-tangles; devices which Shakespeare used habitually. Wars, treacheries, tortures and the like, add to the entertainment, but always graced with flowers of speech, with a grand finale of love and virtue rewarded and a double marriage bringing down the curtain.

All this sounds obsolete: but the euphuisms and conceits, which were the fashion in Elizabethan literature, are given a personal magic by Sidney, as they were by Spenser. He graces them with wit, as when he says of his princesses that when they undressed at night 'they impoverished their clothes to enrich their bed'. Like Spenser also, he was possessed by visual sensibility and enthusiasm. He used pictures, tapestries, all tactile things, to enhance his imagery. To read *Arcadia* is like walking in a great garden, such as that of Wilton where the book was written. Statues and arbours, lawns and coppices, decorate his prose, with here and there a punctuation of lyrical verse. All appeared in this artificial landscape with overwhelming frequency and lavish placing. The book certainly overwhelmed Sidney's contemporaries. Its influence was immediate, affecting even the sombre, mighty genius of Shakespeare, and surviving through the following century to dictate the convolutions of the Metaphysical School of poets, the best of whom was Abraham Cowley, whose conceits displaced the simplicity of Herrick, at least for a while.

Sidney's personality, the whole man, was strong enough, however, to be fully conscious of his own weaknesses and vagaries. He had more disciplined work to do after writing *Arcadia*. The deep and unifying emotion of his love for Penelope Devereux was more than a literary convention, as was Dante's for Beatrice and Petrarch's for Laura. He turned to the restrictions of the sonnet, as a good Catholic turns to the confessional; to bring his wandering mind to a halt.

The sonnet had fallen somewhat out of favour for some decades since in Henry VIII's time it had been brought into English verse from Italy by Sir Thomas Wyatt, a Kentish man (1503–1542) and Henry Howard, Earl of Surrey (*c.* 1517–1547). Its first appearance in book form was in the rare publication known as *Tottle's Miscellany*, consisting of 'Songs and Sonattes written by the right honourable Lord Henry Howard late Earl of Surrey, and other'. Both these gentlemen altered the Petrarchan rhyme-scheme which divided the sonnet into two sections, of eight and of six lines. They used the rhyming couplet at the end, and it was this innovation which became usual with the greater sonneteers, after the decades of its gestation: Shakespeare, Spenser, Marlowe, Drayton, Daniel and the thousands who were to follow them. Milton returned to the Italian form, but ran the octave into the sestet with powerful effect, leaving no pause between the statement and the reflection upon it, as the fully formal sonnet should. Not until the nineteenth century was that purity restored, by an Italianate English poet, Dante Gabriel Rossetti.

Sidney, popular and influential because of the success of his *Arcadia*, next adopted the sonnet form and thus restored it to general use. The two forms, the English and the Italian, are most vividly described by the Victorian critic William Sharp:

The Shakespearean sonnet is like a red-hot bar being moulded upon a forge till—in the closing couplet—it receives the final clinching blow from the heavy hammer: while the Petrarchan, on the other hand, is like a wind gathering in volume and dying away again immediately on attaining a culminating force.

Sidney had become more forceful, and he chose the form that emulated the hammer-blow. But he still could not forego the flowers of fancy and antithesis, the tropes and verbal ingenuities. They were assumed as naturally as the elaborate clothes of the period. But in the first sonnet of his long sequence of *Astrophel and Stella* (himself the first, Penelope Devereux the second), he makes several statements that are harshly self-disciplinary, the most striking of which is 'my truant pen'. That is indeed a bringing of himself to task! But he does not altogether succeed, except in adopting an attitude of withdrawal from society. He remains the courtier, the soldier, and the diplomat, trained to the restrictions of those vocations, rather than surrendering to the unguarded candours of the lover. One feels that Queen Elizabeth's jealous eye is watching the young couple, and that amid all their woodland protestations they are looking over their shoulders at that royal menace, with all that it demands of self-surrender and undivided loyalty.

Sidney, however, did not witness the success of his *Arcadia*, for it was not published until 1590, four years after his death. Nor was the sonnet sequence made public during his lifetime, for in 1583 he had married the daughter of Sir Francis Walsingham, who was then the Queen's secretary, and *eminence grise* standing behind Lord Cecil. Sidney had been knighted early in that year, but his marriage offended the Queen because she had not been consulted beforehand. This quirk in her character, a secondary condition, perhaps, of her physical as well as her symbolical virginity (her principal weapon in international diplomacy), was constantly being overlooked by her courtiers, in spite of the risks involved.

Sidney wanted to go to the Low Countries in 1584, where Spain was again rampant, after having William of Orange assassinated, but still the Queen held back from giving her soldiers, admirals and freebooters open commission to declare war on Spain. But an 'incident' in which an English merchant ship was attacked in a Spanish harbour enabled the war party to overbear the Queen's hesitancy, and she authorised Sir Francis Drake to prepare an expedition to attack the West Indies. Sidney, with his friend Fulke Greville, went down to Plymouth secretly, hoping to be enrolled and to get away before the Queen noticed their absence from Court. But Drake, looking upon these two gallants as land-lubbers of little use for his purpose, informed the Queen of their presence in his shipyards. She wrote, commanding their return, but Sidney's servants intercepted the carrier and returned the letter to Elizabeth. Her second command was more thunderous!

The result of this incident was that Sidney really got his own way, for he was appointed Governor of Flushing, and in November 1585 he left England for the Netherlands to take up his appointment. A fortnight after his departure, the Queen graciously became godmother to Sidney's infant daughter. This was a characteristic example of her genius for commanding loyalty.

Sidney's uncle, the Earl of Leicester, still near to the Queen's secret heart, was put in command of the army, but he lingered at home, and

Sidney had to appeal to him to bring reinforcements. He came without them, bored by the whole business of the campaign, and the prospect of winter conditions in Holland. So the winter passed and nothing happened until the spring, when the Spaniards, under their experienced general the Duke of Parma, opened the season with an attack designed to command the Rhine delta. Sidney counter-attacked with an effort to relieve the besieged town of Grave. The war flared up, and Sidney was fully engaged. He could not leave, in May, to attend the funeral of his father, old Sir Henry.

With the help of Dutchmen under Maurice, son of the murdered Prince of Orange, Sidney captured the town of Axel, and thus kept the Spaniards from reaching the coast. But Flushing was still in danger, and if this port fell, the ever-dreaded invasion of England was likely to be realised. Leicester wanted to make a stand at Arnhem, until more troops were sent over from home, but they never came. After another council of war, it was decided that the town of Zutphen should be attacked. Parma was warned of this and sent a force with food and arms to help defend the town. A Colonel Sir John Norris was seconded with a regiment of horse and foot to intercept this convoy. Through an early morning mist the sound of hooves and wheels grew louder just as Leicester, with Sidney and other staff officers, joined Norris and his troops. Leicester retired, but Sidney remained, with two friends who were already wounded in earlier battles, the one being thus unable to wear full armour, and the other only one boot and no thigh-piece. Sidney, urged by his oddly conceived notions of chivalry and romanticism, decided that he must be at no greater advantage in battle than his comrades. So he discarded his own metal thigh-pieces.

As the mist cleared, the battle began, with the English cavalry charging the convoy. Fierce hand-to-hand fighting followed, and Sidney's horse was shot. He remounted another, and re-joined the mélée, to receive a shot that shattered the bone in his unprotected thigh. He was led back, a mile and a half, to camp, after the incident which is now one of the world-famous examples of chivalry, compassion, and self-abnegation. Loss of blood gave him a raging thirst, and on the way back he asked for water. When it was brought him, he noticed that a soldier being carried alongside him was also in need. Fulke Greville records the immortal saying, 'Thy need is yet greater than mine'. The good friend added 'and when he had pledged the poor soldier, he was presently carried to Arnhem.' This place received heroes again in 1942. I know one, a doctor, among those dropped by parachute, who operated without a break for 72 hours in the open air, amid the battle, before being taken prisoner. That too must be cited as an act of total self-control.

What Sidney must have suffered during the 25 days that he lingered, in submission to the torture from the surgeons, is an experience few people, other than those in the Far East, could endure today. It was thought that he would recover, and the Earl of Leicester wrote home that the worst was over. Sidney's wife, his two brothers, and a priest named Gifford, came out to him. He made a will, leaving his lands and revenues to his family. Then he died.

The news was carried round the civilised world, and the Dutch asked for the hero to be buried in Holland, under a regal monument. But it was decided to bring his body home, after embalming it. It was carried to Flushing and put aboard his own ship *The Black Prince*. On 5 November, the ship berthed near the Tower of London and the body was taken to a church in the Minories. There it lay for a while because of some legal debate about his debts, and the burden on the family estate following his father's recent death. His father-in-law, Walsingham, paid off enough on account, in twentieth-century fashion, for the funeral to proceed. It appears that Walsingham, despite his high position in the royal service, was permanently impoverished by his determination that his son-in-law be buried without any blot on his reputation.

The ceremony was delayed until February 16th, and a gossip of the period, what today we should call a newspaper man, wrote that throughout the country 'it was accounted a sin for any gentleman of Quality for many months after, to appear to Court or City in any light or gaudy apparel'. The procession wound its way to old St Paul's Cathedral, whose aisles were draped in black. The body was buried under the Lady Chapel, behind the High Altar, and a double volley of musketry was fired from St Paul's Churchyard. Fulke Greville, his friend and first biographer, ordered his own tomb to bear the simple description of his greatest honour, 'Friend to Sir Philip Sidney'.

All vanished in the great Fire of London, eighty years later. No, not all! Even Sir Philip Sidney's writings are rarely read, the man remains, offering in perpetuity, that cup of cold water, which, like the widow's cruse, is prophetically refilled.

Philip's brother Robert, nine years his junior, served with him during the war in the Netherlands, and returned there again in 1596, after diplomatic service in Scotland and France. His contribution, as a Kentish born character, was thus similar to that of his elder brother. He was appointed to the Governorship of Flushing, a post which he held for five years, until the accession of James I, when he was recalled to London. James favoured him, and although he was heir to the Earl of Leicester, immediately raised him to the peerage as Baron Sidney of Penshurst, in 1603. Two years later he was again honoured, and became Viscount Lisle. This title is held by the present-day owner of Penshurst Place.

The title of Earl of Leicester had become extinct in 1588 when Robert's uncle, Queen Elizabeth's favourite, died. It was revived in 1618 and added to Robert's honours. By marrying twice and having a large family, he ensured the long connection of the Sidneys with Penshurst. There he lived quietly in his later life, maintaining the family tradition of scholarship and interest in the arts. He was Ben Jonson's patron. His son, also named Robert, who succeeded to the titles and the estate, fostered Charles the First's children there after the Civil War and the murder of the King. His eldest son Philip favoured the Parliamentary side during the war, and this may account for the younger royal children being sent to Penshurst for awhile during the subsidence of the social and political turmoil after 1649.

This second Earl of Leicester had 15 children by his wife, daughter of a Percy, Earl of Northumberland. So the family proliferated, marrying always into the nobility; the Cecils, the Pelhams, the Spencers, surviving in the Weald of Kent like a fragment of the ancient Forest of Anderida.

One of the sons of the family, Algernon Sidney, born at Penshurst in 1622, was also a Parliamentarian, like his elder brother. He was endowed with the characteristic talents of the family, for politics and soldiering. He rose to command a Division in Fairfax's Army and fought at Marston Moor, where he was badly wounded.

He was principally, however, a political man, and for most of his life he was in and out of Parliament, a passionate advocate of its increasing prerogatives, intriguing against the Tory ascendancy and theorising on behalf of Whiggism and its advocacy of an aristocratic oligarchy and a strict limitation of the power of the Crown. Naturally, he was distrusted by Charles II, especially as he spent so much time in the Scandinavian countries and confusing his intrigues there with visits to France and Italy, where he played the part of the English Eccentric (a phenomenon always amusing and sometimes a dangerous figure in world politics, as for example, Lady Hester Stanhope, Byron, Wilfred Scawen Blunt, and the late T. E. Lawrence).

He was a bold privateer, a Liberal before his time, hot tempered and prone to trouble wherever he went, but able, until the last error of judgment, to escape the consequences of his obstinacy and rashness. Thus, when he was appointed one of the Commissioners for the trial of Charles I, he removed himself to Copenhagen to avoid taking part. From there, however, he condoned it. He was the sort of free-lance with whom you never know where you are, though you know that he is likely to add a pinch of salt to enhance the spice of life. So he made friends as well as enemies, but in the end they could do him no service, not even the King of Sweden who believed him to be a statesman and gave him rich presents. He was a scholar, loved nature and especially birds; a strain from the stock of his famous kinsman. He was tall and overbearing, and no obsequious respecter of persons. He too quarrelled with his contemporary Lord Oxford, while gambling with him at the Hague, and was with difficulty restrained from a duel. Thereupon he came back to Penshurst and wrote an *Essay on Love*.

But he was soon back in politics, at the restoration of the Long Parliament, and we find him over in France, via Brussels, where he had his portrait painted by van Edmondt (still to be seen in Penshurst Place). His was a temper akin to that of Milton in the writing of the *Aeropagitica*. It combined egoism with idealism, a mixture which tends to make a man practise what he preaches, and damn the consequences. Thus, while in France, deeply involved in plans to bring a regiment of ex-Commonwealth soldiers over to fight for the Hapsburg empire, though being at the same time under consideration for a pension from Louis of France, the 'Sun King', he was asked by that autocrat to give the royal stable a horse belonging to him. Algernon Sidney shot the horse, saying 'it was born a free creature, had served a free man, and should not be mastered by a king of slaves': a true statement, but not one normally to be uttered by a professional diplomat.

The end to his outrageous originality came with his involvement in the rebellion of the Duke of Monmouth, and the Rye House Plot, in which Lords Russell and Essex also lost their lives, the latter by suicide. Sidney was also arrested and sent to the Tower of London, on a charge of High Treason and conspiring against the life of King James II. His past history as an active Parliamentarian was prejudicial to a fair trial, especially as one of his judges was the notorious Jeffreys, whose name is still anathema in the West Country. Algernon Sidney insisted on conducting his own defence, and spoke with nobility and eloquence: but James was frightened by the conflagration of which his brother's bastard was the kindling-wood, and he accepted the advice of Jeffreys to refuse a petition from Sidney.

Algernon's last act was to write *An Apology*. It did not explain why he had managed to get himself embroiled in a rebellion whose purposes were contrary to his own life and principles. He was beheaded in the Tower on 7 December 1683, aged sixty-one, and his body was brought home to be buried at Penshurst, where the only serene periods of his life had been spent, amongst the birds and woodlands, the gardens and farmlands which he had loved as much as Sir Philip had done. Both men were of the same nurture and formative environment.

The literary gifts, and the acquisition of scholarship, in the Sidney family, were shared by its womenfolk. Sir Philip had four sisters, three of whom died young. The fourth, Mary, was married, not very happily, to the second Earl of Pembroke, and spent her married life at his noble house Wilton, outside Salisbury. There she held intellectual court, as I have described, making her home a private university where she entertained, and sustained, many famous writers of the Elizabethan glory. Her scholarship was wide, in Latin, Greek and Hebrew. Her deepest love was for her brother Philip, with whom she worked on the book *Arcadia*. After his death, she revised the book, with additions, and re-published it in 1598, the year in which she also published her brother's collected poems. She followed this with a homiletic book, long ago planned with Philip, called *Discourses on Life and Death*. It was an attempt to assuage the grief which she still could not contain, even after the passage of twelve years.

Two years later she wrote a tragedy in blank verse called *Antonie*, and followed this with a version of the Psalms, some of which had already been put into verse by Philip. She could not escape from his influence, though she worked hard at literary tasks, and maintained a bounteous friendship with many writers, first amongst them the divine Edmund Spenser, who dedicated to her his *Ruins of Time*, as his contribution to Philip's memory. She must have been pleased, though it made the wound bleed afresh, to be assured by Spenser that 'both in shape and spirit she was much like her brother', and that 'his goodly image lives in the divine resemblance of your face'.

The poet Daniel, a popular sonneteer, came as tutor to her son at Wilton, and he dedicated to her his sonnet sequence *Delia*, amongst other works. Two other poets whose fame has survived the dust of time, Thomas Nash and John Donne, came to Wilton. Donne, that powerful innovator of con-

versational rhythms into verse forms, became a close friend of this woman
whose mental powers matched his own. When she died in 1621, another of
her protegés, William Browne, wrote the perfect epitaph.

> Underneath this sable hearse
> Lies the subject of all verse,
> Sidney's sister, Pembroke's mother:
> Death, ere thou has slain another
> Wise, fair and good as she,
> Time shall throw a dart at thee.

Another daughter of the family, Dorothy Sidney, was born in 1617. She
too was to become immortalised, more happily than her brother Algernon.
Though born at Sion House, Brentford, she spent her early life at Penshurst,
until her marriage to the Earl of Sunderland. The poet Edmund Waller, of
Groombridge, only a few miles from Penshurst, fell in love with her, or
pretended to, though he was a widower and eleven years her senior. He
called her 'Sacharissa', because of her sweet character, and wrote a lyric
addressed to her which is fragrant in many anthologies:

> Go, lovely Rose!
> Tell her that wastes her time and me
> That now she knows,
> When I resemble her to thee,
> How sweet and fair she seems to be.
>
> Tell her that's young
> And shuns to have her graces spied,
> That hadst thou sprung
> In deserts where no men abide,
> Thou must have, uncommended, died.
> Small is the worth
> Of beauty, from the light retired . . .

but that is enough of the song to reveal that Dorothy Sidney did not credit
his love. Nor did her family, who looked for higher rank and wealth, and
saw, perhaps, a flaw in his character which revealed itself much later in life,
when Dorothy, widowed, asked him for more tributes in verse, and he
replied 'When you are young again, Madam, and as lovely as you were
then'.

The Earl of Sunderland was killed at the Battle of Newbury in 1643,
when his wife was pregnant with a second son. She retired to Penshurst,
where for nine years she lived as a widow, bringing up her two sons and

also fostering the children of the martyred King Charles. Her generous and wise character endeared her to them. In addition, she made herself responsible for the folk in the neighbourhood of Penshurst, so many of them impoverished by the economic aftermath of the Civil War.

In the course of this public work she met one of the Kentish gentry, whose gentle and benevolent personality so impressed her that she married him, and thereby lost caste amongst some of her aristocratic peers. He was Sir Robert Smith, of Sutton-at-Hone, an ancient house of the Knights Templars, near Dartford. Class distinctions were so powerful then, partly as a reaction of the blood-stained 'levelling' processes of the Civil War, that even the unworldly Dorothy herself spoke of marrying this good man 'out of pity'. Dorothy Osborne, whose correspondence with her future husband Sir William Temple reveals some of the personal problems created by the war, could not be tolerant of this Countess who stooped to marry a baronet whose activities were modest and local. But Dorothy Osborne's criticism of her was not for marrying below her station in Society; it was for *condescending* to do so. 'I think I shall never forgive her one thing she said to him, which was that she married him "out of pity" ', and Dorothy Osborne had come from a Royalist family!

The second marriage was also a happy one, but it was also short, for both the husband and the son born of it were dead within eight years. When her daughter Lady Halifax died, she left Penshurst and went to live at Rufford, the seat of her son-in-law, where she looked after her four grand-children. Her portrait by Vandyck, at Penshurst, perpetuates her endearing beauty, something not too flawless, and therefore the more appealing.

Christopher Marlowe

It is inevitable, in recalling the literary figures native to Kent, to refer again and again to the course taken by the Renaissance as its great tide flowed northwards to the more remote reaches of the Old World. The Elizabethan writers who, by the mystery of genius in their work, have become immortals, were all taken in that tide, drawn to Italy and France, and after that influential ebb, returned to their native land, having suffered a cultural 'sea-change'.

Fortunately, I do not have to discuss Shakespeare in this connection, as he is not a native of Kent. Whether or not he ever went abroad is always in dispute, but in character and philosophy, as well as technique, he is an outstanding example of the artist working during that turbulent century after the Renaissance, buoyant upon the Reformation, had broken all bounds in general speculation upon the nature of the universe, of man's place in it, of his pre-nativity and his final destination.

Shakespeare, with humour and equability tempering his powerful pessimism, 'out-topped all knowledge' with the astounding force of his vocabulary. Matthew Arnold's sonnet on his genius suggests that he may not have been aware of the authority of his own use of words, and of what they implied in the matter of personal experience in so many walks of life. I am thankful to have escaped the task of trying to enlarge on that judgment: but so universal is Shakespeare that he has to appear momentarily in this gallery of Kentish immortals, apart from his own references to the county, such as the unforgettable speech about Dover Cliff and the 'dangerous trade' of gathering samphire carried on there; an occupation which I suspect he had in mind as an allegory of his own occupation, the making of poetry.

The more immediate reference to Shakespeare, however, is that he was born in the same year, 1564, as another poet who, on 6 February, was the first-fruit of a marriage between a Canterbury Cordwainer (shoe-maker), and the daughter of a rector of St Peter's Church in the town, who had been dispossessed of his living during the reign of the Catholic Queen Mary, because he was a married priest. The infant's father was John Marlowe, or Morley, and he was a craftsman of substance, an alderman, a typical example of the rising middle-class which, given rein by the increasing secularisation of education, was ousting the comparatively illiterate nobility from its monopoly of power, both economic and political. Earlier in the century, two men of this class had emerged to be, temporarily, rulers of the country, Wolsey and Thomas Cromwell. Previous to them, one Henry Chichele, a lad from Higham Ferrars in Northamptonshire, had become Archbishop of Canterbury and founder of All Souls', Oxford, that *cor cordiam* of intellectual aristocracy.

So frequently in the emergence of a master-mind, or spirit, from this stolid commercial root, the requisite sensibility is supplied by the mother, of more 'gentle' birth. (We have, in the present age of a belief in equality, to put that description in parenthesis). It was so with Chichele, and also with Christopher Marlowe. Catherine Arthur, his mother, had been born into a clerical household, and gave her son's infant environment some quality of intellectual consciousness. But we dogmatise on these matters only at our peril. The fact that her father was driven from his rectory during the short Papist revival may have fixed her character in a mould of obstinate puritanism, which she could have inflicted on her family. That would account for much of Marlowe's revolt against all religious faith during his few tempestuous years of adult life.

Christopher was perhaps the first of all scholarship boys. He benefited by turncoat Cranmer's love of scholarship, which prompted that unhappy Archbishop to put some of the monkish funds seized by his Master King Henry to found scholarships at King's School, Canterbury. 'But let the ploughman's son enter the room', was his explanation for this experiment in democracy. In a poem called 'A History Lesson', I dealt with one consequence of this educational development. It ends as follows:

> Some few citizens of Canterbury
> Were quick to profit. A shoemaker's son,
> Born beneath the shadow of Bell Harry
> And Anselm's modest tower, sang with the others,
> Gentlemen's sons, squires' boys, any
> 'Apt to learning' as harsh Cranmer phrased
> This one provision for the singing scholars.
> Oh merciless posterity, before
> You judge that Prelate for his cruel deeds,
> Faggot and stake and cruel mutilations,
> Think of the act which set a boy to sing
> Free of the cordwainer's last, free of the dark
> Alley, free to learn the craft that summoned
> Tamburlaine and Helen, free to swim
> The Hellespont with Leander, free to launch
> A thousand ships and burn the topless towers
> Of Ilium in a verbal holocaust
> That set the torch blazing in Shakespeare's hand.

For it was Marlowe who preceded the greater master in the use of blank verse for making dramatic dialogue. We do not know much about his activities at King's School. Indeed, his whole life is a tangle of contradictions and conflicting reports. But he must have shown precocious ability, for he proceeded from school to Cambridge, on another scholarship given by Archbishop Parker. He entered Corpus Christi College, where he took his B.A. degree in 1584, and his M.A. three years later. The academic Thomas Seccombe claims that Marlowe matriculated in 1571; but that would have been at the age of seven. It is an improbable suggestion, even for a time when boys were sent up to the two universities in childhood, at the age of twelve. But there is a vast gap between seven and twelve, in the timeless opening chapters of human life.

A notable school-fellow at King's was Richard Boyle, who took to law and became a great landowner in Ireland and was made Earl of Cork. A later scholar there was William Harvey, the great doctor and natural philosopher of comparable power to Newton. Harvey has had more celebration in his home-town of Folkestone than Marlowe has had in Canterbury. His birthplace. Fortunately, a Mayor of Folkestone during three sessions over the past two decades, Alderman John Moncrieff, urged to curiosity by the noble statue to the Doctor which stands on the sea-front, put his interest to civic use by organising local pride and promoting some ceremonies to express it. He found his efforts taken up by the Harveyan Society and

Medical Councils all over the world. So public consciousness in Folkestone is now prepared for the quatercentenary of Harvey's birth in 1978, when that great doctor's work, described in another chapter of this book, should again be held in universal remembrance.

Marlowe's unorthodox character and spirit of revolt showed themselves while he was still up at Cambridge. A Fellow and tutor of his college, one Francis Kett, may have had some influence in leading him into the byeways of the rapidly widening territory of Renaissance scholarship. Like so many who leave religious conventions in which they have been brought up, this man dabbled in mysticism, and probably, like Faust, in diabolism. He was later burnt at the stake for heresy. As this was in 1589, Marlowe would have known of this act of extreme persuasion, only to be hardened in his own rejection of the savagely affirmative views of the Establishment.

Marlowe's terms up at his university were marked by frequent truancies, which for long remained unexplained, and also puzzling because they appear to have been overlooked by the college authorities. In the nineteen-twenties, however, the American Professor Leslie Hotson, while researching at the Public Record Office, a repository of incalculable depths, found certain papers relating to the enquiry into the death of Marlowe. Hotson was a singularly lucky researcher, for he also came by chance upon the letters written by the poet Shelley to his wife Harriet, and impounded into Chancery during legal proceedings after the breakdown of the marriage.

From Hotson's discoveries, it seems that Marlowe's disappearances from College during term time were frequently due to his being abroad in the Low Countries, on some errands proposed by Sir Francis Walsingham, the founder of a well-organised Secret Service department in the pay of the Crown. How Marlowe got himself thus entangled has not been fully ascertained. He was possessed of a powerful personality, mettlesome and adventurous. His scholarship in Latin was outstanding, and his translation of Ovid's *Amores*, a work likely to attract much popularity, was in process while he was still at Cambridge. His version showed at once the magnetism of genius. Here was poetry with a difference, the like of which had not been known since Chaucer dominated the prosody of our language.

He drifted away from Cambridge before he was 24 years old, drawn by recognitions and successes which were at that time coming to the world of letters, and thereby giving it the first promise of professional status. Actors such as Richard Burbage, and an actor-manager and impresario such as

Edward Alleyn, were shortly to become established figures, anticipating Shakespeare's career in the making of fortunes in the theatre.

Marlowe's principal activity, whatever else he may have been engaged in, was now the art of poetry, and particularly dramatic poetry that at once found its mark. He attached himself to the Lord Admiral's Company of Players, managed by Edward Alleyn, who had already made a reputation as an actor of the women's parts in the plays of the period. The fact that women were not allowed to act accounts for the curiously reticent sexual reference, or at least demonstration, in Elizabethan drama. This determines the clarity of tone, the gesture of formality, which permeates even the most bloody of plots. It was a quality hard to describe, yet it may be due to the simple fact of the legal requirements of the Elizabethan theatre.

Marlowe met Thomas Kyd in London, and found a congenial rebel. This playwright was the first to recognise the growing public demand for a literary art that should attempt to combine the many demons of energy let loose by the New Learning, the revolt against Catholic authority both temporal and theological, the changing economic structure of society through the growth of urban commerce and industry which was so rapidly overtaking rural culture and wealth. The tales of gods and heroes from Greek and Roman sources; the romances of chivalry from Italy and France; the home-grown knockabout rustic plays devolved from medieval religious allegories, all had to be turned to account in order to give a sense of familiarity to the audiences who filled the courtyards of the inns, and the few adventurous theatres, where plays were given to the English folk of the sixteenth century.

Thomas Kyd (1558–1594) supplied this need with the first melodrama, a play called *The Spanish Tragedy*. Like the later poet, Milton, he was the son of a London scrivener (the equivalent of a solicitor), and he was educated for the law. He followed the classical devices of Seneca, philosophical dialogues rather than actable plays, presenting life as a pageant of disaster to be endured only by the cultivation of stoicism. Princes, love-stricken women, jealous rivals for the joys of love and power, murder, suicide, grief and insanity; all these ingredients are so skilfully kneaded into *The Spanish Tragedy* that the play dominated the Elizabethan stage for a generation, its popularity prolonged by some patching up at the hands of Ben Jonson.

It was the talk of the town when Marlowe came to London to try his fortune in this now recognised profession of play-writing. He saw what the public could take in this matter of confused melodrama. But he had his own poetic genius to propitiate, and also he had, maybe almost unconsciously,

to reveal his own perversities of character, his views on moral values, learned
in pride which had uprooted him from the fidelities of his humble birth.
He brought also to his first drama certain propositions of a destructive
philosophy and cynicism acquired in his mysterious truancies abroad during his terms at Cambridge.

He was driven by the *folie de grandeur* of the self-made man who attributes his success to his own efforts rather than to the 'destiny that shapes
our ends'. Thus he turned with relish of narcissist fixity, to a theme, the
career of a Mongolian shepherd who by the might of his own egoism became
the emperor of the known world. *Tamburlaine* was written in two parts, a
method which Shakespeare must have appreciated in his plans for the
historical chronicles. *Part One* appeared in 1587, the year that Marlowe
finally left Cambridge.

He was 23 when this play hit the Town. Here was something new; a
drama that favoured the villain and glorified violence, cruelty and the lust
for power. The forces for evil which had been held in check by the pretended ascendency of Christian charity, under the authority of the Church
of Rome and the even stricter teachings of the Reformists, were now lauded
in poetry whose range of imagery, extravagance of epithet, and rhythmic
force, had never before been known in the English tongue. It had all the
dogged vigour of the earlier folk-dramas with their alliterative rhymings,
but it added to their farmyard realism a delicacy and musicality that be-
mused the audiences and doused their moral indignation, should it protest
at the evil which this young poet presented and so outrageously justified.

The successful combination of these contradictory qualities resulted in
a captive audience, whose appetite for melodrama was satisfied, and the
heavy meal washed down with this wine whose bouquet indicated a vintage
poetry. Even today, the reader or playgoer of even moderate verbal sensibility, sits like Bajazeth, the Emperor of Turkey, captured by Tamburlaine
and imprisoned in a cage. He speaks to his crazed wife, who has cried out
against the tyrant,

> Let all the swords and lances in the field
> Stick in his breast as in their proper rooms!
> At every pore let blood come dropping forth,
> That lingering pains may massacre his heart,
> And madness send his damned soul to hell!

Bajazeth answers, and what he says may be used as an allegory of the power
which this Christopher Marlowe exercised upon gentlefolk and groundlings

alike in the Elizabethan theatre. Nor has the demonic magnetism of his verse lost its attraction four hundred years later. Here speaks the universal captive.

> Ah, fair Zabina! we may curse his power,
> The heavens may frown, the earth for anger quake;
> But such a star hath influence in his sword
> As rules the skies and countermands the gods
> More than Cimmerian Styx or Destiny:
> And then shall we in this detested guise,
> With shame, with hunger, and with horror stay,
> Griping our bowels with retorqued thoughts,
> And have no hope to end our ecstasies.

Blank verse, as a medium that was to combine poetic rhythm with that of actuality in the welter of everyday life, had not much further to go in its development. Shakespeare was to take it up where Marlowe left it, and to give it both greater variety within the possible permutations of the pentameter, and enrich it with even more subleties of syllabic music.

Marlowe, like his 'Barbarous and bloody Tamburlaine', could be capable of more gentle emotions, which he personified in Zenocrate, daughter of the 'Soldan of Egypt', with whom Tamburlaine fell in love, and whom he married; an amelioration which much affected his plans for conquering the world, after 'threatening it with high astounding terms', a technique which the young poet so triumphantly employed, boasting to lead his audiences

> From jigging veins of rhyming mother-wits
> And such conceits as clowning keeps in pay.

Those are the opening lines of the play of *Tamburlaine the Great*, and they direct the course of this arrogant and self-assured young man's career, whose fatal weakness was the tempestuous conceit that would not learn to exercise discretion and tact, two qualities of absolute importance in the other field where (thanks to Leslie Hotson's researches) we have learned that Marlowe frequented during the absences from Cambridge, and later when his life was sufficiently hazardous in the vagabondage of the theatre.

Marlowe's reference to 'rhyming mother-wits' was a challenge (he was a compulsive challenger) not only to the un-tuned drama of the folk, seeded out of the religious morality plays of the previous two hundred years, but also to the more conscious artists who immediately preceded him, and those who were his contemporaries, most of the latter university products more academically conventional.

Before *Tamburlaine* was performed in 1587, John Lyly, the verbal dandy of the Elizabethan age, had produced at least five plays: George Peele (a courtier and therefore amateur) had written *The Arraignment of Paris*, to amuse the Queen; Kyd had made his mark with *The Spanish Tragedy*; Norton and Sackville had been still earlier with their pedantic *Gorboduc*. Indeed, since the Queen's accession, at least seven plays had been presented before her each year, so that about a hundred and fifty plays preceded the coming of *Tamburlaine*. Thus Marlowe had once again a large world to conquer. He succeeded with as much bravura as he had done in history, in fiction as in fact. The poet and critic Edward Thomas, in his Introduction to the Collected Plays of Marlowe in *Everyman's Library*, says that *Tamburlaine*, by reason of its success, instantly found a detractor, who wrote of 'idiot art masters who intrude themselves to our ears as the alchemists of eloquence, who (mounted on the stage of arrogance) think to outbrave better pens by the swelling bombast of braggart blank verse'. This suggests that Marlowe's aggressive character was already storing up trouble for him. The critic may have been Greene, well-named as the intellectual and academic snob who attacked Shakespeare.

This 'braggart blank verse', however, had an organic grandeur in its syllabic constructions and sequences which gave Shakespeare a precedent for releasing his own musical genius. Here is an example.

> Nature that framed us of four elements,
> Warring within our breasts for regiment,
> Doth teach us all to have aspiring minds.

The turn of thought and the instancy of the images is Shakespearean. But Marlowe wrote those lines. He also had an additional sonority which sounded through English poetry until its overtone reached Milton's ears. Listen to these two examples, also taken from *Tamburlaine*:

> Zenocrate, lovelier than the love of Jove,
> Brighter than is the silver Rhodope,
> Fairer than whitest snow on Scythian hills,

and the second example is still more indicative of Milton's Handelian musicianship:

> Of such a burthen as outweighs the sands
> And all the craggy rocks of Caspia.

It is not only in these chromatic depths of tone that Marlowe pioneered.

He also speeded up the pace of English verse, his passion and his energy, some of it evil in its genesis, rushing the measures along in a rapid fugue through which the Anglo-Saxon syllables take on an Italian fluency. The only poets who have induced such comparable pace into our prosody are Shelley and Swinburne. But I must not linger too long on literary technique, for some readers of this book, which by reason of its miscellaneous theme must discuss characters and interests from many walks of life, will agree with the pretended cynicism of Marlowe himself who said, in this same youthful play,

> And 'tis a pretty toy to be a poet,

a sentiment likely to be felt by a word-weary veteran in the art of letters, but not by a young man with the world at his feet.

Marlowe made the most of that 'pretty toy', though in giving himself mainly to the demands of the Elizabethan theatre, he had not time to contribute much purely lyrical verse. We know of only two poems, but both are superb, though the second and more ambitious he left to be finished by a much more scholarly practitioner, George Chapman. The short 'Come live with me and be my love' is frequently anthologised, and needs only my reminder here of its purity of tone in the manner of Theocritus. The second, *Hero and Leander*, is possibly the more revealing of Marlowe's unique genius because it was only a fragment.

The difference between the two parts is instructive. Chapman, with his learning, his steady patience (which carried him through his hexametric translation of Homer's *Iliad*), lowered the temperature of Marlowe's incandescent lines, as they lit the Hellespont that always divides lover from lover. He introduced a moral, as though it were a Bailey bridge, to make the junction, though the theme of the tale was one of severance. Yet he was a disciple of the genius whose poem he completed. It was as though Southey should complete *Kubla Khan*. The sympathy with his master was there, but instead of the divine arrogance, there was only the self-conscious academic snobbery of intellect.

The only work of art comparable with Marlowe's fragment, is Botticelli's *Primavera*. The method of both masters is that of a heightened visual consciousness, as though both wore powerful lenses. See what I mean, in the following lines from the opening of the poem:

> About her neck hung chains of pebble-stone,
> Which, lighten'd by her neck, like diamonds shone.

> She ware no gloves; for neither sun nor wind
> Would burn or parch her hands, but, to her mind,
> Or warm or cool them, for they took delight
> To play upon those hands, they were so white.

Compare that with Botticelli's painting of the strands of hair, blown out by the springtime zephyr. The music of substances is eloquent in both; distilled sensuality.

However, that was not the way which Marlowe's genius and fortunes went. He short-circuited the processes of the spiritual condenser, and gave his abilities to further playwriting, all of them adding to his prestige in his few remaining years of life. Outstanding among them was his version of the Faust legend, *The Tragical History of Doctor Faustus*. The choice of theme again is significant of the reigning passion in Marlowe's personality. It was pride; and for him it proved to be most emphatically one of the seven deadly sins, by destroying his capacity for wisdom and intellectual control of himself and the situations into which his service under Walsingham brought him. The last words of the play are a prophecy of his own downfall. Faust is snatched by Satan, to whom he has sold himself, for the gift of all knowledge. But at the last, crying 'I'll burn my books', he vanishes, and a chorus declaims

> Cut is the branch that might have grown full straight,
> And burned is Apollo's laurel-bough,
> That sometime grew within this learned man.
> Faustus is gone, regard his hellish fall,
> Whose fiendful fortune may exhort the wise,
> Only to wonder at unlawful things,
> Whose deepness doth entice such forward wits
> To practice more than heavenly power permits.

All that, the self-condemnation, after the glorious achievement in this marvellous poem-play that Goethe and Swinburne both saluted as a supreme masterpiece! They did not exaggerate. The marriage of dramatic intensity to poetic verse of the purest possible music endures throughout. The scene where Mephistopheles conjures the re-embodiment of Helen of Troy at Faust's request, is almost hackneyed by repetition of the lines

> Was this the face that launched a thousand ships
> And burnt the topless towers of Ilium?

I cannot leave this aspect of Marlowe's genius without quoting the rest of that exclamatory intoxication. Faust kisses the mirage, still unaware of the

Devil's deceit, and utters the following soliloquy, which is as supreme a piece of verbal perfection as anything written in English verse.

> Sweet Helen, make me immortal with a kiss.—
> Her lips suck forth my soul: see, where it flies!—
> Come, Helen, come, give me my soul again.
> Here will I dwell, for heaven is in these lips,
> And all is dross that is not Helena.
> I will be Paris, and for love of thee,
> Instead of Troy, shall Wertenberg be sacked;
> And I will combat with weak Menelaus,
> And wear thy colours on my plumed crest;
> Yes, I will wound Achilles in the heel,
> And then return to Helen for a kiss.
> O, thou art fairer than the evening air
> Clad in the beauty of a thousand stars.
> Brighter art thou than flaming Jupiter
> When he appear'd to hapless Semele;
> More lovely than the monarch of the sky
> In Wanton Arethusa's azur'd arms;
> And none but thou shalt be my paramour!

The conjuring play of vowels in that passage was not only perfect, it was also a pioneering perfection, a model for poets and critics ever since. Shakespeare at once seized on the linguistic possibilities displayed by his exact but more precocious contemporary.

Recognition of Marlowe's mastery has never flagged. Hear what Edward Thomas, in the twentieth century, has said about *Faustus*. 'Into this subject Marlowe could without hesitation or obstacle put the whole of himself, his intellectual subtlety and experience, his love of beauty, of power, and of luxury. He used the legend with only just so much of the paraphernalia of the supernatural as was easily and almost universally credible in his day; and he made Faustus a human individual student of that age, with a shade of rusticity—one can imagine him with an accent as probably Marlowe had the accent of Kent—which adds to the intense reality of the whole, to the beauty and dalliance of the central part, the kissing of Helen, the snatching of the Pope's dish, and to the terrible splendour of the end. High mighty line—mighty in its movement as in its content—was at its proper task in expressing those "brave translunary things" '.

That was written by a critic whose own poetry was deliberately composed in opposition to such grandeur, preferring the minor keys of quiet contemplation, expressed in hushed understatement. Swinburne, more in the manner of Marlowe, both in extravagance and speed as a poetic character, sums up his thunderous critical essay on the young master in the following paragraph.

The place and the value of Christopher Marlowe as a leader among English poets it would be almost impossible for historical criticism to over-estimate. To none of them all, perhaps, have so many of the greatest among them been so deeply and so directly indebted. Nor was ever any great writer's influence upon his fellows more utterly and unmixedly an influence for good. He first, and he alone, guided Shakespeare into the right way of work; his music, in which there is no echo of any man's before him, found its own echo in the more prolonged but hardly more exalted harmony of Milton's. He is the greatest discoverer, the most daring and inspired pioneer, in all our poetic literature. Before him there was neither genuine blank verse nor a genuine tragedy in our language. After his arrival the way was prepared, the paths were made straight, for Shakespeare.

So much for Marlowe's achievement. But what about his premature destruction? He was murdered on 30 May 1593, in an upper room of a house, probably a bawdy house, in Deptford kept by a woman named Mistress Bull. The district was within the royal precincts of Greenwich Palace, where even the drawing of a sword was forbidden. The punishment for duelling and other violent conduct was death.

The circumstances of the supposed drunken brawl in which Marlowe came to blows with three men and was killed with his own dagger being turned against him and stabbing him through the eye, have never been taken at their face value. The reason for these doubts has been that the three men, after arrest and some questioning, or pretence of questioning, were pardoned. Their names were Robert Poley, Ingram Frizer, and Nicholas Skeres. Ingram Frizer, the man who in self-defence against the enraged poet turned the dagger and thrust it into Marlowe's brain, was no mere boon companion. It appears that he had been concerned, in 1581, in an elaborate international plot between the French, the English and the Turks, to seize Malta from the Catholic Order of the Grand Knights, who held the island as an outpost of Spanish power.

England had been quietly infiltrating soldiers into Malta. Drake and Hawkins took part in organising naval preparations. The English 'agent', working from the English College in Rome, was this Ingram Frizer. He, with Robert Poley, were in the employment of Sir Francis Walsingham, who had also employed Marlowe on the recommendation of the Minister's brother Sir Thomas Walsingham, who was an admirer of Marlowe and frequently entertained him at his house in Chislehurst. It was in Chislehurst Church that Marlowe was alleged to have been buried. An American academic persuaded the authorities to open a grave there, only a few years ago, on the presumption that a solution of the mystery of the poet's death would be revealed. Nothing was found.

Hotson's more historically orthodox researches in the Public Record Office, however, suggest that the quarrel was not accidental, incident to a drunken brawl amongst four buddies, or maybe even strangers. What more probably was the cause of the murder was that Marlowe, since his under-graduate days in Cambridge, had been gainfully employed in the service of Sir Francis Walsingham's Secret Service Office. This would account for his frequent absences during term time, without being asked to account for them. With his extravagant personality, his intellectual arrogance aggravated by his humble birth and financial circumstances, he would have constand need of money to augment the meagre scholarship which had carried him to the university, where he mixed with his social betters, only to find most of them inferior in ability and ambition.

Success in London as the leading playwright after the production of *Tamburlaine* and *Faustus*, with the other handful of plays, including his *Edward II*, which was yet another model for Shakespeare, only increased Marlowe's appetite for grandeur. He was patronised by Sir Walter Raleigh, also a poet, but a dangerous patron because of his atheistic ideas, poisonous fruits of the Renaissance. What Marlowe learned he used with as much publicity as his genius could summon. Not only ideas but practices, imitating the ways of life of the 'glory that was Greece' were attributed to Raleigh, and thence to Marlowe. Neither made any secret of their wildness.

The danger was that Marlowe, through his service under the Crown, knew too much to be allowed to indulge in indiscreet conduct, and still more indiscreet boastings. What followed was a decision by his masters that he must be silenced. That is the more probable cause of the scene in Mistress Bull's upper room, where a supposed irrelevant drunken brawl was staged, and Marlowe's double career brought to an end.

For the Canterbury Festival in Coronation Year, 1953, the corporation commissioned me to write a play for performance in the courtyard of St Augustine's Abbey, outside the old walls of the City. I used the story of this son of the town, and I domesticated it as far as possible, in order to locate it more closely. I brought in the whole Marlowe family, with its history from Christopher's birth to his death, making the last occasion coincide with the marriage ceremony of his younger sister. I took poetic licence for much of the story, and introduced a royal visit by Queen Elizabeth, which brought the overweening young genius to the presence of the Queen; an audacious bit of stagecraft that got his father into trouble with the jealous aldermen of the City, after the departure of the royal party. The last Act of the play shows the wedding festivities of Christopher's younger sister. The noisy gaiety is suddenly silenced by a heavy thudding at the door of the parental home. The intruder is Chapman, the scholar-poet. He has come to break the news of Marlowe's death.

Throughout the drama, numerous Canterbury worthies play their parts. Their names are taken from registers of the sixteenth century. One of them is Laurence Applegate, a tailor, and also a toper. Throughout the play he speaks in hexameters, to give the effect of pompous and somewhat maudlin sentiment. But he was present, as a close neighbour, at the scene of the boy's birth. Now, at the end, he is also in the home of the Marlowes, and he hears George Chapman (speaking in blank verse of characteristic solemnity) say this,

> Listen, you wedding guests, here's an example
> Of those divinest phrases which he beat
> Like leaf of gold beneath the craftsman's mallet.
> Hark to what he says of a bride's coming,
> Words that befit his sister's marriage day,
> Her sweet appearance where she stands before us
> Entitled to her triumph and the joy
> We must not darken with the shadow of grief.
> Listen, friends, here are Christopher's words
> Picturing the Goddess of Love herself,
> Fair Venus, now embodied in this bride.
> *'Upon her head she ware a myrtle wreath,*
> *From whence her veil reach'd to the ground beneath;*
> *Her veil was artificial flowers and leaves,*
> *Whose workmanship both man and beast deceives:*
> *Many would praise the sweet smell as she past,*
> *When 'twas the odour which her breath forth cast;*
> *And there for honey bees have sought in vain,*
> *And beat from thence, have lighted there again.'*

The poor, grief-stricken father is incredulous, but at last he realises the genius of his son, and cries

> My son wrote that, Sir ? Those are Christopher's words ?
> That's good and sober sense enough.

> You heard them, Mother? And you girls?
> The boy is standing in the room, it seems:
> Is with us after all . . .

Chapman, still somewhat sententious, takes up the old man's reaction, and proclaims,

> The poet stands in all the rooms of the world,
> And is an ever present figure watching there
> Noting the traffic of our human hearts.
> You cannot banish him by death. His voice
> Sings on, making the world he celebrates
> Triumphant over the grave. Hero and Leander,
> The lovers in this poem, will survive
> The massive stones of Canterbury Cathedral.
> Such is my prophecy, who stands for Christopher
> Upon this wedding day. Let us proceed.

His advice is taken, and the celebration winds down to the final benediction by the parson. But old Applegate must have the last words, though they come from his cups. The bridal procession has moved out to the street, leaving him alone. He pours yet another cup of wine and advances toward the audience, raises the cup, and then speaks the epilogue.

> Ladies and gentlemen, we are the eternal audience.
> We are younger than we seem, older than we look.
> We have attended the birth of the poet Christopher Marlowe.
> We have seen his coming of age, we have witnessed foul murder.
> All is not done. Whether you be from Canterbury
> Or from the furthest corners of the English world,
> You shall be Christopher Marlowe's audience for ever.
> Here is a mystery beyond our understanding.
> Accept it as you will. I raise this cup of wine
> To symbolise the miracle that we have seen;
> The Canterbury boy, the shoemaker's son
> Changed to Apollo. It needs the wastrels of the world,
> Such as I am, to spot these dubious procedures,
> That lack official sanction, being the playful gestures
> Of the Olympian Gods in all their wantonness.
>
> (*He raises the cup again*).
>
> All's in this glass, the caprice and the genius.
> Water becomes wine, as at the feast in Cana.
> Drink this, said God, at the sacrament of inspiration.
> Of this, immortal souls are made. Immortal souls

Who hear the Sons of Morning singing. Christopher Marlowe
Is of that choir, his voice a grace-note to our Canterbury.
(*He tosses off the wine, stumbles and subsides upon the bench
as he murmurs his last line.*)
Amen, I say to that. Amen, and God have mercy on us.

I may have taken some liberty in thus using Leslie Hotson's theory about
the cause of Marlowe's death, but the probability is there. The killer had
worked in Malta. Marlowe wrote a play, *The Jew of Malta*; a strange
tragedy, which suggests close acquaintance with violence and intrigue. As
a slave says in one scene,

> Why, was there ever seen such villany,
> So neatly plotted, and so well performed?
> Both held in hand, and flatly both beguiled?

There was much *villany* in Marlowe's short life. But there was also much
music.

The Stanhopes

THE STANHOPE family, like the Sidneys and the Sackvilles, were intruders from above, into the indigenous gentry of Kent. Their power, and nation-wide connections and interests, did much to open out the county to the more general activities and culture of the kingdom, and the period during which the seven successive Earls of Stanhope flourished was particularly enhanced by their distinction as scholars and statesmen.

The family settled at Chevening over 250 years ago, and the seven generations of the family who have lived there have been markedly house-proud, giving inventive and imaginative attention to the maintenance of the house and estate. The death of the seventh Earl in 1967, without an heir, brought the title to an end and left the great house vacant. Such noble domains can no longer be maintained by individual owners out of the pro-ceeds of farming the land within their enclosure. It has been suggested that Chevening should be taken over by the State as a permanent home for the Princes of Wales. I should think that it would be more appropriate as the official home of the Dukes of Kent, thus helping to restore to the county, or preferably the duchy, its former concise character as almost 'A Little Kingdom', as I called it in a book of that title.

Chevening is within 20 miles of the centre of London, but its situation toward the end of the Westerham valley that runs east and west out of Surrey along the northern part of the Kentish Weald, has made it a geo-graphical site that has diverted modern development of main roads and suburban intrusion. It is now isolated somewhat by these twentieth-century rural changes around it; so much so, that unless the estate as a whole is given to some definite purpose, it must inevitably disappear piecemeal under the rising tide of democracy, with its gentle but inexorable wavelets. The architectural character of the house is regal, suited to be the home of a royal but constitutional figure so closely associated with the county, and symbolical of it.

The house has long been an organic feature in the history of Kent. It owes its name to Adam de Chevening who settled there early in the thirteenth century, but it passed from that family in 1551 to a John Lennard, who also held land in the neighbourhood at Sundridge, Knockholt and Halstead. These Lennards were lawyers, members of a profession that began to proliferate under the Plantagenet kings and the sophisticated growth of the Church as a landowner. The profits made by the lawyers account for the detestation of these black-gowned professionals expressed in the whole of folk literature, and in the treatment of them and their skilfully-gotten gains whenever the hapless people rose in short-lived revolts.

In spite of latterday encroachment of suburbia, the Westerham valley, that western reach of the Kentish weald along the ancient Roman settlement of Titsey over the Surrey boundary, has kept a touch of poetic beauty, an enhancement which nature composes here and there through the scripture of geography. Travelling eastward further into Kent, between the North Downs on the left-hand and Toys Hill and Ide Hill on the right, we feel a sense of a natural seclusion, which survives, ghostlike, even though the road through the villages between Westerham and Riverhead is blatantly motorised. We feel that somewhere, to left and right of us, the landscape still remains secretive, where the young Darenth stream creeps, and woods rise toward the downland on our left and the sombre domes of the two hills on our right. The road through the valley, as also branch lanes off it on the left, are abruptly turned at the walls of Chevening estate, and discreetly led round its periphery. May that prohibition remain for ever.

It was one of these Lennards who, by taking a long lease of Knole, kept the poet-statesman Thomas Sackville from inhabiting it. Though Queen Elizabeth had bestowed it on him in 1566, he could not take possession until 1603 (see page 81). The Lennards, who by marriage had acquired the title of Lord Dacre, moved to Hurstmonceaux; but they continued to be buried at Chevening. It was a Lord Dacre who pulled down the earlier house at Chevening, and rebuilt on the site. Sir John Summerson, that meticulously accurate writer on the history of architecture, has verified that the new mansion was designed by Inigo Jones. It is designed on the grand scale, but with lyrical lightness.

There the Dacres lived, until the grandson of the man who employed Inigo Jones lost his fortune. He married an illegitimate daughter of Charles II and was created Earl of Sussex. He succumbed to the vices of Charles's Court life, and following his death in 1715 (after a long and penurious retirement to Chevening) his daughters sold the estate two years later to James Stanhope, the first Earl, who had distinguished himself, first as a soldier fighting in the confused and purposeless wars in Flanders and the Peninsular, occasioned by the dynastic rivalries of the ornamental but pernicious dynasties of the Hapsburgs and the Bourbons, who did nothing but harm to their centuries-long hold on the unfortunate people of western Europe.

After that martial career, James Stanhope came home and at the age of forty, married a young heiress named Lucy Pitt, thus making a connection that later was to advance the family fortunes and power. He took to politics, in the Whig interest, and at once was transfixed by a few barbed arrows from Jonathan Swift. But he was as ruthless and headstrong, as well as brave, in his political life as he had been on the field of battle. So on the death of Queen Anne, when it was thought that the Tories might use military force to thwart the Hanoverian succession and restore the Stuarts, Stanhope was advanced as the man to prevent this *coup d'etat*.

Accordingly, when King George I arrived, Stanhope was made Secretary of State and a Privy Councillor. As such, he conducted most of the negotiations in Europe during the uneasy lull between wars, where the Low Countries and Austria, France and Spain, growled at each other from within the uncertain frontiers of their harried and starving territories. He also fought so well at home, both against the Tories and within his own party, the Whigs, that by the time George I returned to Hanover, Stanhope was in control of the government.

When Stanhope bought Chevening in 1717, he and his wife Lucy at once began to 'modernise' it, Inigo Jones's original being by that time not quite in the latest architectural fashion. It was Lucy, daughter of the rich nabob Thomas Pitt, who undertook most of the alterations. They were so various that the work was still in progress when the first Earl died. His public duties, which included the difficult and delicate job of bursting The South

Sea Bubble, kept him away from home, either in London or abroad. The Duke of Marlborough was old and sick, and Stanhope had therefore to take charge of the Army.

During the exposure of the South Sea Company Stanhope took a strong line and proposed that the estates of the people responsible for the swindle should be confiscated, in order somewhat to relieve the victims. He was, of course, attacked in the House of Lords by one of the peers implicated. His anger was so great that he had a stroke, was carried home, and died next day, on 5 February 1721. He was brought to Chevening for burial. His wife gave birth to twins later in the year, and survived him only by two years. His tomb in Westminster Abbey, designed by William Kent and erected by Rysbrack is as eloquent in stone as he was in office as the leading statesman during the opening of the Hanoverian period of our history. The Prussian ambassador in England described him as 'the only Englishman I know who has a truly comprehensive spirit'. He was certainly a man of great vitality, and this characteristic remained with his descendants for five generations, in one form or another, augmented by the equally powerful genes which Lucy Pitt imported into the family.

The combination produced a son, the second Earl, who was only seven years old when his father died, and nine when he lost his mother. It may have been this bewildering experience that made him a shy, introspective character. He remained diffident all his life, subdued by a premature acquaintance with death. His grandfather, Thomas Pitt, who became his guardian, died after fulfilling that important office only for the next two years. A brother and two sisters died while he was still a youth.

After the death of his grandfather, Philip Stanhope's guardianship was undertaken by a cousin, Lord Chesterfield, a literary dilettante who tried to dissuade the boy from following his own bent, which was mathematics. This could not have helped to reduce the diffidence which hid such remarkable abilities that later in life Stanhope became one of the leading mathematicians of his time. When he was sent on the Grand Tour, that most valuable feature in any educational method, he showed little interest in the pictures, sculptures and buildings which he was intended to study. He turned inwards, to a study of theology, metaphysics, and the subject for which he so obviously had a genius, mathematics. He made such progress in this last that when he returned home to Chevening, there to set up house with his sister Lucy as doyenne, he was elected to a Fellowship of the Royal Society.

He married late, at the age of 32. The woman of his choice was also mature, the twenty-six year old Grizel Hamilton, grand-daughter of the Scottish Lord Haddington. She brought no money to the marriage, but a gentle and loving character, wholly harmonious with that of the absent-minded and socially shy mathematician. Country life at Chevening suited them both, and Stanhope was for long desultory in his attendance at the House of Lords. Only when his cousin, William Pitt, rose to power, did Stanhope rally to represent the family in its public life. All the Stanhopes were remarkable for their family loyalty, and it included the Pitts, relatives on the female side, through the sweet character of Lady Lucy, whose domestic interests dominated her outlook on life, and made the daily regime of the great house of Chevening as intimate as that of a cottage.

Here is an extract from a letter which she wrote to her brother after attending the festivities for George III's Coronation: 'Mamma has wrote you in the enclosed letter all that has passed, how well we came off; the bairns behaved like two angels, as well as possible in every respect. They weed three times, but gave little trouble as they never went further than the passage and did what they had to there without any scruple. . .', and so she goes on about getting home and putting the children to bed.

The elder of those two boys was delicate, and a few years later he died of consumption in Switzerland, where his parents had taken him. It is significant that both parents went, leaving the younger boy at Eton. The whole family was desolate after the death of this young Lord Mahon, the heir, who as he was about to expire, dictated a letter to his brother Charles, urging him 'never do anything which you wish to hide from anybody, for you can hide nothing from God; never tell an untruth, be honest and good in every respect, and never mind naughty boys laughing at you for being so'. Such sentiments savour of the humble piety of the lower-middle class of the eighteenth century society, where the evangelising of Wesley and his followers was doing so much to alleviate the poverty and deprivation of the majority of the population.

This genetic tendency to democratic outlook and sentiment, however, could not wholly differentiate the aristocratic family from the orthodox *hauteur* of their peers. The scientific and eccentric third Earl, that same Charles who received the pious letter from his dying brother, was later to renounce his youngest daughter Lady Lucy Rachael Stanhope, when she eloped with the family apothecary, a Thomas Taylor of Sevenoaks. Liberal opinions did not extend to a toleration of that alliance, though the Tory kinsman William Pitt helped the young couple by giving Taylor the post of controller-general of Customs.

Another member of the family, the Lord Chesterfield referred to above, famous for his letters of advice to his illegitimate son by a Frenchwoman, did not even profess to share the liberal Whiggish views and habits of his kinsfolk. He was a highbrow and solitary figure, always in opposition to the party in political power, even though he served in it. He was a self-sufficient man, frozen within his own icy pride. When Samuel Johnson wrote the line 'Toil, envy, want, the patron, and the jail' as being the lot of the writer, the patron whom he had in mind was Chesterfield, who had snubbed him in the matter of encouragement in the making of the great Dictionary. His code of manners and moral values was worldly but exquisite, and he put it on record in the series of letters written to his son. His fame rests solely on that paternal exercise, one which, as might be expected, the young man refused to profit by.

The brilliant and genial second Earl Stanhope died in 1786, aged 72, and his homely wife lived on until her 93rd year, in the Dower House at Ovenden, where she busied herself collating the family archives, welcoming her grandchildren, and by every other means maintaining the family unity and harmony.

She wrote letters, and one addressed to the gardener at Chevening ends, after a long discourse on protecting the pear garden from visitors, with a sentence which today might well be displayed by *The National Trust* and other benevolent landowners at the entrance to their properties:

You have been long enough at Chevening to know how all ought to be and to keep encroachers in awe which is sometimes necessary though always with civility of course to teach them manners.

I have already hinted that Charles, the third Earl, broke out of the traces of warm affection which hitherto had kept the family united. He showed this difference in boyhood, for his mother wrote about him, 'His father has hopes he'll do very well. I hope for the best but dare not flatter myself too much, too well knowing what a cruel disappointment is, I try to prepare myself for the worst, and daily think what may happen'. Her foreboding was to be fulfilled by events, for he turned out to be an irritable eccentric, precocious and versatile intellectually. He inherited his father's mathematical genius, and put it to practical use by inventing various instruments. During his early years he lived in Geneva, where his brilliant intellectual gifts made so great an impression that he was invited to become one of the City Council. This experience inclined him to democratic principles and small-town individuality, which, added to his personal idiosyncracy, made him an odd-man-out when he entered the political world of his own country.

Though he married the sister of William Pitt, his kinsman, he fell out with his brother-in-law when that brilliant pragmatist introduced legislation that smelled of Toryism, and favoured open opposition to France. He turned for a while from politics to give himself to science, and more inventions, such as an improved printing press, optical lenses, canal locks, calculating machines, and the writing of a book called *Principles of Electricity*. His gaunt, lanky figure became a prop for the cartoonists of the day, notably Gillray, who fastened not only on his public life but also on his stormy relationship with his children. For he became a domestic tyrant, a know-all who was always right. By his first wife, Hester Pitt, he had three daughters. The youngest escaped by marriage. The eldest, named Hester, broke away from the paternal tyranny by going to live with her grandmother, escaping both from his erratic temper and the discomforts caused by his perpetual tinkerings with the structure of the house at Chevening. The conflict between father and daughter was a case of Greek meeting Greek, for they were alike in their arrogant self-sufficiency and power of domination; Churchillian traits.

Hester's subsequent career was to make her the most immortal member of the great family, and I shall deal with that after setting the rest of the Stanhope background. This could not be done, however, without recourse to the history of the family written by Aubrey Newman, a Fellow of the Royal Historical Society. His book is more than an academic exercise. Every character in it comes to life, animating the detailed scholarship with human energy, warmth and variety. Readers who want to know more about the Stanhopes will enjoy Mr Newman's *The Stanhopes of Chevening*, as it moves through seven generations, down to a gentle serene closure as impressive as a summer sunset.

The third Earl's career may appear to have been unsavoury, from my paragraphs above. It had more positive qualities than I have suggested. He was a powerful character, and his inventions were not all eccentric. He improved the development of steam-ships, introduced the idea of steam carriages, two pioneer contributions whose developments have revolutionised human society. Revolution was his watchword, and where he saw it at work, he added his own weight to the venture, as in his adaptation of James

Watt's discoveries, and his financing of Wilson's invention of stereotype in printing.

His son and successor, the fourth Earl, went to the other extreme, reverting to a serene and gentle way of life, but without enclosing the family in an ivory tower. On the contrary, he opened Chevening to the public, thus fore-running our way of life in the twentieth century, where the owners of almost every great house in the country sit at the receipt of democracy, apologetically making a small charge to help toward the cost of repairing the inevitable depredations caused by thousands of pairs of feet and curious fingers.

Philip Henry was as full of vagary as his father, and one of his contradictory traits was his rigid Toryism, due to his grateful fidelity to his uncle William Pitt, who had received him and helped him when he, like his sister Hester, left home to escape their father's wayward tyranny. In his lifework, he was anything but a stiff Tory. He was a pioneer in organising charity foundations. He proposed and sponsored the foundation of the National Gallery, for his interest in the arts was practical, as was shown in his care of the estate and the interior of Chevening.

These interests were passed on to the fifth Earl, a noble character who chose a wife of comparable temperament. This couple vindicated the system of aristocratic government. They did nothing but good with their wealth and their social ascendency. The Earl, also a Philip Henry, was a historian whose fame during his lifetime was exceeded only by that of Macaulay. He took a leading part in most of the new Societies founded during the nineteenth century toward the amelioration of human and other barbarism and discomfort, as our civilization became more conscious of its own defects. He introduced legislation for the passing of the Copyright Laws, thus offering a viable profession for men of letters.

The sixth Earl, after minor efforts in the Army and in politics, relapsed into conventional country gentlemanly interests, running his estates in England and Ireland benevolently but without remarkable verve, though more than supported by his vivid wife, a great hostess and patroness of musicians.

The last, and seventh Earl, James Richard, was more distinguished, and we know what an active political career he had. He was a selfless gentleman, like his grandfather. When Churchill took over the Premiership in 1940, he found Stanhope not dynamic enough for modern wartime conditions. Ruthlessness was needed, and Stanhope did not possess it. Perhaps the vitality was running thin, as usually happens in families descended in affluence from one outstanding founder, though Churchill was an alarming exception to this possible genetic frequency.

But gentleness is a great virtue, especially today now our way of life tends to treat it as a light hidden under a bushel. The last Stanhope's valediction, in leaving Chevening to the nation, was a characteristic gesture. It may make his name as permanent as that of his kinswoman Hester, though 'the evil that men do lives after them; the good is oft interred with their bones'.

It is probable that, if individual fame is likely to survive the holocausts of the twentieth century, and the illimitable possibilities of the twenty-first, the one member of the Stanhope family most likely to be remembered is Lady Hester, eldest child of the third Earl. And she does not deserve it. She did nothing outstandingly evil, to ensure immortal infamy, but in her personality she had all the satanic attributes, as Milton portrayed them. She was high-born, endowed with great physical beauty so elusive that no two people could agree about its uniqueness: she used people mercilessly and discarded them when they had served her purpose, or if they objected to her selfish demands. In society she was an explosive virago, contemptuous and insolent even when acting as official hostess to her uncle, William Pitt, the Prime Minister. She lacked aesthetic taste, and owing to the eccentric Jacobinism of her eccentric father, the third Earl Stanhope, she was indifferently educated, and might without exaggeration be called a thick-skinned philistine. In her later life, all these dubious attributes of character reached such tumidity that she became an ineffectual monster, shut up within her own insanity as well as within her ruined monastery hidden amongst the mountains of Lebanon.

That is the negative aspect of this woman whose career has put her amongst the most famous of her sex: Helen of Troy, Cleopatra, Ruth, Catherine the Great, Elizabeth the First, and Florence Nightingale. I have given this selection of comparisons because Hester Stanhope also possessed qualities in some distorted degree, for which all of these were famed, each in her particular genius. Her physical beauty has been recorded, as was that of the Helen whose face 'launched a thousand ships': she loved, voraciously, as Cleopatra loved: she was on occasion as cruel as the Russian Empress: she had judgment of character and political consciousness as had Queen Elizabeth: she could be as administratively efficient and fearless as Florence Nightingale, using her menfolk as relentlessly to her dynamic purposes. Yet in the end she achieved nothing enduring, except her own notoriety, which is almost as powerful as that of the legendary Scheherazade.

The 'good that was interred with her bones' can be less easily and briefly portrayed. It has been done, and done objectively, by the biographer Joan Haslip in her study of this strange woman, published in 1934, a piece of work so detailed and picturesque that it is not likely to be superseded. Before Miss Haslip's enquiry, nobody had taken the trouble to ferret out the mobile complexities of the way of life in the Middle East; the feuds, superstitions, barbarous civilities, hideous cruelties, and miniature political networks amongst this wreckage of ancient Biblical kingdoms, into which this powerful Englishwoman intruded, and held mythical court as 'Queen of Jerusalem', a fantasy whose origin is uncertain, but in which both she and the Arabs acquiesced.

Lady Hester was born on 12 March 1776 at Chevening, and lived there until 1800, long after her two sisters and her three half-brothers had fled from the eccentricities of her madly doctrinaire father and the icy personality of the step-mother, Louisa Grenville, who took the place of Lady Hester's mother (sister of William Pitt) a year after her death in 1780.

That death was the first adverse influence upon the girl's development. Her father's pre-occupation with science, engineering and the general improvement of the human race did not enable him to compensate for the cold indifference shown by the second Lady Stanhope toward her step-daughters and also her own sons. Hester spent much time with her grandmother, Grizel Stanhope, who tried to balance this unfortunate upbringing by over-indulging the child's passionate temperament. The combination of contrasting environments at Chevening and Burton Pynsent, near Sedgemoor, her other grandmother's home, fostered the schizophrenic division in her nature.

Her father did not wholly neglect her. He replaced her governesses by a tutor, and himself interrupted her education from time to time by instructing her in his jacobinism, the political philosophy which had made him break his allegiance to his brother-in-law Pitt, and adopt the republicanism of the revolutionists in France.

The result was to add bewilderment to the girl's inherited oddities of character. Like most children, she rebelled against her father's theories and eccentric practices, while absorbing much of them into her subconscious mind. The division of her personality thus began at an early age, with the inherited traits always dominant. She was imperious, passionate and proud.

She went her own way in spite of the parental efforts to mould her. She mothered her sisters and half-brothers, who during their childhood accepted her benevolent tyranny, grateful at least for some show of love, which neither of the parents offered. Even later, when her sisters had departed into marriage, and her brothers into their respective careers, her influence survived, though the eldest brother, Lord Mahon, and the youngest James, were later to deprecate her adventures and strange conduct. Nevertheless, they came again and again to the rescue of her wild financial crises.

Her middle brother Charles was perhaps most deeply attached to her, and it was while he was living with her and James in a house in Montague Square in London that she met General Sir John Moore, Charles' chief and friend. Both brothers fought in the Peninsular Campaign and Charles and the General were killed at the disastrous Battle of Corunna, while James suffered a nervous breakdown due to his experiences there and his grief over the loss of his brother and his friend.

Hester's short acquaintance with Moore, while he spent so much of his free time at Montague Square, caused her to fall in love with him, though he gave her no encouragement. Thus the disaster, a double brereavement, added further to the hardening of her character, which already had suffered twice from her acquaintance with death, first that of her mother when she was an infant, and secondly when the death of William Pitt robbed her of his extra-paternal love, and her exalted place as his hostess at 10 Downing Street. As for the set-back to a more passionate love, she had already had that experience during the exciting years with her uncle, when she fell in love for the first time with her cousin Lord Granville Leveson-Gower, an ambitious diplomat who realised that her personality would be no asset to his career, and who therefore jilted her and went off to Moscow as Ambassador.

That first love-affair was staged in the most exalted setting of her life, at least from the conventional social point of view. But before she went to live at Downing Street, she was to have a period almost of retreat after the nervous strain of life at home, where rebellion against her father and stepmother was combined with indiscriminate friendships around the countryside and in London.

The mental and emotional discomfort of life at Chevening after the departure of her sisters and brothers was endured for some time, but in 1820 she gave up the battle, and accepted the invitation of her other grandmother, Lady Chatham, and went to live with her at Burton Pynsent, to be indulged, as I have suggested, with such freedom that the contrast with the restraints and irritations of life at Chevening exaggerated her developing idiosyncracies. She was already a good horsewoman, and now rode madly around the Somerset countryside on a powerful black mare, unaccompanied by groom or chaperon, scandalising the local gentry, and acquiring amongst the rustic folk the beginnings of those legendary attributes which were to increase during the rest of her life, until the woman was lost in the myth.

Her paternal grandmother, the gentle Lady Grizel, who had maintained a correspondence with Lady Chatham largely about the interests and doings of the young Hester, was piqued by her grand-daughter's departure to Burton Pynsent, and the correspondence between the two grandmothers ceased. This break shows how extraordinary was the personal magnetism of the girl, who in spite of her wilful temper and imperious behaviour wherever she might be, and in whatever company, even that of Royalty, attracted so unbreakable a devotion. This power was to remain with her throughout her life. She was never without at least one faithful devotee.

Lady Chatham's death brought to an end this almost idyllic period. It also, fortunately, ended a comradeship with another cousin on the Pitt side of the family, a wild character named Lord Camelford. He was a physical giant, crude and violent, in revolt against a gentle, pedantic father, and following rather the character of the original nabob Pitt who founded the fortunes of the family. Camelford was one of the most notorious of the Regency bucks, and he ended his career of gambling and general dissipation by being killed in a duel in 1804, to everybody's relief, especially his superiors in the Royal Navy, a profession in which he had played merry hell, and but for his aristocratic connections would have been court-martialled and executed for various crimes, including that of murder.

William Pitt, Hester's uncle, had always been a good friend during her long feud with her father. Since her grandmother's death left her homeless, Pitt invited her to come to Walmer Castle, while he was out of political office. On his regaining the Premiership, he took her with him to Downing Street as his official hostess. His bachelordom during office had been an inconvenience, and he did not believe that Hester's complete lack of social tact, and her frequent rancorous and outspoken criticisms of important people and delicate political situations, could add to that inconvenience.

The relationship between this middle-aged bachelor and the almost terrifying young woman, already fully mature and authoritative at 28, was one of the wonders of the age. That age was steeped in scandalous conduct and rumours of scandal, but not a spot touched these two who reigned at Downing Street, each replete with idiosyncracies that in every respect cut across the grain of current fashion. Pitt gave his niece the paternal affection which she had missed throughout her life. In return, she loved him as a daughter, and combined this devotion with the motherliness which she had given to her brothers. She nursed him through his constant invalidism which manifested itself in frequent attacks of gout and was to kill him a year later, after the agonising uncertainties about his country's safety, until Nelson ended them at the Battle of Trafalgar. During that year of domestic collaboration, Hester put no curb on her tongue, nor did she disguise her interest and inherited ability in the art of politics. Her savage witticisms at the expense of her uncle's ministers as well as his opponents, echoed and re-echoed round Parliament, the clubs and drawing-rooms where policies and reputations were made or relinquished. She caused Pitt and Canning to fall out, largely because she was jealous of their mutual interest in Latin and Greek literature, which her lack of education prevented her from sharing.

It was during this powerful but dangerous period of her life, that she fell in love with Lord Granville Leveson-Gower. Pitt saw that humiliation faced her, and he sent the young man off to St Petersburg as Ambassador, knowing that ambition and not love was the young man's motive for his association with Hester.

Hester lacked the smallest element of reticence in her nature, and her grief was confided even to Leveson-Gower's worldly-wise mistress, Lady Bessborough, who had warned the young man that in flirting with Hester he had been playing with fire. The conflagration was seen throughout Mayfair, Whitehall, and the great country houses of the nobility. It was even rumoured that Hester's emotional disturbance was due to the fact that she was with child.

By the time that Lord Granville returned to England however, the fire had died down. Hester's sexual infatuation was lost in a more genuine, a much deeper grief. William Pitt was dying, and her love for him was both spiritual and substantial. She nursed him at the end, and his last request to Parliament was that as his niece had worked for three years as his personal secretary and hostess, during the period when England was in peril from Napoleon's ascendancy in Europe and the revolutionary political system which the 'little Corporal' imposed wherever he conquered, some permanent recognition should be made of her devotion.

For once, national gratitude survived a statesman's death. Hester was voted a pension of £1,200 a year for life. Its value would be ten times that of a similar income today. Even so, Hester fostered a grievance, and henceforth state of mind dominated her character. Her father was still estranged from her, so she could not return to Chevening, even had she so desired. She rented a house in Montague Square, and for a year or two domesticated there with her two younger half-brothers, Charles and James, who tried to enliven her with the company of the fellow officers from their regiments. But this was a dull substitute for the brilliant company that had surrounded Pitt and his ministers. Further, she had been used to feudal riches, and was not even conscious of the middle-class tradition of economic tidiness and thrift. She had no sense of proportion in money matters; was alternatively mean and lavish, according to her whim and temper, an aristocratic habit which she never outlived.

Neglected by high society which had fawned upon her even though she flagellated it during her few years of power, she tried the experiment of retreating from human contacts, by taking a house in the Welsh mountains, where she could nurse her sorrow at the loss of her brother Charles and General Sir John Moore at the Battle of Corunna. But 'once bitten, twice shy' applies to the experience of grief as well as to other of life's discomforts. Hester's character was growing harder as blow followed blow, humiliation after humiliation. Her practical capabilities, apart from her contemptuous indifference to the realities of finance, became more marked. Her farmhouse in the Wye valley was smartened up, and she lived an artificial rustic life there, with women servants and male grooms, and encouraged home industries amongst the Welsh peasants. She did not, however, relinquish her political interests, which she kept up to date through her wide and intricate family connections, her brother James acting as scout.

The experience renewed her vitality, and she soon began to crave for a similar but stronger medicine. In 1810, she went abroad with James, and a young, newly qualified doctor named Charles Meryon, a curiously docile but ambitious person who was to remain completely mesmerised by her, escaping and being drawn back, until the last stages of her life when her lapses into delusions and fits of raging insanity finally drove him away. She was never to return to England.

Her adventures from that time until her death twenty-nine years later, have become legendary, and have placed her among the immortals of history.

She went first to Gibraltar, to find that her fame preceded her. She was besieged by the closely crowded society there, and would have left at once, had not another arrival attracted her attention. He was the rich and reckless Marquis of Sligo, who was in trouble for some misdemeanour toward the British Navy. He had with him a friend, also rich, named Michael Bruce. Both were in their early twenties, and their handsome looks and gay demeanour amused the now world-weary and disillusioned Lady Hester, smouldering in her grievances against the conventions and hypocrisies of high society, although she had left that environment for ever.

Michael Bruce, twelve years her junior, was an amiable *nouveau-riche*, dazzled by his own wealth, which was enabling him to make close contact with the nobility, a process of infiltration which had been active throughout society since the seventeenth century. Bruce found Lady Jester doubly attractive; by her name and reputation, and by her physical uniqueness. She was tall, immensely dignified and dominating, her features familiarly reminiscent of those of her famous uncle, the late Prime Minister. Her biting wit stimulated the young man.

His attachment to her was ensured by the departure of her brother James, who was recalled to his regiment. Lord Sligo also had to depart, summoned before the Admiralty to account for some minor transgression.

Lady Hester, recovered from her depression and lapse into middle-age dowdiness, responded to young Michael Bruce's gallantry so overwhelmingly that he discovered himself as a man, and was surprised to find himself to be the first to deflower this virgin spinster. They left together for Malta, accompanied only by Dr Meryon (patronised also by Bruce), and Hester's companion, a gentle and educated Miss Williams, another magnetised attraction equally as helplessly entangled as Dr Meryon in the future adventures and fate of their employer.

After some months in Malta, the lovers departed for Greece, whither Lord Sligo had preceded them. On their arrival at Zante, Bruce wrote to his friend Sligo suggesting that he should join them. The fact was, he found Lady Hester's temperament so wayward and unpredictable that he was alarmed. The close quarters and lack of privacy on the boat had caused Lady Hester to play the part of the great lady, though this was inconsistent with her open advertisement of the love affair at its beginning in Malta. Further, on landing in Greece, Bruce found that Hester was totally uninterested in history and archaeology, which were his hobbies. The united party travelled around Greece, making the acquaintance of the various Turkish governors, finally to settle in Athens, where Lady Hester and Bruce took a house together and entertained, amongst a cosmopolitan set, the picturesque figure of Byron, which Hester first saw diving naked into the harbour as the boat approached Piraeus. He visited frequently, but a clash between these two dominating personalities was inevitable. Lady Hester found Byron handsome enough, but thought his poetry mere verse-mongering, and said so. She also disputed his statements in conversation, and finally decided that his eyes were too close-set, a sign of viciousness.

Byron was equally disillusioned. He thought her to be over-bearing, and he left Athens for Patras in order to escape from her sharp tongue. He wrote to his friend Hobhouse from that refuge, saying

I have seen too little of the lady to form any decisive opinion, but I have discovered nothing different to other she-things, except a great disregard of received notion in her conversation as well as conduct. I don't know if this will recommend her to our sex, but I am sure it won't to her own. She is going to Constantinople.

Her arrival there, to display openly her illicit alliance with Michael Bruce, and to command social contact with the Sultan regardless of the intricate social niceties of the Ottoman Court and way of life, alarmed the British Minister, Stratford Canning, a strait-laced young diplomat. He was overawed by her famous name and relationship with the Government at home. He was relieved, temporarily at least, when Lady Hester took a house along the coast of the Bosphorus. The love affair did not thrive there. The icy winds that blow through the Bosphorus attacked Hester's chest, and she relapsed into invalidism. Sligo and Bruce escaped to Smyrna, after some sharp conflicts between Hester's pride and Bruce's conceit. The boy of twenty-two even had dared to denounce her 'extraordinary ignorance'. It is certainly odd that in spite of her passion for travel around the Mediterranean and the Middle East, she showed no knowledge of or interest in the literature, arts and history of this cradle of western civilization.

During his absence, Bruce had been thinking over the awkward situation into which he had been dragged, not unwillingly, by this passionate love affair, which was proving to be mainly physical. He was very rich, and could sustain Lady Hester, though she dealt with financial matters as though she were administering a small nation. But he still believed her to be uncommonly beautiful in her regality. So he went back to her and proposed marriage, in spite of his father's objections.

To his chagrin, she refused. Friends and family were drawn into the discussions, and brother James took strong objection to such a misalliance. The uncertainty dragged on, while Lady Hester defiantly publicised her liaison more and more widely, deploying her perverse temper recklessly as her character matured and hardened. In addition, she continued to flout the official policy of the Diplomatic Service in its dealings with the Greeks and the Turks, dictated by the permanently ominous power of Russia looming in the background.

The lovers, by their unwillingness to solve the problem one way or the other, were being driven further and further from social acceptance at home. They were becoming refugees, in much the same way as Byron and Shelley, not because of their conduct, but of their open display of it and the theories which they invented to justify it.

The lovers set sail to spend the winter in Egypt, but were shipwrecked on the way, on a rock off the island of Rhodes. Lady Hester took command during the crisis, for the crew were incompetent and her own followers frozen with terror. They were finally brought ashore, but lost all their luggage and Hester's little pet dog. All that was saved was a bag of money and a miniature of Sir John Moore. The money served to buy clothes, and it was from this incident that Lady Hester took to the habit of wearing Turkish dress. That was another step nearer her final severance from England, but not from her imperious way of life.

The picturesquely attired couple were received in Egypt with full honours by the reigning tyrant, Mehemet Ali, who though he had risen from humble origin, on a tide of blood, exhibited the grace and royal technique of an hereditary monarch. After a month spent in Cairo, enlivened by visits to the Pyramids, and the acquaintance of selected members of the English colony, Lady Hester and Bruce left for Jaffa, where again they took a house together, excluding even the faithful Dr Meryon, whom Bruce found to be pedantic and a bore. Hester's lavish expenditure in gifts and bribes, with which she sugared her imperious demands, was largely supplied by Bruce. He was beginning to be worried about his finances. In addition, Hester was becoming more eccentric, as a result of taking up the study of astrology, and being informed by a crazy fakir that she was destined to be crowned as Queen of Jerusalem.

This prophecy so excited her that she decided to go to the Holy City, and she set off in state, with a company of janissaries commandeered from the Governor of Jaffa. The journey was a triumphant progress, for her fame had spread throughout Arabia. She was said to be completely fearless, and it was even doubted that she was a woman: so splendid and intimidating a figure must be super-human. As she encountered Arab chieftains, one by one they made oblation and entertained her in their tents with ceremonial hospitality, and feasts that must have kept Dr Meryon busy.

At Nazareth she fell off her horse and was obliged to rest for a week, during which she met the famous German explorer Burckhardt, whom Bruce introduced to her. This encounter further annoyed her because Bruce's worship tended to be diverted to his professional traveller and archaeologist, who had won the confidence of the Turks and Arabs without bribing his way around their territories, as she had done, mostly at Bruce's expense.

After a cruel winter spent at Hamah, on the banks of the river Orontes, Lady Hester determined to fulfil one of her most persistent ambitions, which was to visit Palmyra, the almost fabulous city which in the third century A.D. had been the capital of a small kingdom splintered from the Royal Empire by its queen, Zenobia, a beautiful and strong-minded woman whose intelligence and capacity for benevolent rule appealed to this Englishwoman as embodiments of her own capacities. Zenobia had revolted against the Roman domination, as Hester believed herself to have thrown off the rules and conventions of her own country.

So once again the *caravanserai* set forth, at considerable expense. And again Hester's personality dominated the wandering folk of the desert. She took to calling herself 'Queen of the Arabs', and consulted her books of astrology with increasing credulity. Her arrival and reception at Palmyra confirmed these delusions.

It was inevitable that the love affair should become irksome to both parties. Bruce, sufficient in his own conceit, realised that Hester was withdrawing more and more into the world of her own fantasies, and that the financial cost of following her there was threatening to exhaust even his great wealth. He and she had spent four years together, and he was becoming increasingly an appendage. But it was Hester who decided to make the break.

No sooner had he gone than Hester fell victim to a widespread outbreak of plague in the Middle East. It affected her brain, and though she recovered, her mind remained damaged, and was subject to outbreaks of violent temper. Delusions hovered there like birds of ill omen. The story of the remainder of her life is a sad one. She retreated from normal human contacts, finally to immure herself in the ruins of a monastery hidden within the convolutions of the mountains of the Lebanon, under a height known as Djoun. She saw less and less of her own countrymen, though she kept remote contact in order to finance her repairs of the ruin, whose interior she restored into a semblance of some fairy palace described in the stories of The Arabian Nights.

Dr Meryon was sent home, where he married, but he could not break the spell, and he went out to be with her almost at the end of her life, leaving her still alive, and still able to treat him as a servant of doubtful ability. To the very last, her powerful personality made itself felt throughout Arabia, largely by the legend which had accumulated round it. Her letters, mostly fulminations growing ever more delirious, to her relatives in England and to successive Prime Ministers and Governments, came home like echoes of dying thunder.

Those echoes still reverberate around the landscape of history, as time withdraws it to a more insignificant horizon. But we hear the sound today, and are drawn back, as to the teasing attraction of an enigma, to the power and misused genius of this woman, who is likely to be the only member of the great Stanhope family to be remembered, along with Zenobia of Palmyra, and other immortal queens of whose grandeur and authority she partook, though in fact she served no useful purpose.

William Harvey

IT CAN be argued that all human activities, practical as well as theoretical, spring from the consciousness of some sort of philosophy within the mind of man. The famous words of Descartes, 'I think, therefore I am', imply this, and can be extended into 'I think, therefore I act'. I recall an amusing demonstration of this. It occurred many years ago when I was sitting at work in my study, while a journeyman was fitting a slow-combustion stove in the fireplace. He was not garrulous, and did not interfere with my writing. At the end of his task, however, he stretched himself, stiff after crouching, turned to me and said, 'Now, sir, would you like me to explain the *philosophy* of this stove ?' I was delighted. I was all attention, though my concentration on his instruction was diluted by the flow of thought aroused by the nice touch of folk-pedantry in the unexpected use of the word 'philosophy.'

But why not ? The craftsman was right; he was speaking out of an inherited, unconscious tradition going back to the Middle Ages, indeed to pre-historical ages, when any form of applied, acquired skill, was believed to be a god-given power. It was called a 'mystery'. This closeness between speculation and function has given a kind of sanctity to every practitioner, in whatever field. Do we not still speak of 'priest-craft' in connection with theology, that most ancient and primitive continent of abstract thought ?

It is not surprising, then, that the art and science of medicine should have had a particular affinity with philosophic exploration down the centuries, and that the first medical practitioner, the half-mythical Aesculapius, and Aristotle, the first truly inductive philosopher, should have become tutelary figures in the history of medicine. Even today, with medicine ramifying into an infinite number of specialisations, the symbolical figure of Aristotle survives as a reminder of some unitary concept toward which the most advanced pathology, psychology, neurology, and even the mechanics of surgery are suggesting a mutual interdependence.

So great a profession, by reason of the social and personal power it offers to its practitioners (even under a National Health System), by very reason of its roots in philosophic enquiry, has offered scope for infinite quackery; but the 'bedside manner' is not to be easily dismissed. It too is deep-rooted in the intuitions of past practice, the belief that mind and body are an organism which is still a mystery that connotes the unity of all things.

These thoughts of a layman are by way of introduction to the task of preparing the canvas on which to paint the portrait of one of Kent's most universally revered sons, William Harvey, whose discoveries in the science of philosophy created a revolution in medical knowledge. He stands with Newton, Darwin and Einstein as a creator of a new epoch in human knowledge.

He lived at a time, during the reigns of King James I and King Charles I, with eight years of the Commonwealth, which might be called the tag-end of the Renaissance, a cultural period in European history comparable to our own, with everything in the melting-pot; everything questioned, much overthrown, much invented and tried out in politics, religious belief and practice, domestic habits and mechanisms; wild conjectures in the extension and application of knowledge; confusions and clashes consequent upon all these elements in human life.

Science was coming of age, and rebelling against the parental control by theology. It was beginning to take on more and more authority in the world of medicine, and to question that of Aristotle and Galen, the two outstanding classical demiurges of the profession. That profession in its methods was still comparable to the practices of the African witch-doctors who function today, not without occasional success. Even its great figures, such as Paracelsus (about whom Robert Browning wrote one of his most characteristic long poems), John Caius and his master Vesalius, Fabricius who was Harvey's master at the University of Padua, all of whom were explorers with varying degrees of scientific attack in their work, continued to condone and practise medical treatments of horrifying ineffectuality and cruelty. But these survivals of what can only be called witch-craft persisted through the nineteenth century. Wherever there is no certainty of factual knowledge, charlatanism slips in, often disguised as contemporary fashion.

William Harvey was born in Folkestone into a family deeply rooted in Kent. It was a commercial family which since the reign of Henry III had been prosperous. A Sir Walter Harvey was Mayor of London at the time of that king's death. William's father, Thomas Harvey, was well-to-do, for he held properties around Folkestone, at Newington, Arpinge, and other hamlets, which had been in the family for several generations and were to come into William's hands, he being the eldest son. Thomas married twice, both his wives being from a family named Haulk, of Hastingleigh, that remote and charming little village lost in the Downs some ten miles inland from Folkestone. They too were prosperous, and the conjunction of the families consolidated the substantial setting in which the boy began his career.

He was born on 1 April 1578, and the date of his baptism, five days later, is recorded in the Canterbury Cathedral Register, though the ceremony was held at the Church of St Mary and St Eanswith. Little is known about his infancy in Folkestone, but it is likely to have been a happy one, supplying the basis of a steady temperament, which was to counteract an inherited tendency to outbursts of aggressive anger. He did not suffer opposition gladly, though he had to put up with it for some few years after the publication of his first book which exploded in the medical world as did Darwin's *Origin of Species* in that of the theologians over two hundred years later.

He had two sisters, one dying in childhood, and six brothers, all of whom prospered, especially Eliab, born some twelve years after William. Eliab, with three of his brothers, traded with the Middle East, and rode on the tide of prosperity due to the importing of coffee beans from Turkey. This newfangled drink had been introduced into England during the later part of the sixteenth century, and within a few decades it became so popular that the first 'coffee-houses' appeared. These institutions were frequented by merchants and later by courtiers, writers, and news-gatherers who wrote the broad-sheets which were the forerunners of the newspaper.

The Harvey brothers traded in all manner of spices and other oriental merchandise, and were thus in a position to take advantage of the ever increasing demand for the coffee bean. William appears to have been supplied by the family with this expensive luxury, his favourite indulgence. John Aubrey, in his *Brief Lives*, which book includes the first account of William Harvey's life, says that 'he was wont to drinke coffee; which he and his brother Eliab did, before Coffee-houses were in fashion in London.'

When Harvey's will was proved, it was found that he left certain items to a niece, 'excepting my coffee pot'. This suggests that the silver coffee-pot was highly treasured by him, and that he desired it to go to the brother with whom he so frequently enjoyed the drink that, as was recorded at that time 'comforteth the Brain, and Heart, and helpeth Digestion'. The diarist Evelyn, that great maker of gardens, wrote in 1637 'there came in my time to Balliol one Conopius out of Greece. He was the first I ever saw drink coffee, which custom came not into England until thirty years after'.

The family home of the Harveys, known as The Post House, in the middle of Folkestone, was both domestic and business headquarters. It must have teemed with life, for all the children were born there, to mingle during childhood with clerks and apprentices, agents and customers, thus acquiring a firsthand knowledge of human nature.

The mother's family, the Haulks, was also mercantile. A cousin was Alderman and Sheriff, and served as Mayor during 1610–11. He led a trainband of archers in Canterbury in 1588, one of his young fellow militiamen being John Marlowe, father of Christopher Marlowe.

The ménage offered a fertile setting for the boy's mind and character. His position as the eldest child gave him self-confidence and the technique of authority, valuable attributes toward the making of a successful career. Unlike Marlowe, he did not have the strain of seeking a scholarship to the King's School in Canterbury, and later another one to a Cambridge college. He was entered as a commoner to King's School at the age of ten, and in 1593 he entered Caius College, Cambridge. He was nineteen when he took his Arts degree, having already chosen his vocation in medicine. There is no certainty about what led to this. Maybe those first ten years before going to Canterbury offered him a freedom close to earth, for much of the time was spent on the family farmholding at West Dane. In those days the Weald was still heavily wooded, in spite of the demands for charcoal to smelt the iron in the soil, and for timber to build the ships that carried our wool and cloth, or provided the rudiments of a Royal Navy. The primaeval Forest of Anderida was mainly of oak, a wood so appropriate for all these purposes that Queen Elizabeth's Government had to impose an Act rationing the felling of timber.

Wild life abounded, to stimulate an intellectual curiosity already becoming a conscious passion, the determination to find out how nature worked, in all its vast and mysterious variety.

He chose the right College in Cambridge, for in 1567 Gonville College had been reorganised by its dynamic Master, Dr John Caius, and renamed as it is today, with a bias in its curriculum toward medicine. The career and doctrine of Caius must have influenced Harvey, for both remained reverent toward Galen, in spite of their divergence from much of his medical dogma. Both continued their studies at Padua University, the most reputable centre for medical science in Europe during the sixteenth century. Caius is said to have lodged with the famous anatomist Andreas Vesalius during his terms there. This great teacher was later to be Harvey's.

Caius returned to England determined to get more facilities for furthering the study of anatomy. He obtained a Charter which granted Gonville College the bodies of two criminals every year, after their execution. It is significant to note that after dissection, the remains were duly buried after a religious service attended, with reverence, by the Master and Fellows of the College. This is a nice example of the way of life still made coherent by the Christian belief in the sanctity of the individual. At least, that was the philosophic idea behind the ceremony.

Harvey spent two years at Padua, and profited greatly, for he found it to be both cosmopolitan and democratic. It was ruled more by its students than by its dons, and thereby attracted scholars from all over Europe, and especially from other ancient universities in Italy such as Bologna, the oldest, where the anarchic and despotic local governments of the so-called free cities created too disturbing an environment for scholastic work. Even in Padua, however, there was frequent trouble among the students, owing to their different pursuits and national origins.

The variety amongst his fellow students was useful to Harvey. It widened his interest in every field of cultural affairs. Though his Latin prose was consistently, throughout his life, criticised as clumsy, he could use it freely to express himself, and as he wrote his two most important books in this *lingua franca*, they quickly attracted the notice of scholars in all the universities of Europe, so that he became famous (or notorious to some ultra-conservative practitioners), and his theses widely proclaimed and accepted. At that time, scientific disquisition had not been purged of literary and imaginative phraseology. I doubt, indeed, if this divorce took place until the twentieth century, with the rapidly increasing medical knowledge that demands day by day new nomenclature which has created a jargon intelligible only to the specialist. A hundred years ago, Darwin wrote of his discoveries in a prose that is still a cultural vehicle in which the general reader may travel. So did Lyell and Huxley. Thus it was that

Harvey, in writing his set of rules for the student of Anatomy, phrased the eleventh of them as follows, 'To serve in their three courses according to the hour-glass, 1. the lower belly, nasty yet recompensed by admirable variety, 2. the parlour or thorax, 3. the divine banquet of the brain'.

That 'divine banquet of the brain' has a Shakespearean ring. It also rings a bell for the present-day psychiatrist.

Harvey returned to England in 1602 a fully qualified Doctor of Medicine with the degree of Padua University. He settled in London, and two years later married the daughter of Dr Lancelot Browne, who had been Physician to the late Queen Elizabeth and was now similarly serving the newly arrived King James I. This was a judicious as well as an amatory move.

We do not know much about Harvey's wife, in spite of the fame of her father. Her husband rarely mentioned her, but the fact that she had a tame parrot occasioned from him a picturesque passage of prose which begins 'My wife had an excellent, and a well instructed parrot, which was long her delight; which was now grown so familiar, that he was permitted to walk at liberty through the whole house: where he missed his Mistress, he would search her out, and when he had found her, he would court her with a cheerful congratulation. If she had called him, he would make answer, and flying to her, he would grasp her garments with his claws and bill, till by degrees he had scaled her shoulder; whence he descending by her arm, did constantly seat himself upon her hand'. That may be a frivolous quotation, but it is another example of the literary idiom of the seventeenth century, which Harvey used naturally when writing in English, and therefore in character, so pronounced that it shines even in a translation of his Latin by another hand. I could not have quoted it were the passage not included in the masterly, detailed biography by Geoffrey Keynes, who is the outstanding example in our day of that combination of philosophy, the arts and medicine, which I described above as the cultural norm of earlier centuries. He is a famous surgeon, the most erudite editor of the poetry of William Blake, while amongst other literary achievements his book on Harvey presents a vast mass of material clearly organised and presented.

Dr Lancelot Browne failed to get his son-in-law attached to the Court as one of the King's physicians, but later Harvey succeeded through his own brother John, who was by that time Yeoman of the Bedchamber to James I. William's position at Court survived the King's death, and he found not only professional favour with Charles I but a personal friendship founded on mutual cultural interests, especially in science.

Apart from his political obstinacy, and a belief in the ancient but absurd myth of the divine right of kings, Charles I was a cultured and sensitive man, faithful to his friends if devious to his opponents. The results of this temperament were to affect William Harvey's career, for during the Civil War the faithful physician stayed with the King, and carried on professionally from the Court while it was domiciled in Oxford. This fidelity caused Harvey some embarrassment during the early stages of the Commonwealth tyranny. Only his patent honesty and ability saved him and enabled him to return to the two fields which he had been forced to neglect while attached to the Court of King Charles.

Those fields were St Bartholomew's Hospital and The Royal College of Physicians, where throughout his career he played a part consistently appreciated by his colleagues, in spite of his somewhat choleric temperament and his outspoken inability to suffer fools and charlatans patiently.

None of these qualities, however, would have made him one of Kent's immortals, had he not possessed something more. It was the imaginative genius that commanded all his work, and especially his steady researches and experiments into the physiological structure of all living organisms. This passion took hold of him in boyhood, and it remained dominant throughout his life, whatever the circumstances likely to distract him from that concentration of mind and interest which is the principal symptom of genius, in whatever form that formidable power may express itself. For example, at the Battle of Edgehill Harvey was put in charge of the King's sons, the Prince of Wales aged twelve, and the Duke of York aged nine. John Aubrey, the first and contemporary biographer of Harvey, in his book *Brief Lives*, describes this adventure: 'During the fight, the Prince and the Duke of York were committed to his care: he told me that he withdrew with them under a hedge, and took out of his pocket a book and read; but he had not read very long before a bullet of a great gun grazed on the ground near him, which made him remove his station'.

That coolness and steadiness of purpose is characteristic of the man. It brought him to the top both in the Hospital and the College, and it gave his two books the authority which overrode the opposition at first excited by their revolutionary contents, and drew acceptance from the medical faculties in every part of the western world.

St Bartholomew's Hospital was a survival of a medical hospice founded by a monk named Rahere, within the Priory at Smithfield, in 1123. The primitive hospital survived the great takeover bid of Thomas Cromwell when he 'nationalised' the monasteries in 1539. Six years later it received a Royal Charter which enabled it to continue its benevolent work as a teaching hospital. It does so today. Harvey remained as Physician to the Hospital until his death some forty years after his appointment. Through his clinical work there, and his tenure of the Lumleian Lectureship at the Royal College of Physicians, he was able both to expand his researches into the physiological structure of the human body (as well as other organic life) while reporting to his students and colleagues on 'the work in progress'. Thus the ground was prepared for the publication in Frankfurt of his great work in 1628, when he was forty years old. It was written in Latin, with the laborious title *Exercitatio de motu cordis et sanguinis* (which can be understood even by a non-Latinist).

In his years of work toward this challenging statement which, in brief, is that the blood-stream of all animals functions within a confined system pumped from the heart, which sends the blood with its life-maintaining content of oxygen through the arteries, back through the veins to the lungs where it is re-oxygenated, and so the heart again, where the process is repeated. This definition of a miracle was as simple and fundamental as Galileo's that the Earth was round, and as Einstein's short Equation stating the principle of Relativity. All three discoveries re-directed the whole system of thought within their several fields, and indeed beyond those fields, for they affected philosophy in general, the whole concept of human knowledge, and the symbolism of religious faith.

During the years while Harvey was experimenting, he was helped by his favourite student and friend Charles Scarburgh, who also employed a pupil, a boy of fifteen named Christopher Wren, who was already expert in making models of various anatomies of the human body needed for use in the lecture theatre. It is significant of something unexplainable other than that of a divine process, that creatures of genius, like birds of a feather, tend to flock together. Maybe it is because they speak the same inaudible language, which the Greeks called *nous* and we call intuition. When such congregation of brain-power occurs, something world-shaking always takes place. It is magnetism of human consciousness that builds a civilization. Scarburgh was to have a distinguished career, and to be knighted, as well as succeeding Harvey as Lumleian Lecturer at the Royal College. Wren was to mature as a prime example of the all-round genius, comparable to Leonardo da Vinci, creative in many fields: mathematics, astronomy, administration (he was Master of the Mint)—and he designed and built St Paul's Cathedral.

Si monumentum requiris, circumspice is engraved on his tomb there. Such
men of universal mental grasp and authority cannot be thus continent of
knowledge today. Goethe was the last of them. After Goethe's time, knowledge has so proliferated and colonised that no individual can comprehend
the whole, nor even that of his own field of inquiry.

Harvey's position at Court involved him in many extraneous activities.
He accompanied the Earl of Arundel (a faithful patron who wholly believed
in his ability) on an embassy in 1636 to try to persuade the Emperor of the
misnamed *Holy* Roman Empire to restore the Palatinate to King Charles's
nephew the Elector Louis; a mission which failed. The journey took
Harvey to many great cities in the Empire and Italy; Vienna, Prague, Linz,
Venice, where he met scholars and doctors, to realise that his fame had
gone before him. He met Descartes and found that the famous philosopher
welcomed his theory of the circulation of the blood as a practical proof of
the validity of the method of empiricism in his own *Discours de la Methode
pour bien conduire sa Raison.* That being so, it is odd that Francis Bacon
should have remained persistently antagonistic to Harvey, both as man and
philosopher.

As we have seen, in his own country the prophet was not without
honour. The poet John Donne, who as King's Chaplain must have met the
King's Physician, was scientifically minded, as his poetry demonstrates in
so many of its exploratory themes. This may have been due to the fact that
the poet's step-father John Syminges, was President of the Royal College of
Physicians. Two Kentish characters were also willingly subjective to
Harvey's revolutionary discovery. Dr Robert Fludd, four years Harvey's
senior, was born at Bearstead in 1574, son of Sir Thomas Fludd, Treasurer
of the Cinque Ports. This interesting man turned from theology to mysticism and finally to that curiously persistent cosmological dogma known as
Rosicruciansim. It exists todays, and has a considerable fascination for
persons who want to comprehend the universe as an orderly, almost a
biological structure. The brotherhood has always aroused marked opposition from orthodox thinkers, both in science and theology. It may have been
the biological symbolism inherent in the Rosicrucian cosmological nomenclature which made Robert Fludd see in Harvey's discovery of the contained
circulation of the blood, a welcome 'proof' of this neat, mystical *credo.* The
fact that it persists today, amidst our universal climate of scepticism,
suggests that its followers find in it a means of 'continued mutual love and
affection among themselves'. Those words are taken from the deed of gift

by which Harvey bequeathed to the Royal College of Physicians his estate at Burmarsh in Kent, inherited from his father, for the endowment of an annual oration. This was in addition to 'a noble building of Roman architecture comprising a great parlour or conversation room below and a library above' together with the books to fill that library, and with specimens of instruments used in the surgical branch of medicine.

Another man of Kent who subscribed instantly to Harvey's theory, and who became a close friend, was Sir George Ent, born at Sandwich in 1604. They met in Rome during the mission with Lord Arundel. Ent was also an M.D. of Padua. He remained intimate with Harvey until the great man's death, and has left on record a description of him during a visit in 1650, when Harvey was 72:

I found him with a cheerful and sprightly countenance investigating, like Democritus, the nature of things. Asking if all were well with him, 'how can that be', he replied, 'when the State is so agitated with storms and I myself am yet in the open sea? And indeed, were not my mind solaced by my studies and the recollection of the observations I have formerly made, there is nothing which would make me desirous of a longer continuance. But thus employed, this obscure life and vacation from public cares which would disgust other minds is the medicine of mine'.

That visit by Dr Ent was made at Combe, in Surrey, where Harvey spent the last years of his life, exiled from within twenty miles of London by the Commonwealth Government, because of his former close association with Charles I. His rooms in Whitehall Palace, that now vanished congeries of buildings where Milton as Cromwell's Public Relations Officer was to be housed, had meanwhile been searched by the barbarous rather than fanatical soldiery which is always the bestial weapon of warfare, with the consequent destruction or pillage of his furniture and the lifelong collection of his notes, manuscripts, and anatomical models, many of the last made by Christopher Wren.

A year after Dr Ent's visit, Harvey published his second book, *De Generatione Animalium*. It completed the monument to his worldwide fame. It consisted of 72 chapters, discussing the phenomena of the generative processes of all animal life, and of physiological structures and articulation. This also was written in Latin, but an anonymous translation into English appeared in 1653. In some respects, this work carried him still further toward our ever-widening conceptions of the origin of physical life, and with even more unaided originality.

The idea of the circulation of the blood had been vaguely conceived by both Aristotle and Galen, and throughout the sixteenth and seventeenth centuries Renaissance workers in the medical field had been adding hypotheses that built up to make the bridge which Harvey crossed so sure-footedly. But his almost mystical research into the composition of the blood whose circulation he had already mapped, and of the part it played in attaching the germ-cell of life after the conjunction of the sexes, was an adventure comparable to that of Newton 'voyaging through strange seas of thought, alone'. It makes him a peer of that great genius.

The fact that Harvey left surgical instruments as part of his bequest to the library of the Royal College of Physicians does not signify that he was unorthodox in his attitude toward the cultural class-distinction between the physician and the surgeon. It is one which lingers today, as we see by the social survival of calling a physician 'Dr' A, and a surgeon 'Mr' B. That is the only difference now. Otherwise, it is the surgeons who get the publicity, while the physicians tend to work as 'backroom boys'.

While Harvey was Physician to Bartholomew's Hospital, he drew up a charter of sixteen regulations which severely differentiated between the function and responsibility of the physician and the surgeon, the latter being treated as no more than a barber mechanic working under, and in the presence of, the doctor. This brought him into conflict with the Barber-Surgeon's Company, whose title reveals the low status of this half of the medical profession at that time.

He was equally authoritative with the druggists, who hitherto had been confederate with grocers. He was instrumental in the setting up of a chartered Society of Apothecaries in 1616, constituted and functioning under the Control of the Royal Society of Physicians. Thus the whole medical world was organised on a class basis according to what were considered cultural and philosophic principles. The surgeon and the dispenser were not necessarily Latinists, for example. They were not expected to be of scholastic education and distinction. The demands and expansions of our contemporary National Health Service have extended that easement even to physicians, as part of the general levelling down of cultural acceptance.

Harvey had two other close friends in the Royal College of Physicians who enthusiastically accepted his theory of the circulation of the blood, and did so at once, supporting him during the period when his general practice suffered, and he was treated as a crank by many colleagues. These two doctors were father and son, both named Baldwin Hamey. The elder had come from the Low Countries to be physician to the Earl of Essex, during the latter years of Queen Elizabeth's reign. He was persuaded, however, to accept the same office for the Tzar of Russia, but when he got there he found that his duties also constituted being Chief Poisoner. Boris Godunov also coveted his services. Two years passed before he was able to escape from the Russian Court, and during that time he wrote a series of letters to his son in London, mostly in Latin and some in Greek. They lay in the library of the Royal College of Physicians until after the last World War, when they were discovered by the Librarian, Dr John Keevil. This gentleman had been a naval surgeon, and had won the D.S.O. for conspicuous bravery during the war. He was a small, neat, gentle scholar. He translated the letters and edited them, with his own learned and lively commentary, in two volumes which were published by Geoffrey Bles, a fastidious imprint. The story of Hamey Junior is told in the second volume, *The Stranger's Son*. It makes a valuable compendium to Geoffrey Keynes' biography of Harvey. The two books cover the history of the Royal College during the seventeenth century. It is the story of the angel-winged science of medicine emerging from the ugly chrysalis of superstition.

Harvey was necessarily concerned with much of that superstition. Though the Royal College had been founded in 1518 by Linacre, the following century and a half had not given it time enough to purge itself of most of the dreadful practices taken over by the profession from the still prevalent witchcraft with its foul 'medicines' and butchery. Harvey was obliged by royal command to investigate many cases of the practice of witchcraft, but invariably he contrived to avoid condemnation of the women accused. He was a humanist, and he deplored the cruelty of the general run of humanity, which during the seventeenth century was aggravated by the state of Europe while the Thirty Years' War raged. During his travels abroad on the several missions in which he played a professional part, he recorded what he saw in middle Europe, where the ravages were so bad that the folk were reduced to living like animals. His recoil from the barbaric chaos was like that of his predecessors Erasmus and Melanchthon, who had reacted with similar disgust against 'man's inhumanity to man', a way of death in life which no degree of enlightenment appears to mitigate, as we see in the world today.

In the course of the ages, civilization has equipped itself with a vast and various machinery to combat this unaccountable savagery, which is more horrible than that of the vulture and the wolf, because it is practised with unction and self-consciousness. We have Law, but the Law can be an ass. We have religions, but religions can be fanatical and more cruel than lust. We have the arts, but they can be amoral. Medicine alone works with dispassionate benevolence toward the betterment of our human condition.

Those of its profession who fulfil the Hippocratic Oath by the discipline of a cool scientific knowledge combined with a wider, philosophic sensibility, stand at the head of the evolutionary process by which we must believe mankind to be advancing, in spite of the obscuring evidence to the contrary. There is no nobler human being than the great doctor. One of the greatest of them is William Harvey; not only because of his revolutionary discoveries and research as physiologist, but in his day-to-day practice as a doctor and his administrative work in St Bartholomew's Hospital for forty years, and in the Royal College of Physicians, where he is still a tutelary figure.

He died in his eightieth year, on 3 June 1657, of a paralytic stroke, and was buried in his brother Eliab's family vault in the Essex village of Hempstead, near Saffron Walden. A more appropriate resting-place would have been in Canterbury Cathedral, as it were in the bosom of Kent, his mother-county.

William Pitt

IN THE autumn of 1754 the great Lord Chatham, the statesman who towered above the venal politicians of the mid-eighteenth century, bought for the comfort of his increasing family a country house sufficiently near to London for him to spend as much time as possible there, while still in office. The house was called Hayes Place, set in charming common-land in Kent, some twelve miles from London. The fluctuating fortunes of the Pitt family, especially in financial matters, were at that time on the up-grade, because the Duchess of Marlborough had left Chatham £10,000 in her Will, as a mark of her esteem for his defiance of Prime Minister Robert Walpole, the cynic who believed that 'every man has his price', and by that political philosophy was responsible for much of the corruption of the Governments during the reigns of the first three Hanoverian monarchs.

That legacy from the formidable Duchess of Marlborough was not the only eccentric mark of esteem shown to Chatham for his noble and disinterested service to his country, so pronounced as to be almost fanatical. Some twenty years after the gift, a country gentleman unknown to Pitt, named Sir William Pynsent, died and left his whole estate in Somerset to the statesman whom he revered. It was worth some £3,000 a year. These legacies, however, were not enough to make up for Chatham's refusal to practise simony and other fashionable devices for making fortunes while in political office. The only member of the Pitt family who possessed financial acumen was the grandfather of the statesman. He was Thomas Pitt, the

Governor of Madras, one of the nabobs who, either in or out of the service of the East India Company, milked the Indian States and came home with vast fortunes. Thomas secured a sound foundation for his family in this way, and cemented it the more firmly as he was about to leave India with his booty, by buying, at risk, an uncut but enormous diamond for a few thousand pounds. He superintended the cutting of it in England, and sold the polished stone to the French royal family for over a hundred thousand pounds. He made more money out of the chippings. None other of his descendants appears to have inherited his financial genius. They were either persons of strict integrity, or plain fools lacking the necessary sense of reality in money matters. Even Chatham and his still greater son William Pitt junior were not free from this weakness.

That son is one of Kent's contributions because in 1759 he was born at Hayes Place. Like many of the family, he was not physically robust. He inherited from his father, the Great Commoner, a tendency to gout. At the time of his parents' belated decision to marry, Chatham, in breaking the news to his friend George Lyttelton, wrote that he had to offer his bride 'a fortune very far from tempting and a health shattered and declined'. He was forty-six. Hester Grenville, daughter of the noble family whose seat was at Stowe, was thirty-three. So the marriage was a late one, and not well-cushioned. But it proved to be happy, for Lady Hester was a woman of character and good commonsense, as we have seen from the account of her protection of her grand-daughter Lady Hester Stanhope. Without her reputation for those good qualities, Chatham would never have been able to command the help of various bankers, particularly Coutts, during the periodic financial crises of his career.

William Pitt the younger was the second son of this belated marriage. He was born on 28 May 1759, ten years before the man whose downfall he was to engineer by his adroit foreign policy and his superhuman patriotism, a work and an energy which together were to bring him to his grave nine years before his achievement ripened and Napoleon was defeated in 1815.

The boy was a prodigy, and the chief pride of both his parents. He exhibited patriotism as the infant Mozart exhibited a genius for music. When he was seven years old, his father was created Earl of Chatham. The child's acceptance of the news has been recorded. He said 'I am glad that I am not the eldest son. I want to speak in the House of Commons like Papa.' Perhaps his father's achievements, and the spirit hovering over the events of contemporary history, may have had some mysterious influence on the child's infant years. Macaulay has pointed out that in Pitt's first year in this world,

every month had its illuminations and bonfires, and every wind brought some messenger charged with joyful tidings and hostile standards. In Westphalia the English infantry won a great battle which arrested the armies of Louis XV in the midst of a career of conquest; Boscawan defeated one French fleet on the coast of Portugal; Hawke put to flight another in the Bay of Biscay, Johnson took Niagara; Amherst took Ticonderoga; Wolfe died by the most enviable of deaths under the walls of Quebec; Clive destroyed a Dutch armament in the Hugli, and established the English supremacy in Bengal; Coote routed Lally at Wandewash, and established the English supremacy in the Carnatic. The nation, while loudly applauding the successful warriors, considered them all, on sea and on land, in Europe, in America, and in Asia, merely as instruments which received their direction from one superior mind. It was the great William Pitt who had vanquished the French marshals in Germany and French Admirals on the Atlantic—who had conquered for his country one great empire on the frozen shores of Ontario and another under the tropical sun near the mouths of the Ganges.

Is it hyperbolical to suggest that the patriotic energy and administrative genius of such a man must have overflowed into the personality of his second son, the first son and later inheritor of the title being such an inadequate vessel?

William Pitt was dogged by poor health all his life, and he was a sick child. At the age of 14, always a difficult period over the hurdle of puberty, he was undersized and weighed only six stone. He had not been to school, for it was feared that the barbaric rigors of Eton would be too much for him. His tutor, however, was well chosen, a classical scholar from Pembroke Hall, Cambridge, named Wilson. This good man educated him from the age of six until he was fourteen. During those years he also studied with his mother, and precociously became conscious of the fundamental value of possessing a good speaking voice, deliberately trained to make the fullest use of the music of language. He caught this valuable habit from his father, of whom Scott Holland, one of the many biographers of the Pitt family, said that 'he never talked but always conversed'. This instrument of rhetoric, so important as a social asset, especially to people in public life, was used by Pitt throughout his career with a bravura that commanded admiration even from the victims whom it was destroying. His tutor's training in the classics of Greek and Latin literature, with his own passionate interest in that of his native tongue, gave him a large armoury of reference on which to nourish his genius for oratory (an art which is suspect in our modern world, which prefers statitistics and balance-sheets).

At the age of seven he wrote to his father in Latin. At eleven, he began a letter to him as follows, 'From the weather we have here I flatter myself that the sun shone on your expedition, and that the views were enough enlivened thereby to prevent the drowsy Morpheus from taking the opportunity of the heat to diffuse his poppies upon the eyes of the travellers'. His father replied in similar Handelian numbers, saying that wasps formed 'an ambuscade of Pandours' and that the horses were 'coursers of spirit not inferior to Xanthus and Podarges'. Such a form of communication as that would only arouse a bewildered giggle in a present-day child, and be called dishonest affectation by its schoolmasters. Style in writing, and technical proficiency in speech, are regarded today as anti-equalitarian, and we find public-school boys and actors and actresses cultivating the accents of the illiterate mob, for fear of being thought 'superior'.

Neither Chatham nor his prodigious son ever had such a fear. They both believed in their superiority, and practised to maintain it. And they succeeded. Like Pericles in fifth-century Athens, their ascendency had to be challenged by an opposition required by the democratic system of government, but the gesture was little more than mechanical. Each went to his death, and to burial in Westminster Abbey, mourned without qualification as the saviour of his country. The unanimity of national feeling was exactly like that which was expressed, worldwide, at the death of Winston Churchill, another figure aware, like Pericles and the Pitts, of the power of the art of oratory even in a democratic society.

With his sister Harriet, the young William wrote verse and plays in the manner, but lacking the substance, of Johnson's *Rasselas*. It was good training. It laced the intellectual fibre. As his tutor Wilson said, on relinquishing his eight years of preparing the boy for reception into Pembroke College, Cambridge,

Mr Pitt is not the child his years bespeak him to be. He has now all the understanding of a man, and is, and will be, my steady friend through life. He will go to Pembroke, not a weak boy to be made a property of, but to be admired as a prodigy; not to hear lectures but to spread light. His parts are most astonishing and universal. He will be fully qualified for a wrangler *before he goes*, and be an accomplished classic, mathematician, historian and poet.

So at 14 this paragon went to Cambridge, accompanied by his own tutor, and alas, by the hereditary gout, which struck at him as soon as he met the harsh climate of that otherwise enchanting place. He was brought home by his nurse and did not return to Pembroke until midsummer of the following year, 1774. The doctors' prescription for his recovery had been copious drinking of port, a regimen which he followed for the rest of his life. It seems to have kept him going, as fuel for a temperament always functioning at concert-pitch. His college tutor, a Dr Pretyman, was instantly subjugated, as had been Wilson, and also remained his friend. Pitt was to die in his arms, after the death-stroke of the news of the Battle of Austerlitz. Pretyman, under the name of Tomline, wrote the first biography of his idol. I cannot recommend it, because I have not read it; but later biographers are unanimous in condemning it as dull.

During his terms at Cambridge, his political appetite was fed by public events, for England's most disastrous blunder was bearing its poisonous fruit. We were in process of losing our New England colonies, thanks to a combination of the obstinate stupidity of King George III and the ineptitude of this Prime Minister, Lord North. Young Pitt, enclosed within his own political genius, and unable to mix with his fellows and release his passion through sports, was tortured to learn of his sick father's efforts to put matters right, through his still powerful influence in the House of Lords. The effort was to form a new Government that would reconcile the country to the just demands of the colonists. Chatham spoke for the last time, in a burst of seemingly contrary arguments, urging loyalty to the King, opposition to France, and agreement with our own folk in America. But he collapsed in the act of speaking, and was carried out of the House.

His sons hurried to Downing Street, where Chatham was living in one of the houses since vanished. The family took him down to Hayes Place, where he died on 11 May 1778.

Because of Chatham's stand over the War of American Independence, the King ungraciously refused to be represented at the State funeral of the Minister who had supported him so loyally, and done more toward the security and enlargement of British power than any statesman since Cromwell.

Chatham's heir was absent with his regiment, so the chief mourner had to be his second son, William Pitt. The biographer Holland Rose says

Few of the beholders had any knowledge of his manifold gifts; and the crowds which gazed at the stately procession, as at the burial of England's glories and hopes, could not surmise that the slim figure following the hearse was destined to retrieve the disasters of the present and to link once more the name of Pitt with a great work of national revival.

That is nobly said of a noble character who stands, with Dr William Harvey, as an example of human genius fully extended. These two master minds were certainly Kent's greatest contribution, because of the range of their intellectual consciousness, their force of will in the exercise of it, and the nobility of their moral characters. Their more fitting historical placing would have been fifth-century Greece, with Pericles and Anaxagoras.

Chatham's death, like that of Churchill in our time, was not a national disaster, because both men's work was done: nor can it be said to have disrupted William's life, in spite of the grief which drove him even more deeply into himself. The effect of the loss was to release him from tutelage. He had taken his Degree two years before his father's death, and had been in the habit of coming up from Cambridge to haunt the House of Commons, listening and learning both the technique of Parliamentary procedure, and the issues with which it was perpetually concerned.

He decided to read law, as a necessary equipment for the career on which he had been decided since he was an infant of seven years of age. He entered himself at Lincoln's Inn, and took chambers in Stone buildings, the most gloomy end of an otherwise enchanting college. To this day Lincoln's Inn keeps a little of its medieval character. I lived in Old Square before the last war, and every September I used to go down into the garden and collect mushrooms from under one of the seats in the north garden. On winter nights I was admonished by the forebodings of an owl. The seclusion there, set in the midst of London's—of England's—governmental life, must have offered Pitt a period of intense application to his studies, an enlargement in the outer and more practical world of his work at Cambridge.

He needed that armoury, for his task was to be a heavier one even than that which his father had handled. From the moment he entered political life, he had to face outbreaks of violence at home, and the combination of France, Spain and the rebel states of America in a war soon to be stepped up under the ferocious military genius of Napoleon. Pitt tried his hand first as a candidate for Cambridge, but was defeated. His Cambridge friend, the Duke of Rutland, recommended him to Sir James Lowther (the patron of Wordsworth) who held the disposal of eleven pocket boroughs. The young man was offered one for Appleby, a place which he never visited. He took his seat in the House of Commons in January 1781, to begin a career which has no equal in Parliamentary history. He was in his twenty-second year.

Lord North, a gross figure with the cynicism of Walpole but lacking his ability, had been in office for eleven years, and was to be kept there by King George for more than a further year, during which 'the nation seems to have fallen into a deep sleep', as Sir Samuel Romilly said in his reformist criticism of the Government's indifference toward the news of the British defeat at Yorktown, which meant the loss of our American colonies in New England. The only concern of the administration was with the suppression of the clamour for Parliamentary reform and the abolition of pocket boroughs. The Gordon Riots and the antics of the unsavoury reformer John Wilkes had created such public panic that the King was able to rule almost as a despot, Parliament having sunk into such disrepute.

Pitt hovered between the Parties, and quickly showed his hand, which was to introduce reform into the composition and procedure of Parliament. The combination of subtlety and simplicity with which he maintained that campaign at once showed his amazing ability. He carried on the battle with high spirits and even gaiety, in spite of his indifferent health. His geniality was deep-seated, both in his personality and in his culture. In the midst of the struggle, he was always above the battle. Wilberforce, a man of great force of character as we know from his achievement in carrying through the legislation for the abolition of slavery, said of Pitt that he 'was remarkably pleasant and cheerful, full of wit and playfulness, neither, like Mr Fox, fond of arguing a question, nor yet holding forth like some others. He was always ready to hear others as well as to talk himself'.

Fox was Pitt's most powerful opponent as an orator and a Parliamentarian, representing the more revolutionary views for achieving reform. But the whole conflict during those years of threatened violence, like to spread from events in France, continued throughout Pitt's political career. An increasing restless and more powerful proletariat was hammering on the walls of privilege, and with this ceaseless noise behind him, Pitt had to organise the country to withstand the growing power of France, which the Little Corporal was welding into the formidable force that over-ran western Europe and even at the time of Pitt's death was still glaring at us from across the Channel.

Lord North, that surly stumbling-block, resigned in 1782, and a resolution passed two years earlier that 'the influence of the Crown has increased, is increasing, and ought to be diminished' was put into effect. It was providential, for as G. M. Trevelyan says 'If the personal government of George III and of his children after him had been protracted into the next century, the democratic and reform movements of the new era, finding themselves opposed by the King as their chief source of conservative resistance, must have become anti-royalist and very probably Republican', thereby introducing oligarchic forms of political corruption from which the picturesque snobbery of the system of constitutional monarchy saves us, at least in some degree.

After North's resignation, life in Parliament boiled violently. Out of the turmoil, the thin young man of twenty-five years of age, still a newcomer though supported by the gigantic reputation of his father, emerged cool and decisive. In 1783, after a period in which party loyalties went to the wall, Pitt took office as Prime Minister.

He was still a Reformer, and remained so until the rise of Napoleon caused him to realise that the instant need of the country was to convert itself into a fighting machine. Churchill did precisely the same in 1940. Pitt stood by the King and the unwritten Constitution, and Fox became his chief opponent and most formidable debating rival. In the first ten years of his premiership, his achievement, as summed up by Trevelyan, was

to reconstitute the finances of the country, restore its prestige at home and abroad, begin to rebuild a new British Empire on the ruins of the old, modernise and secure the governments of Canada and India. After Walpole's example, he reconstituted the power of the Prime Minister in the State as the true governor of the land, not the mere instrument of the royal will. He finally fixed the British conception of the Cabinet, as a responsible and united body, dependent on an independent House of Commons.

He made the Tory party an instrument of progress, as we have hopes of seeing it in action again during the second half of the twentieth century, under the leadership of another Kentish-born leader.

All his life had been preparing him for this purpose. Never was a genius so consistent, gathering its forces by eager but patient method toward a whole concept of statesmanship, in finance, law, culture and moral authority. And his instrument for effecting this was the art of oratory which he had perfected from infancy. Hear how Macaulay describes his mastery of that art:

At his first appearance in Parliament he showed himself superior to all his contemporaries in command of language. He could pour forth a long succession of round and stately periods, without premeditation, without ever pausing for a word, without ever repeating a word, in a voice of silver clearness, and with a pronunciation so articulate that not a letter was slurred over. He had less amplitude of mind and less richness of imagination than Burke, less ingenuity than Wyndham, less wit than Sheridan, less perfect mastery of dialectical fence and less passion fused together than Fox. Yet the almost unanimous judgment of those who were in the habit of listening to that remarkable race of men placed Pitt as a speaker above Burke, above Wyndham, above Sheridan and not below Fox. His declamation was copious, polished and splendid. In power of sarcasm he was probably not surpassed by any speaker, ancient or modern; and of this formidable weapon he made merciless use. In two parts of the oratorical art which are of the highest value to a minister of state he was singularly expert. No man knew better how to be luminous or how to be obscure. When he wished to be understood, he never failed to make himself understood. Nothing was out of place; nothing was forgotten; minute details, dates, sums of money, were all faithfully preserved in his memory. On the other hand, when he did not wish to be explicit—and no man who is at the head of affairs always wishes to be explicit—he had a marvellous power of saying nothing in language which left on his audience the impression that he had said a great deal.

Gibbon had something to say in confirmation of this power which Pitt demonstrated, and maintained until his death from exhaustion, over the Parliament and over the country. 'Since my leaving England', Gibbon wrote,

in the short period of last winter (1783) what strange events have fallen out in your political world! It is probable, from your present connections, that we see them with very different eyes; and, on this occasion, I very much distrust my own judgment. I am far too distant to have a perfect knowledge of the revolution, and am too recently absent to judge of it with impartiality. Yet let me soberly ask you on Whig principles, whether it be not a dangerous discovery that the King can keep his favourite Minister against a majority of the House of Commons? Here indeed (for even here we are politicians), the people were violent against Fox, but I think it was chiefly those who have imbibed in the French service a high reverence for the person and authority of Kings. They are likewise biassed by the splendour of young Pitt, and it is a fair and honourable prejudice. A youth of five-and-twenty, who raises himself to the government of an empire by the power of genius and the reputation of virtue, is a circumstance unparallelled in history, and, in a general view, is not less glorious to the country than to himself.

The rest of the story of this man, his turn to Toryism and machiavellian manipulation of the national purse toward the strengthening of our national defence on land and sea, and to the support (or bribing) of the floundering European monarchies to bring them together for the single purpose of defeating Napoleon, as Churchill went out after Hitler, is public knowledge available in a vast historical literature, and I need not repeat it. His behaviour in private life is presented in the previous chapter of this book, dealing with the Stanhopes. The fact that the almost maniacal egoism of Lady Hester Stanhope was subjected to a pure and devoted love for Pitt, which ministered to him in his days of power and triumph, and nursed him during his last days, when he lay worn out by the singleness of his purpose to defeat Napoleon, but assured of victory by the news from Trafalgar; all this is a testimony to his magnetic power.

In spite of the character of lofty arrogance, attributed to both him and his father by some critics, he remained a simple and fundamentally modest man. His last public utterance was at the Lord Mayor's Banquet nineteen days after Nelson's victory, which was the turning point in the war with France. Pitt was then very ill, but he rose to respond to a toast which described him as 'the Saviour of Europe'. He said in reply, still audible in spite of his physical weakness, 'I return you many thanks for the honour you have done me, but Europe is not saved by any single man. England has saved herself by her exertions, and will, as I trust, save Europe by her example'.

He had yet something more to say. They were his last words, murmured as he died, at daybreak on 23 January 1806, the twenty-fifth anniversary of his entering Parliament. His nephew James Stanhope was leaning over him, and heard 'Oh, my country! How I leave my country'. So wide a passion is a strange rarity, at such a moment when an individual soul is at the point of departure from this life on earth, as a person. He had never married, but was devoted to his family, the Pitts and the Stanhopes. But the wider range of his emotional life was this which embraced a whole nation. Only genius is capable of that, as we see it emerge in great artists, statesmen and saints; a vast power of impersonal attachment which is awe-inspiring, even intimidating to lesser mortals.

James Wolfe

I HAVE not been able to say much about William Pitt, Senior, the 'Great Commoner', the Earl of Chatham, because his birth elsewhere than in Kent places him outside the scope of this book. The history of the Pitt family, however, is comparable to that of the Sackvilles, in that both produced, in a father and son, two men of great personal genius which included political, cultural and military ability of so authoritative a quality as to make a permanent mark upon the history of Britain. The Seven Years War was won largely by Chatham's immediate and personal control of the military strategy, an interference from outside the War Department that often opposed the orthodox planning of the professional soldiers.

The most marked example of this was his commissioning the young Colonel James Wolfe as commander of the campaign in Canada, over the heads of senior officers, two of whom, Brigadiers Townsend and Murray, were to resent the imposition and to do their best after Wolfe's death to deny him the credit for the great victory which brought Canada within the embrace of the British Empire, and so unified our control in North America that later the New England colonists decided to break away and form a republican United States. Pitt's acumen in recognising Wolfe's still unstretched genius resulted in no less than that reshaping of national relationships in the eighteenth century, with subsequent consequences in world history of unlimited duration.

A considerable monument of literature has gathered round Wolfe, and his own *Instruction to young officers* remains as a classic textbook on the geometry of warfare. Outstanding amongst the books on his life and achievement is the biography by Robin Reilly. It is a work of devoted scholarship, beautifully utilised to tell a comprehensive story that balances the portrayal of character with the narration of events. The account of the taking of Quebec is a masterpiece of military history. The author's detachment in judging the character and abilities of his hero, weighing them against his physical and social deficiencies, gives the reader confidence and a sense of having met Wolfe in real life.

The Wolfe family was Celtic in origin, the name being traced back to Wales, and to Ireland. It seems to be a convention for our British armies to be led by generals of this warlike race. I need not labour the obvious in mentioning one or two who played leading parts in the two world wars of the twentieth century. From Cromwellian times there are records of Wolfes as outstanding soldiers. The last of these precedents was James's father Edward who in 1710, at the age of 25, had reached the rank of major. He fought in Flanders under Marlborough, and in Scotland during the Jacobite rising of 1715. He was substantially stationed in York where he met and married, in his fortieth year, a girl of twenty named Henrietta Thompson, daughter of a landowning family of substance. She was tall and thin, and had a receding chin and eloquent eyes. All these physical attributes she was to pass on to her children, and particularly to her elder son.

That son was not born until more than two years after the marriage, by which time the retired Colonel Wolfe had come south, and bought a house in Westerham, Kent, thus enabling his son James to be a participant in *Kent's Contribution*.

The house is a Tudor building, almost facing up the bye-road at the bottom of the village leading to Hosey Common, Ide Hill and Toys Hill, and westward thence to Chartwell, now another monument to a member of a family immortalised by military prowess. That southern ridge of the Westerham valley is a lovely stretch of country, with views across the Weald to the coastal downs. In 1725 the peacefulness of the wide valley, and the mid-weald hills closing it southwards, must have been absolute. It endured until the age of the motor-car in our own time, and even now it has its moments, as though space and serenity are recollecting themselves, mourning their diminishing silences.

Colonel and Mrs Wolfe settled there in 1726, and both being sociable people, they soon made friends, amongst whom were the vicar and his wife.

It was during the colonel's absence on some semi-professional purpose (for he still held his commission), that Mrs Wolfe felt the intimations of child-birth. The vicar's wife, a Mrs Lewis, took her up the hill to the vicarage, where on 2 January 1727 she gave birth to James Wolfe, and stayed there for nearly a month until strong enough to return home to *Spiers,* as the Tudor house was called. *Spiers* is now in the hands of the National Trust, and can be visited. At the top of the village, on the triangular green below the path leading to the church, stands a statue of Wolfe. There is another at the top of Greenwich Park, near the Observatory, with the hero pointing his raised sword toward Canada.

A year later James was presented with a brother, christened Edward, who later was to follow the same profession. Both children were delicate, prone to colds and general debility due to constitutional weakness in the lungs, another inheritance from their mother. Robin Reilly's book quotes Mrs Wolfe's recipe for counteracting this family complaint:

Take a peck of green garden snails, wash them in beer, put them in an oven and let them stay till they've done crying; then with a knife and fork prick the green from them, and beat the snail shells and all in a stone mortar. Then take a quart of green earthworms, slive them through the middle and strow them with salt; then wash them and beat them, the pot being first put into the still with two handfulls of angelica, a quart of rosemary flowers, then the snails and the worms, the agrimony, bears feet, red dock roots, barbary brake, bilbony, wormwood, of each two handfulls: one handfull of rue tumerick and one ounce of saffron, well dried and beaten. Then pour in three gallons of milk. Wait till morning, then put in three ounces of cloves (well beaten), hartshorn, grated. Keep the still covered all night. This done, stir it not. Distill with a moderate fire. The patient must take two spoonfulls at a time.

Who would resist stealing that as a recipe toward ensuring the enlargement of the British Empire? It serves also to show the detailed thoroughness with which Robin Reilly's biography has been written, and thus excuses my petty larceny.

Owing to the mother's hypochondria, and the poor health of the two boys, they were not sent away to school, but to a private tutor who ran a small school in the village. During the first five years of young Wolfe's boyhood, his father spent much time at home because his regiment was employed in the district on road-making. That appears to be a good scheme for employing the army in peacetime. This Roman method might well be used today, and extended to include the inmates of our over-crowded prisons, thus aiding the national economy and advancing our public works.

When James Wolfe was five years old, the local manor house, *Squerryes Court*, standing in a rising parkland almost opposite his home, was bought by a family named Warde. It is in their possession today. The newcomer was a widower with children, and one of them, named George, six years of age, struck up a friendship with the gawky, red-headed infant. Both wanted to be soldiers, and both were to become soldiers. Even after the removal of the Wolfes from Westerham to Greenwich (which we may consider to have been in Kent at that time), the friendship survived that separation from day-to-day converse. Indeed, it survived until Wolfe's death; visits were interchanged between Westerham and Greenwich. The latter district must have been delightful in the early years of the eighteenth century, with the view from Blackheath over the park to the noble architectures of Inigo Jones and Wren along the river below, and the distant view upstream of London, at that time still a concise city with but sparse intrusion over the south bank of the river. Even today the view is heartlifting, as seen from the foot of Wolfe's statue.

The removal to Greenwich was made in order to send the two brothers to a school established there for the sons of naval and military officers. The boys were fortunate in finding a headmaster with a vocation for teaching, and their education prospered happily. Both boys revered him; and that sort of relationship is an education in itself. James's progress at the school, however, was cut short by international events. England went to war with Spain in 1739, when he was twelve years of age. His father was re-commissioned as a Lieutenant Colonel, and took part in the expedition against Carthagena. He took James with him, as an infant, unofficial ensign.

Spain had broken the Treaty of Utrecht of 1713, by which Britain was granted the right to trade in the supplying of black slaves from Africa to the New World. Spain had begun to encroach on this and other profitable activities by seizing our ships as smugglers. War was inevitable, and large-scale operations were put in hand, in the course of which Edward Wolfe was promoted to Adjutant-General. Father and thirteen-year-old son set off for Portsmouth together, but there the whole expedition was held up by general muddle, mainly due to swindling contractors. The fleet lay at Spithead from August until October, with the troops in close confinement aboard. The delicate boy, with his inherited tendency to tuberculosis, fell ill, and to his great grief, he had to be sent home. Even the return to so congenial a school could not assuage his chagrin.

The war muddled on, with so little success that the government of

Robert Walpole, that tough East Anglian cynic, lost the confidence of the nation, and he had to resign, in 1742.

In that year, three after the first setback to a military career, the fifteen-year-old James Wolfe was commissioned as an ensign in the Twelfth Foot, and so began the career to which he had dedicated himself, with his friend George Warde, at the age of six. Nor was he entirely a novice, for his passionate devotion had led him to close study in addition to the good services of the military school in Greenwich. He was already a marked character, six foot tall and thin as a lath, red-haired and pale, with keen blue eyes fanatical in their brilliance. He was shy but friendly, and people liked him and admired his singleness of purpose. It made him a professional amongst amateurs, as were most military men in this country at that time. Only Frederick the Great in Prussia had evolved a professional army, strictly trained and disciplined. Our only discipline in both the army and navy was brutality by dilettante officers toward an illiterate rank and file.

The Twelfth Foot (the future Suffolk Regiment) was sent out to the Low Countries, where Ensign Wolfe put his theoretical knowledge of logistics efficiently into practice at the Battle of Dettingen, after a cruel winter of inaction. That period of ennui, however, was relieved by the reunion with his friend George Warde, who had been gazetted as a cornet of dragoons. The boys met in Ghent, and took advantage of the pleasures of the town. Neither the environment of the flat country, nor the juvenile minor dissipations, improved the boy's poor physique, but he was able to move with his regiment in the February of 1743, cheered by the arrival of his brother Edward, who had also contrived to be commissioned.

The enemy consisted of French, Spanish and Prussian armies, for King Frederick was in temporary alliance with France, a momentary conjunction in that dreadful *olla potrida* of European conflict which had been boiling since the seventeenth century. King George II hampered the British forces by his anxiety about Hanover, his other kingdom, which neighboured Prussia. He was present at the Battle of Dettingen, the layout of which had been skilfully prepared by the French Command. Even so, the very uncertainties of the British progress enabled our army to muddle through the trap set by the French, but at great cost of life, both human and equine.

James had become acting Adjutant during the battle, and both his and his brother's conduct were commended, and James was promoted Lieutenant. The campaign developed, and after some months another promotion brought James a captaincy in the King's Own Royal Regiment. From that time onward, the speed of his advancement in the army is comparable to that of Mozart in the world of music. Never was there such an infant prodigy in military history, with the exception of Alexander the Great.

In the October of 1743, brother Edward succumbed to the fatigue and exposure of the campaign. He died of tuberculosis at the age of sixteen, a tried but physically ill-equipped soldier. James was similarly handicapped. For the rest of his life he was subject to dire sickness, a combination of rheumatism, gravel in the kidneys, and the dreaded disease in his lungs. It is to be remembered that throughout what was to follow the bright achievement showed with all the more brilliance against this sinister background of doomed health.

His brother's death hit him badly, but the letter that he wrote home to his mother was that of a soldier rather than of a son. He was already hardened to his profession, and for the rest of his short life he wore this armour of rigid self-discipline, subjecting emotions and personal inclinations to the requirements of his studies in the history and science of warfare, and his duties which became increasingly demanding on his time and attention with each promotion. His mother wanted him to come home on leave after Edward's death, as he could well have done. But he remained at the front in Belgium, determined not to let private and personal concerns delay his professional progress.

When at last he did get home, it was not for long. The rebellion of the Jacobites under the incompetent leadership of the Young Pretender broke out in 1745, and James, by now a favoured cadet of the Duke of Cumberland, was commissioned Brigade-major, and marched north to take part in the fighting at Falkirk and Culloden. He stayed in Scotland with the army of occupation, and so completely by this time had he conditioned his mind and conscience to the mechanics of militarism, that he saw no wrong in Cumberland's savagery in the so-called 'punishment' of the Highlanders, whether or not they, as individuals, had taken part in the up-rising. The oppression was no exceptional treatment. When has the aftermath of war ever been otherwise, during the immediacy of defeat?

Still under Cumberland's baleful benevolence, Wolfe returned to the campaign in Flanders, and at a battle at Val was again commended by the Duke, and shortly after promoted to a majority in 1749, this being followed a year later by a further step to Lieutenant Colonel, with which rank he continued to serve in Flanders and later in Scotland. His health was not improved by the climate of Scotland, where he served for some years, and he was given leave for six months, which he spent in Paris, solemnly learning to dance, and attending the salons of the great ladies, with the intention of improving his social technique. This joyless martyrdom he undertook as a necessary adjunct to his military status and intended further progress as a soldier. His letters reveal this naive single-mindedness, and also his theoretical interest in the ladies. There are hints that he was more practical in his approaches to the women of the town.

While in Paris, he met Philip Stanhope, the natural son of the Lord Chesterfield, neighbour of Wolfe's parents in Blackheath. It was this son who received the famous set of letters of advice on social deportment, and how to become a man of the world. The letters have survived, but they failed to prevent the son from sinking into obscurity. Another person whom he met was an ensign named William Hamilton, aged twelve. This lad was later to become the British Ambassador in Naples, and to marry the famous courtesan Emma, Nelson's unfortunate lover, who provided the infatuated hero with a daughter who subsequently married the vicar of Tenterden and led a sedate life. A faded photograph of the clerical couple, wearing stuffy mid-Victorian clothes, may still be seen in the vestry of Tenterden church.

This interlude in Paris did not improve the physical condition of the ambitious young soldier. We learn that he had some teeth stopped with *lead* while there, thus adding more poison to his wretched body.

He returned to his regiment, which was stationed in Dover Castle, where he was to spend two years restoring discipline and training to the ranks, and doing his best to prevent his young officers, most of them older than himself, from marrying prematurely and thus breaking their single-minded devotion to the regiment.

From Dover, the 20th Foot, which by the magnetism of his personality Wolfe had honed up to razor-sharp efficiency, was sent to Exeter, where the Jacobites were stirring up the half-starved peasantry. This move interrupted his tentative courtship of a young gentlewoman named Elizabeth Lawson, who failed to respond. But romantic passion never carried Wolfe away. As he wrote of this repulse, 'It took away my stomach for two or three days, and made me grave, but time, the never failing aid to distressed lovers, has made the semblance of her a pleasing, but not a dangerous object. However, I find it best not to trust myself to the lady's eyes, or put confidence in any resolution of my own'. As this young woman was a Maid of Honour at Court, it is possible that even in love, Wolfe doctored his passion with ambition.

It appears that Wolfe's experience in Paris now served him well, for his strict military character had found some added graces which enabled him to command the dangerous situation in the West Country without undue harshness. He made social contact with the Jacobite families there. Even so, as he wrote home, 'It begins to work a little favourably but not certainly, because the perverseness of these folks, built upon their disaffection, makes the task very difficult'.

These civil problems, however, were swept away by more serious concerns, much to the joy of the dedicated young professional soldier who had now given ample proof of his ability to command troops with a considerable efficiency comparable to that of Field Marshall Montgomery in our century. Both held to the same scientific principle: maximum discipline and close control, always with the intention of minimum losses.

The serious concerns were the renewal of war in Europe, in 1757. Wolfe served as a staff officer in the opening of the campaign by the expedition to Rochefort. It was a failure, but the authorities were persuaded that had Wolfe's tactical plans been followed, our attack would not have been driven off. His reputation was not affected, and in the following year he was further promoted to Brigadier-general and set out to attack the French possessions in North America. The objective was to capture Louisburg, the French stronghold over the smaller islands at the entrance to the estuary of the St Lawrence River. This was to be the opening gambit of a long-term policy which William Pitt the elder, as Minister for War, was trying to develop, against the obduracy and stupidity of the Prime Minister, the Duke of Newcastle, and the majority of his Government. Pitt was the only member of it who foresaw the importance of the still unknown interior of North America, which the French were already marking out, by a series of fortifications, round the Great Lakes and down the rivers to New Orleans.

Wolfe served under General Amherst, and in the final assault on the town he led the troops, and took the glory. He was the hero of the day, and when he returned home on leave, again owing to a breakdown in health, he was publicly acclaimed. He contrived, however, to fall in love for the second time, while taking the waters at Bath. The lady was named Katherine Lowther, and her brother was amongst the richest men in the country. But Wolfe was now a figure to reckon with, and fame had justified his air of authority, and added a flourish to his social deportment.

His courtship was successful, and the young couple became engaged.

Wolfe was also more affluent, for during this long stay in England, he had been appointed Quarter-master General in Ireland, a post which carried a large remuneration. He resigned from it only because his military genius once again took command of his common-sense. The soldier dismissed the self-seeker, and even the lover. He returned to the war in America, fully aware of Pitt's determination to drive the French out of complete control of Canada and an encirclement of the New England States.

During the celebration in his honour, he had dined with Pitt, and it was on this occasion that the great statesman recognised the potential force in the young man, and picked him as the instrument most likely to bring a daring policy to fruition. Thus, shortly after the engagement to marry Miss Lowther, Wolfe left England again and arrived in Louisburg in time to sail with the expedition on 1 June 1759, which was intended to force its way up the St Lawrence, and make contact with Amherst who was bringing up his forces from New England and approaching Montreal, by this meeting to encircle the French and destroy their plan to penetrate southward to New Orleans and command the whole of North America. The stake was a huge one, as Pitt realised. With the French defeated in the New World, the situation in Europe would be favourable to Britain and her allies. Pitt's policy would be vindicated, and he would be in a position of strength to oust the mediocre Duke of Newcastle from the Treasury and take command himself, as a statesman justifiably convinced of his destiny.

Wolfe's promotion to Brigadier had been only provisional, while on service in Canada during the siege of Louisburg. The Duke of Newcastle was dubious about substantiating the appointment. He told the King that he believed Wolfe to be mad. A man of his bumbling personality could not appreciate the forceful monomania of genius. The King made his famous reply to this suggestion: 'Then I hope he will bite some other of my generals'.

Wolfe appears to have done so, for as soon as he was given the full command of the expedition setting out from Newfoundland, a dual military and naval operation, his staff and the troops became inspired, and followed his highly wrought tactical plan with a devotion that was to ensure victory. And this eager submission to his unorthodox procedure was given after the usual protests of the more conventional officers, especially two of them, Brigadiers George Townsend (a social snob and bitter satirist), and one Murray, the inevitable Judas Iscariot type to be found in every organisation or community.

The plan of campaign devised by Wolfe, criticised by his staff because he kept its daily developments so much to himself in order to ensure the element of surprise in circumstances and surroundings where spying was at saturation point, has been written about at great length, and it still is not fully agreed upon as being a masterpiece or a reckless gamble which happened to succeed. The more military science develops as a philosophy of technical means of adaptation, a balancing of equipment to circumstances, the more Wolfe's plan tends to be accepted as a classic model. This fact, together with the international results of his victory, has given Wolfe his place in world history.

The final assault was so sudden and so swift, that we tend to forget that the siege lasted for three months, from June to September, and that behind the elaborate actions and delays lay the threat of the Canadian winter, all too steadily approaching, an invisible army in favour of the French under Montcalm, a highly trained and skilful general working ceaselessly to maintain contact with, and maintain supplies from, Montreal, which Amherst was approaching from the south.

This question of supplies to feed the army was always uppermost in Wolfe's mind. He was a realist, down to the least detail, in the same way as Montgomery before El Alamein. Wolfe's vision was wide-ranging, and in his letters we see the mind of a statesman planning toward large-scale objectives, consonant with those of the master-mind of the man who had picked him for the task, William Pitt.

In general outlay Wolfe's campaign was simple, like most works of genius. It was to spread out his arms and hug his opponent. The risk was, in disposing of his forces along a thin line for some forty miles along the River front, that he was offering Montcalm opportunities for sorties, helped by the terrain, to cut the thin line, isolating the English fleet in the St Lawrence, and giving himself more assurances of contact with Montreal.

British bases were established on the island of Orleans, and on the mainland south of the river at three other posts whence crossings could be made with advantage. The comings and goings between these posts, on land and water, kept the French guessing. So did a remote camp based on the north side of the river about seven miles east of Quebec, downstream at Beauport. The process of enfolding encroachment went on for the three months, and Wolfe still kept his hand secretly on the trigger.

His staff officers grumbled, objected, but maintained their faith in him, with the two exceptions whom I have mentioned. Criticism at home hummed steadily in the background, but Pitt, whose political future depended upon the result of his wholly unorthodox appointment of this young man over the heads of War Office veterans to so vitally critical a post, showed no sign of hesitation about his choice. The weeks passed, with setbacks due to Montcalm's ability, the vagaries of weather, and the demoralising consciousness of the approaching winter and the shortening of daylight. The French appeared to be cool. Montcalm's *sang froid* was almost disarming. There is a story of the establishing of the first point at the tip of the island of Orleans, which was to be the hinge of the great, final leverage. The priest of the island who had left with his flock, addressed a note of apology to the British command, because the vegetables in his garden had gone to seed!

The opening attack on 31 July was repulsed with heavy losses on both sides. This was a dangerous setback for an army under the control of a young general whose tactics seemed to his staff to be equivocal. The disaster might be compared with the tragic experiment during the last world war when the assault was made on Dieppe and Berneval. Was Wolfe's attack a similar experiment before the main assault ? It will be remembered that the attack on the French coast was against cliffs and up gullies, such as that at Berneval. This was comparable to the assaults across the St Lawrence along the heights of the north bank, of which Quebec was the crown.

All sorts of decoy operations were employed during the three months' siege, with skirmishes in which the French gave as good as they got. The British had to learn how to deal with guerilla warfare, as practised by the native Indian warriors conscripted by the French. Textbook theories deduced from centuries of warfare in Flanders against equally conventional military opponents had to be adapted, and on occasion discarded. This necessity strengthened Wolfe's personal ascendency. His own methods were as elastic as those of the Indians. His troops appreciated this adaptability, but his officers did not, and he had to contend with constant criticism, silent maybe, but felt by his acute sensibility. That sensibility was heightened by his deteriorating health. The three diseases of rheumatism, gravel and tuberculosis combined under the aggravation of constant setbacks, anxieties, and the knowledge that he was taking risks which, if ending in failure, would put an end to his career and to the English foothold in Canada, possibly to the war with France in Europe.

In the last days before the final assault Wolfe was bedridden, and the rumour went round that he was near his end. It was more than a rumour, for he was a dying man. By sheer effort of will, a concentration of spiritual power gathered from his lifelong devotion to military science, both in theory and on the field, he rose from his bed on 13 September, the day of decision.

What is so impressive is that the action that day followed the abortive attack made on 31 July. But at every point of approach, a greater weight of armoury was delivered, with the addition of four deceptive feint attacks behind Quebec at the French centre. The bombardment across the river opposite the city was repeated, but this time a crossing was made from the first post on the south bank westward from the main caps of Levi and Orleans, up river.

Opposite this first post was a narrow gully leading from the shore up to the Heights of Abraham. What followed, after some two thousand troops had reached the wooded heights up this gully, was an elaborate but more professional battle. I need not retell it, for it is now recorded, moment by moment, in the military textbooks, and in most schoolroom history books. Robin Reilly's account of it is masterly in its clear narrative, and its estimate of the parts played by Wolfe's officers who commanded the several brigades converging on the plain west of the city, where the main battle closed and the victory was decided. He has written that Wolfe's moves were so precise and deliberately thought-out that the battle could be compared with a game of chess played by a master. He proceeds to explain why, but the gist of his explanation is that Wolfe succeeded in keeping Montcalm guessing at every point, thus creating a confusion and hesitation amongst the French army while, with his smaller forces suddenly united, he drove the attack home.

To the very end he took risks, the most spectacular of which was the final decision of opening fire from the standing square of his troops as the French charged. He waited, and his staff were agonised; but the trust of the men was not broken. They held their fire until their general gave the word. He was already wounded in the wrist and the groin. But he was to be seen, and to be obeyed. The three volleys, at close quarters, broke the French army, killing over a thousand, among them Montcalm.

After the first volley, and the ordered movement forward over several paces to a halt and the second volley, Wolfe was shot in the chest. He was carried back to the rear, where a surgeon attended to the wound. Wolfe's last moments have become as immortalised as those of Nelson. The dying general roused himself to hear the cry 'They run! See how they run!'; he whispered 'Who run?' One of his officers answered. 'The enemy, sir! By God, they give way everywhere!' Thereupon he gave his last command:

'Go, one of you, to Colonel Burton. Tell him to march Webb's regiment to Charles river, to cut off retreat to the bridge.' Life lingered in the diseased and mutilated body for a few minutes. The officers and the surgeon leaning over him heard a few faint words: 'Now I can die—content.'

Townsend took command, and failed to follow up the victory as Wolfe had commanded. In his official report, he referred to Wolfe's death almost as an aside. But his intention to steal the laurels failed. They found their right disposal, and have remained there. They celebrate James Wolfe as a dedicated soldier of genius, whose whole life was given to this dreadful but seemingly necessary profession. Military historians are agreed that Townsend allowed the French to escape, with the consequence that the campaign continued, with further loss of life, and a continuation of all the other miseries consequent on war. Even so, Townsend survived and flourished. Horace Walpole wrote of his 'proud and sullen and contemptuous temper'. It carried him to high office and honours. He became, in the course of his continued military and political life, a Field Marshall and a Marquis, and did not relinquish these and other decorations until he died in 1807 at the age of 84.

Wolfe's widowed mother was refused a pension by the Duke of Newcastle, because his enemy William Pitt had sued for it. But the nation spoke for the dead hero. Again Horace Walpole may be quoted (and he was not often given to sentiment):

The horror of the night, the precipice scaled by Wolfe, the empire he with a handful of men added to England, and the glorious catastrophe of contentedly terminating his life when his fame began; ancient story may be ransacked, and ostentatious philosophy thrown into the account, before an episode can be found to rank with Wolfe's.

Wolfe's body was brought home in H.M.S. *Royal William*, and landed at Spithead on 17 November. It was carried by road to Greenwich, where it lay in state for three days before being buried beside his father. It is not the body but the spirit and genius of the young man which survives, as 'Kent's Contribution'.

Richard Harris Barham

THIS CHAPTER is only a personal interposition, caused by the recollection of a boyhood enthusiasm for a book surviving from early Victorian times into the early decades of the twentieth century. When I was a lad round the turn of the century, *The Ingoldsby Legends* was found in every home, along with *Pickwick Papers*. I see that my copy of those now forgotten Legends, given me by an aunt in 1909, is in The World's Classics, bound in 'Sultan Red Leather', price 1/6d. So it was obviously considered to be immortal. No book was included then in The World's Classics or in Everyman's Library unless it was assured of immortality.

So I hope that I am justified in my choice of Richard Harris Barham, the author of *The Ingoldsby Legends*, as one of the immortals both in Kent who have added a distinctive feature, and a name, to the story of Western Civilization. I hope without making any certain claim, for the course of that story appears to be taking such unexpected turns that not only *The Ingoldsby Legends*, but the whole of European literature, may soon be only academically intelligible to the generations already pressing on our heels.

I have, however, a second motive in writing about Barham, because he was a member of a family which flourishes today, its members scattered around the county of Kent, as were their forefathers during the centuries, typical representatives of that resilient class, the smaller gentry, the knights and squires, whose origins are rooted in the Saxon society which preceded the coming of Norman William in the eleventh century, and whose coherent firmness prevented him from absorbing what I have elsewhere called 'The Little Kingdom' in his Feudal System, as he absorbed the rest of England, demoting the thegns to serfdom, and uniting their farmsteads into huge estates under the Crown, to be handed out to his subject barons.

Osmotic pressure has functioned in history as it does in nature, and the distinctive structure of the land-ownership in Kent has been only partially maintained. As I have tried to show in the chapter on the Kentish gentry and their estates during the Civil War, the taking of sides, for the King or for Parliament, cut through family life; and also by then a few large aristocratic familities had settled in the county during the Tudor tyrannies and the dissolution of the monasteries.

The Barham family, like that of the Derings, is very ancient, though probably not of Saxon origin. Hasted, in his many-volumed History of Kent, suggests that the Barhams were probably of Norman origin, and that one member of it engaged in the removal of 'that turbulent priest' Thomas Becket. He says

Barham Court is a manor or seat in the parish of Barham situated close to the Church. It was probably the court lodge of the manor of Barham in very early times, before it became united to that of Bishopsbourne. And in King Henry the Second's time it was held of the Archbishop of Canterbury as half a knight's fee by Sir Randal Fitzurse, who was one of those four knights belonging to the King's household who murdered the Archbishop, Thomas à Becket, in the cathedral of Canterbury, 1170.

All that has been much in the popular mind since T. S. Eliot wrote his play for performance in the Chapter House, at the instigation of that great man Bishop George Bell, at that time Dean of Canterbury Cathedral. But the play was heavily biased in favour of Becket, and gave no hint that the drama was only an incident in the age-old struggle between king and priest, chronicled in The Old Testament, and in the subsequent history of the whole of Christendom.

This Randal Fitzurse fled to Ireland, and thence to Rome and the Holy Land. The Pope gave him absolution of his crime. Meanwhile, his estate of Barham had been taken over by his brother, who discreetly assumed the name of de Berham. Hasted adds, 'From him it descended in an uninterrupted line down to Bartholomew Barham who did homage for it to Archbishop Wareham, anno. IX, Henry VIII, and in his possession it continued till Thomas Barham Esq., in the beginning of James the First's reign, alienated it'. But the family proliferated, one branch settling at Wadhurst over the county border in Sussex. A member of the family, Sir Nicholas, was sergeant-at-law to Queen Elizabeth. His duties included the prosecution of the Duke of Norfolk in 1571. A later member, Dr Henry Barham, was the author of a book *Hortus Americanus*, published in Jamaica in 1794; a slight reminder to posterity.

At the end of the seventeenth century some parts of the ancient estate were brought back into the family by a Thomas Barham through his marriage with the daughter of a Thomas Harris of Canterbury. She was heiress to the properties of Parmstead (Barhamstead) and Tappington Everard. Four generations later, his descendant Richard Harris Barham was born on 6 December 1788. We know little of his father, except that he was sedentary in his habits, weighed twenty-seven stone, and accumulated a valuable library before dying in 1795, leaving an encumbered estate to his only son, the future author of *The Ingoldsby Legends*, amongst which Tappington Everard plays a considerable part as background.

Both the boy and his mother were in feeble health, and their estate was administered by three guardians, one of whom was a wicked attorney who added the prefix 'mal' to his share in the administration of the boy's inheritance. That was not the only misfortune in Richard's early life. At nine years of age he was sent to St Paul's School, London, famous literary seed-bed. There he made rapid advance in the classics, but no headway with mathematics. This non-polarity is so frequent in the development of high-quality minds that I suspect there must be something wrong with mathematics. It is comforting to think that in future we may be able to leave them in the care of computers, though I fear there may be some error in my calculations on this matter.

Returning to school from Tappington in 1802, when he was fourteen and therefore at an age when that dreaded subject of mathematics begins to loom drearily, still without its more acceptable applications in philosophy, young Barham was nearly killed by the over-turning of the Dover Mail coach. His right arm was crushed. In those days medical aid was rough and ready. He was put, alone, into a hackney-carriage and taken on to London, bleeding steadily. He arrived more dead than alive. On hearing the news, the attorney sent a surveyor to report on the value of the farm buildings, to see to the repair of fencings, to mark out timber for felling, and to look into the term of unexpired leases as concerns in the boy's estate.

Fortunately, the wife of the High Master of St Paul's School took a different kind of practical view of the situation. She prevented a proposed amputation of the damaged arm, nursed the boy back to life and health, and made him her particular protegé henceforth, inviting him to the literary parties given in her home.

Among the regular guests was a leading actress of the day, Mrs Bartley, who also saw in the boy a remarkable aptitude for high-speed versifying and dramatic composition. She taught him the art of speaking. It is an art of which we English are uniquely shy. In Europe and among all Celtic people, the clear and musical delivery of one's native language is regarded as a first principle; the foundation of our culture and our social conduct. In England we regard it as 'showing-off' or as an exhibition of class snobbery. Ask an Italian policeman or peasant the way to your destination, and the reply will sound like a passage from *The Divine Comedy*. The few English folk who do not distastefully masticate their vowels and consonants, are marked men and women; they add a cubit of beauty and authority to their stature. Young Barham, like Pitt the younger, was lucky in this addition to his normal education. It enhanced the whole of his future career, framing, as it were, his natural disposition of bonhomie, lightning wit and genuine benevolence.

His versifying had already attracted attention in school, for a collection of his 'speeches' written for classroom occasions was printed in 1807, and he was thus set upon the way toward his later fame. *The Gentleman's Magazine*, in its November issue, 1808, commented:

These verses, considering them the off-spring of early years, we do not hesitate to say, display much promise of future excellence. They contain many passages which are striking, picturesque, and glowing; while the whole attest a native poetical vein and an harmonious ear.

Listen to an example of that verse, which shows that the young author was not unaware of his future prospects:

> 'Tis true I'm young: perhaps, too, somewhat small;
> But that has been the common lot of all:
> Grave rev'rend sages, heroes six feet high—
> Nestor himself—were once as young as I;
> The sturdiest oak that ploughs the boist'rous main,
> The guardian bulwark of Britannia's reign,
> A sapling once, within its native vale,
> Shrank from the blast and bow'd at every gale.

The 'sapling' was also notorious for his practical jokes, but such was his general character that he became Captain of the School for two years, before going up to Brasenose College, Oxford, where he made an intimate friendship with Theodore Hook which lasted until the latter's death, an event that shattered Barham's genial happiness in his last years. Hook was born in the same year as Barham, and died in 1841, only four years before him. He was a prolific writer, but his reputation survives perhaps more as a wit of lightning-like improvisatory powers, than as a dramatist, essayist and novelist. He was a great clubman at The Garrick Club, which the two friends frequented. His novels introduced a democratic element in *mise en scene* and characterisation which probably influenced Dickens; notably one called *Jack Brag*, published in 1837, when Dickens was just getting into his stride.

Barham had financial difficulties while at Oxford. Brasenose was an expensive college, and he got into a gaming set. He had not learned to distinguish capital from income; and behind this unmathematical lapse lay the vacuum created by that wicked attorney. But Barham was fundamentally a sensible fellow, and he decided to apply to another of his guardians, Lord Rokeby, for authorisation to release some of the trust money to cover the gambling debts. This Lord Rokeby refused to do, but very kindly paid the debts out of his own pocket, wrapped in some shrewd advice. The sugared pill cured Barham, and from that time onward he acted with shrewd realism in all money matters. He was not soon enough, however, to prevent the attorney from depriving the estate of some eight thousand pounds. No doubt the further lesson learned thereby, which caused him to part company with that dubious guide, permanently compensated for his lack of ability in mathematics.

But he became no kill-joy, and his habits during college life were hardly indicative of his future clerical career. There is a story of a conversation with his tutor who had to interview him about his continued absence from morning chapel.

'The fact is, sir' said Barham, 'you are too *late* for me.'

'Too late?' was the astonished rejoinder.

'Yes, sir—too late. I cannot sit up till seven o'clock in the morning: I am a man of regular habits, and unless I get to bed by four or five at the latest, I am really fit for nothing next day'. Characteristically, this impudence was instantly followed by a profuse apology which was benignly accepted. He had about him a blithe ease always eloquently expressed. It must have been a family trait, for it appears in his son's biography, a work in two volumes which might suitably have been contained in one, but for the genial expansiveness with which even the most dramatic and even tragic events are dressed. Thus, in telling how a miscarriage of a letter from the father agreeing to pay the debts of a fellow-student of Barham caused the foolish boy to blow his brains out, the horror is quilted with the following:

It is, however, by no means easy for a young man to stop short in a career of extravagance, without possessing the means of discharging the debts he has already incurred. At the Universities, in particular, his resources are gauged with the nicest accuracy, and the unhappy victim is allowed no peace till all are exhausted. It may be a hazardous matter to lay the hand of legislation upon so delicate a fabric as that of credit; but some restriction is urgently demanded with regard to the disastrous system pursued at Oxford, and though to a less extent, at Cambridge also.

I quote this nice piece of otiosity, because it is a thin echo of the method which its author's father developed into a personal idiom of astonishing elasticity and detached humour. Barham used it as a kind of plastic packaging labelled with his gentle Christian faith, in the apologetic but vain hope of protecting his readers from the dreadful contents of his literary parcels, tales of witchcraft, ghosts, smugglers, poisonings and suicides, all dire potentialities of life on this earth.

That there was no malice in this method, hardly even a hint of satire, is suggested in a character-study of him written by his friend John Hughes, the author of *Tom Browne's Schooldays*, to Harrison Ainsworth a month after Barham's death:

I am perfectly convinced that the same social influence would have followed Mr Barham into any other line of life that he might have adopted; that the profits of agitating pettifoggers would have materially lessened in a district where he acted as a magistrate; and that duels would have been nipped in the bud at his regimental mess. It is not always an easy task to do as you would be done by; but to think as you would be thought of and thought for, and to feel as you would be felt for, is perhaps still more difficult, as superior powers of tact and intellect are here required in order to second good intentions. These faculties, backed by an uncompromising love of truth and fair dealing, indefatigable good nature, and a nice sense of what was due to every one in the several relations of life, both gentle and simple, rendered our late friend invaluable, either as an adviser or a peace-maker, in matters of delicate and difficult handling. How he managed to get through his more important duties is a marvel. Certain it is that they were well and punctually performed in every point relating to cathedral matters, as well as his engagements as a parochial incumbent and priest of the Household, which I believe was the nature of his office at the Chapel Royal.

After graduation, Barham took Holy Orders and in March, 1813, returned to his home county, as a curate in Ashford. A year later he moved to Westwell, near the handsome estate of Eastwell Park. The park is still intact today, but the house has been pulled down. Whenever I drive to Wye, I am teased with curiosity about what goes on in the park, hidden from the twentieth century by the brick wall alongside the road from Ashford to Boughton Aluph, dominated by the one surviving building at the entrance to the estate, a decorative Tudor tower gateway. One of the royal princes dispossessed of his claim to the throne by the outcome of the Wars of the Roses, retired to live in Eastwell Park, and was thus successful in being overlooked by the victors, who might have found his legitimacy to be too dangerous for him to be left alive. There, until his death from old age, he led the life of a scholarly recluse.

Barham found material at Westwell, of which he made a note. It proves that he was already groping his way to the special form of literary career which was to make him famous. Here is the note:

I will begin with a true story of a witch practising her diabolical witchcraft and ventriloquie anno 1574, at Westwell, in Kent within six miles of where I dwell, taken and noted down by two ministers of God's word, four substantial yeomen, and three women of good fame and reputation, whose names are after-written. Mildred, the base daughter of Alice Norrington, and now servant to Will Spooner, of Westwell, being of the age of 17 years, was possessed with Satan in the day and night aforesaid. About two o'clock in the afternoon of the same day there came to the said Spooner's house Roger Newman, minister of Westwell John Brainford, minister of Kinington, with others whose names are underwritten, who made their prayer to God to assist them in that needful case, and then commanded Satan in the name of the Holy Trinity to speak with such a voice as they might understand, and to declare from whence he came.

The Devil, speaking through the girl, confessed that he had been sent by a certain old woman named Alice, with instructions to bring about the death of three people in the neighbourhood. He was then duly exorcised. Later, however, the girl was arrested as an imposter who had used 'ventriloquy'. She received 'condign punishment' for practising the same art as that said to have been used by the Holy Maid of Kent. Barham also made a note about an archer, of the same parish, said to have been possessed by satanic powers, so that he never missed the mark when he shot. He must have been another William Tell, for he 'shot at a penny on his son's head and made ready another arrow to have slain the Duke that commanded it.' One sees the raw material of the *Ingoldsby Legends* accumulating.

In 1814 Barham married Caroline Smart, descendant of a John Smart who was made Garter King-at-Arms in 1449. Two children were born at Westwell, both boys. The younger died in infancy, and soon after this loss the family moved to Snargate, where Barham was made Rector by the Archbishop of Canterbury. He was also given the curacy of Warehorn. These villages, two miles apart, lay on the inland fringe of Romney Marsh, and were thus inhabited by smugglers. At that time this trade was almost a major industry, known as 'The Free Trade'. Barham found them friendly, even when they challenged him riding home at night and thus coming upon them by chance at their nocturnal work, leading horses or trains of donkeys laden with contraband. The churches throughout south Kent were used as depots for such goods. On one occasion a large parcel of tobacco was seized in Snargate belfry, and a keg of Hollands under the vestry table: more grist to Barham's literary mill!

It was a very active mill, mostly taking the form of epistolary verse to his friends and neighbours, inviting them to meals, or relating some local occurrence amongst his parishioners. He was an extremely social character, and he had the faculty for peopling a wilderness. People who know Romney Marsh, even in its presentday state with its once weird remoteness obliterated by bungaloid growth, an atomic power station and a huge holiday-camp, must be impressed by its overall character of solitariness. Even Camber Sands, a few miles east of Rye, their popularity increased by the said holiday-camp, have not completely lost that withdrawn quality, a kind of shyness in nature. Maybe it is due to the fact that the Marsh is a geological newcomer, deposited there by the sea within the last few hundred years.

In the Middle Ages the coast-line came up to Smallhithe, below Tenterden, whose noble church tower was a mariners' guide and warning, since the waters must always have been shallow up that creek, which a conjunction of currents has filled with sand and shingle. What is so astonishing is that within these few centuries, nature has contrived to overlay this deposit with soil so fertile that the grazing there is world-famous for its nurturing of the unique breed of Romney Marsh sheep.

Barham's family thrived there, but he found that his stipend, and diminishing rents from the impoverished estate at Tappington Everard, were insufficient to make ends meet. His lavish hospitality and general benevolence to the poor of the parish also made it necessary for him to augment his income. He was persuaded to this by an accident, recorded in a diary entry dated 13 May 1819. 'Drove William and Dick into Ashford—overturned the gig—broke my right leg and sprained my left ancle [sic]. Mary Anne came back in the chaise with me.' He was immobilised for many weeks, and the resultant boredom drove him to attempt writing a novel. It was called *Baldwin*, for which he was paid twenty pounds. It was stillborn. Still unable to move about, as rheumatism had set in around the wounded legs, he tried another essay in fiction and called it *My Cousin Nicholas*. It was accepted by *Blackwood's Magazine* and sold well enough in book-form to encourage him to seek 'fresh woods and pastures new'.

This resolution was furthered by the illness of one of the children. He believed that the low-lying Marsh, much of it below sea-level, was the cause, and he went up to London to consult a specialist. His son's biography amusingly describes what ensued: 'He chanced to encounter an old friend who was walking along the Strand swinging a letter in his hand. He had carelessly passed the post-office, and taking Mr Barham's arm turned back with the intention of dropping into the box what he had just been writing. It was, he said, an invitation to a young clergyman to come up from the country and stand for a minor canonry then vacant in the cathedral of St Paul's. Simultaneously the question occurred to both—why should not Mr Barham himself become the candidate? His friend had been commissioned to find one sufficiently eligible, but had never thought of addressing himself to his former school-fellow, being under the impression that the latter was well content with his position in Kent. The whole thing was what is commonly called the merest matter of chance. Be that as it may, the intercepted letter was forthwith scattered to the winds, and it was arranged that Mr Barham should return by that night's mail to Warehorn, talk the business over with his wife, and forward his decision within 48 hours.

This he did characteristically enough in a poetical epistle containing

> The Resolution;
> or,
> An Adieu to the Country.'

O, I'll be off! I will by Jove!
No more by purling streams I'll ramble,
Through dirty lanes no longer rove,
Bemired and scratched by briar and bramble.

I'll fly the pigstye for the parks,
And Jack and Tom and Ned and Billy
I'll quit for more enlightened sparks,
And Romney Marsh for Piccadilly.

Adieu, ye woods! adieu, ye groves!
Ye waggon-horses, ploughs and harrows!
Ye capering lambs! ye cooing doves!
Adieu, ye nightingales and sparrows!

Adieu, ye nasty little boys,
So sweetly in the puddles playing!
Adieu, adieu, the cheerful noise
Of grunting pigs and asses braying!

O, I'll begone! at once farewell
To gooseberry wine and pear and codling!
Farewell the sheep's harmonious bell!
Farewell the gander's graceful waddling!

Farewell the compost's sweet perfume!
Farewell rum-punch, nectareous liquor!
Farewell the pimples that illume
The noses of the squire and vicar!

Adieu my pipe! not that of old
By swains Arcadian tuned so gaily.
But that of modern frame and mould,
Invented by Sir Walter Raleigh.

And I'll renounce my dog and gun,
And 'bob' no more for eels in ditches;
The huntsmen, horn, and hounds I'll shun
And I'll cashier my leather breeches!

For me the fox may prowl secure,
The partridge unmolested fly,
Whist, loo, and cribbage I abjure,
And e'en backgammon's lures defy.

At country 'hops', at country balls,
At christening treats no more I'll be!
No more I'll pay my morning calls,
Nor with old ladies take my tea!

Adieu the vestry and the bench,
The rate and justice's approval,
The overseer, refract'ry wench,
Appeal, and order of removal!

The fair, its gingerbread and toys,
Rough roads, deep ruts, and boist'rous weather,
Ye scenes of bliss, ye rural joys,
Adieu! and, Bless ye, altogether!

This unconventional application is quoted at length to show the verbal diarrhoea by which Barham maintained the cleanliness of his moral system. He poured out rhyming verse as an instant reaction to the happenings of his daily life, and it always revealed the significant detail of every situation. He observed everything felicitously, and recorded it thus, rather in the manner minutes later exgurgitate the coloured photograph.

His friends were convinced that his seeming levity in applying for the post of a Canon of St Pauls in verse, and on the assumption that he had already got the job, would of course disqualify him. But they were wrong. On 6 April 1821, the Dean and Chapter appointed him. That meant giving up a permanent home in Kent: but we must not yet forsake him, because his true career and fame still lay ahead, the achievement which was to make him one of the immortals native to the county.

He found a comfortable period-house in Great Queen Street, leading at that time to Lincoln's Inn Fields, but nowadays into Kingsway. I like to think that it may have been the house where the *New Statesman* was born early in the present century; where in a grubby but gracefully panelled back-room Desmond MacCarthy, the Literary Editor, used to stride to and fro amongst a litter of books, talking like Coleridge, wasting his eloquence on whichever of his contributors may have come in to pick up a book for review. That part of central London has been, and is still, a village with a long history of literary activity. A bookman's nostalgic meanderings could well be set there, before the removal of Covent Garden Market changes the whole character and atmosphere of the district that spreads some half mile northward and westward from Fleet Street and The Strand; acres that once shook beneath the footfall of Samuel Johnson, and were watered with the tears of Charles Dickens.

Barham became a lighter figure in that neighbourhood; but it infected him with the literary bug. Within a short time of settling there he was editing the *London Chronicle*, whose first editor was Dr Johnson. He found, however, that his duties as a Canon of St Paul's were no sinecure. They involved much administrative work that filled his daytime hours, so that he had to burn the candle at both ends to further his now fully awakened literary ambitions, latent since boyhood. The editorship came to an end when the *London Chronicle* became merged into the *St James's Chronicle*, a frequent fate with weekly and monthly magazines. But he was actively engaged, in his spare time, with poetic trifles and book reviews in surviving magazines, such as *John Bull*, the *Globe and Traveller*, the *Literary Gazette*, *Blackwood's*, and other periodicals now lost without trace.

His daily habit of work as a part-time writer, depending mainly on a regular professional job, was similar to those of the majority of people engaged in this occupation of producing books and other literary matter. He describes it accurately in his notebooks: 'My wife goes to bed at ten, to rise at eight, and look after the children and other matrimonail duties. I sit up till three in the morning, working at rubbish for Blackwood. She is the slave of the ring, and I of the lamp'. If the product were for *Blackwood's*, it could not have been rubbish, for that dignified and beloved magazine survives today, with a unique reputation for the quality of its contents.

Barham did not neglect his office work, however. He may be compared with an author only 27 years his junior, Anthony Trollope, a civil servant working in the Post Office who rode about the country on horseback as an inspector and made a minor, second immortality by inventing post-boxes, or as they were once called, pillar-boxes. The *furor scribendi* has always found a means of stoking its fires in the civil service, or some such safe harbour. *The Wind in the Willows* first whispered in the Bank of England; Mr Prufrock's proclamation of a new technique in verse was first made from Lloyds Bank. The associations of literature with commerce and administration are infinite, and are likely always to be so, because literature is 'a good walking stick but a bad crutch', one of Coleridge's more concise definitions.

That good friend Hughes, author of *Tom Browne's Schooldays*, from whose obituary encomium I have already quoted, pays a particular tribute to Barham, the officer of the Church:

In proportion as his standing and influence increased in that section of the cathedral church to which he more immediately belonged, their effects were in several unequivocal ways visible for good. It may well be supposed that no corporate body, save the hierarchy of angels, is exempt from occasional differences and discussions. Not that I have any reason to believe that the worthy conclave of which I speak, whose blood is mostly sweetened by the domestic charities of life, deserve that wicked wag Colman's gibe at popish *celibataires:*—

> 'Twold seem, since tenanted by holy friars,
> That harmony and peace reigned here eternally:
> The folks that crammed you with that tale were liars;
> The holy friars quarrelled most infernally.'

But whatever their temporary variances may have been, it is certain that no member of the body was more influential than Mr Barham in promoting, by a happy union of humour and reason, a tone of harmony and gentleman-like feeling in their relations to the chapter, and to each other. I can confidently say that, as his character and merits became better known, he was trusted and consulted by the best and most talented men among the residentiaries as one of themselves.

One of those 'residentiaries' was a Dr Blomberg, who by a lucky chance had been adopted by George the Third's queen as a fosterling, and brought up with the prince who was later to be Regent and then King George IV. The foster-brotherhood survived, and Dr Blomberg thus became a useful friend of Barham in the matter of Royal favour and ecclesiastical promotion. In 1824 Barham was appointed Priest in Ordinary to His Majesty's Chapels Royal, and with the remunerative incumbency of St Mary Magdalene and St Gregory by St Paul. The latter post gave Barham an opportunity to display, instinctively, his remarkable gift for pouring oil on troubled waters.

The two parishes were at parochial war with each other; a sort of quarrel between the two selves of Siamese twins. It was due to a long-standing disagreement about the appointment of a chairman for the vestry meetings. At Barham's first appearance he sat down in the Chair, and there was an uproar of protest. He demanded that a second chair should be brought in and placed by his side. 'Now sir', he said to the leader of the protest, 'You have brought in that chair and placed it here. Let me see you dare seat yourself in it, and within four and twenty hours you shall find yourself in the ecclesiastical courts.' This vague threat, summoned out of Barham's vivid imagination relating to all medieval Church matters, so intimidated the vestrymen that not only was the second chair left unoccupied, but the long-standing enmities disappeared like a morning mist. This achievement was a typical example of Barham's social technique, described by his son as being equipped with 'peculiar tact and conciliatory art'. This natural gift made Barham a successful courtier in the entourage of the indulgent King, and a welcome companion and sweetener in the generally acid literary set. It also tinctured his writings, giving justification to his garrulity and facile rhyming.

Following his appointment to the remunerative posts of the parishes round St Paul's Cathedral, Barham decided to move house into the midst of his duties there and also within the Cathedral. He took a house in the Churchyard by the entrance to the alley in which the Deanery stands. The lane is an airless, dark slope down to the River Thames, even at present. In those days a century and a half ago, it must have been pestiferous. During the eighteen years that the Barham family lived there, five of the children died. These losses were accepted with some degree of equanimity. We hear much of the close-knit family ties in the Victorian Age, with the firm knot of paternal authority and love at the top of each household; but to accept the loss of five of one's children as 'acts of God' and therefore beyond question, tends to puzzle us today, now that the State has taken over most of the responsibilities of the family as the foundation of our social structure.

An instance of what can only be called the grim superstitiousness in this matter of the relationship between parents and children at that period is worth quoting, because it also shows what are the general rewards in the profession of letters. Barham was a member of the Council of the Royal Literary Fund, founded at the end of the eighteenth century to assist poverty-stricken writers, and still doing that good work today. His son's biography records that

Having been instrumental on one occasion in obtaining a donation of thirty pounds for a distressed author, he resolved to make a *detour* on his way home, and inform the poor man of the succour that had been awarded him. The applicant was found in an upper room, containing scarcely an article of furniture: there was no fire in the grate, but in one corner about as many coals as would fill a pint pot. The wife was sitting on an inverted tub, nursing a dying child, and one great source of misery appeared to be the fear that the poor infant would expire without the benefit of baptism. This anxiety was at once removed by Mr Barham, who immediately proceeded to administer the sacrament. The child died on the day following, but the parents were restored by the Society's bounty, and subsequently enabled to regain their position in the world.

The cool sentiment implicit in that little story pervades the *Ingoldsby Legends*, so it may be a family characteristic. It is also due to the general attitude toward children in the nineteenth century, as indeed in all preceding ages where family relationships have been recorded. Was it purely humour that made Barham, at a party given in 1843 by Talfourd (the biographer of Charles Lamb), retort to a lady who had gushed to him, 'I am sure you are

fond of children, Mr Barham ?' His reply was instant. 'Yes, ma'am, I like
them very well—boiled with greens!'

This Struvelpeter kind of ferocity, however, was more a literary device
than a natural attitude toward children. In the long correspondence maintained over many years with the mother of his friend Hughes, there is a
letter describing minute-by-minute agonies of mind suffered by him and
his wife when one of their children was struck down by cholera at five
o'clock one morning. They sat with him all that day, the mother rubbing his
chest 'with a strong embrocation', and the father telling him stories until
at four o'clock in the afternoon he fell asleep:

Poor child!—he never woke again. . . . I received the intelligence, not only
with incredulity, but almost indignation; it was, however, too true. Of what
passed afterwards, I can give you no account—it is a perfect blank in my
memory—the suddenness of the blow was stunning. But a few hours before,
the question had been whether we should take him with us to the theatre, and
now they asked me about his funeral—his *immediate* internment.

The immediacy was urged because there were already 1000 cases of cholera
in the City. Dickens would have made more of that deathbed scene, but I
doubt if he could have expressed grief more sincerely and effectually than
does that pitiable parenthesis, 'it is a perfect blank in my memory'.

Beneath the clubbable *bon viveur*, there lived that quick sensibility which
was expressed yet disguised by his literary facility. Such is the paradox of
human nature.

A prime example of that lightning facility in rhyming is worth quoting. A
boy at Merchant Taylors' School called on Mr Barham one day just before
the breaking-up for the midsummer holidays. The vicar offered to take him
to the theatre that night. The boy confessed that there was some difficulty
in accepting the tempting offer, as he had to write a set of verses on the
subject of Sir Thomas White, the founder of the School. The verses had to
be shown by next morning; if not, there would be trouble. Perhaps the
vicar could help in this matter ? Barham took up a sheet of paper and a
pencil, and without pausing, wrote the following:

> Sir Thomas White
> Was a noble knight,
> Extremely desirous of doing what's right;
> So he sat himself down one beautiful night,
> When the moon shone so bright
> That he asked for no light
> Beyond that of her beams, and began to indite

His last will,—so remarkably good was his sight—
And he charged and bound down his executors tight,
As soon as his soul should have taken its flight,
To erect a good school of proportionate height,
Length, and breadth—Suffolk Lane he proposed for its site,
And its order what architects term composite—
In which all such nice little good boys who might
At the date of their entrance have not attained quite
Their tenth year, should be brought up to read and to write;
Not to give way to spite, nor to quarrel nor fight,
But to show themselves always well-bred and polite,
Keep hands and face clean, and be decently dight
In clothes of a grave colour rather than bright—
At least not so light as remark to excite—
And to make Greek and Latin their chiefest delight;
To be mild in demeanour, in morals upright—
Not to kick, nor to bite,
Nor to pinch, nor affright
Each other by practical jokes, as at night
By aping a goblin, humgriffin, or sprite;
And never to wrong by so much as a mite,
Or a bat, or a ball, or a hoop, or a kite,
Any poor little schoolfellow—Oh, what a plight
I am in after all—poor unfortunate wight!
I can't make my number of verses up quite;
For my paper's expended,
My rhymes too are ended,
And I *can* write no more, for I've no more to write;
So if a line short, I'm in hopes Mr Bellamy
Will pity my case, and not cease to think well o'me.

We are not told what Mr Bellamy, the Headmaster, made of that composition that did with words what only Paganini could have done with his fiddle. It is not surprising that Barham soon found a wider field in which to scatter such a prestigious talent. He was friendly with the publisher Bentley, as he was with most of the literary members of the Garrick Club. In 1837 Bentley published the first issue of his magazine *The Miscellany*. He had roped in the young Charles Dickens, who only four years previously had started his *Sketches by Boz*, and attracted considerable notice when they appeared in book form in 1836. Dickens immediately began *The Pickwick Papers*, which created such a public demand that the whole machinery of the publishing world exploded. Chapman and Hall hardly knew what to do. The only comparable embarrassment in the book world during the twentieth century was that of a small, idealistic publisher named A. C. Fifield, who in 1917 put out a book called *Married Love*, written by the geologist Marie Stopes, a specialist on the nature of coal. The demand for this little book so terrified him that he promptly sold his business to an enterprising traveller for Duckworth, by the name of Jonathan Cape, and retired into the country.

Even the towering vitality and fame of Dickens, however, could not overlay the contributions made by Barham to the new magazine. They were the first of the *Ingoldsby Legends*. Here again the unexpected happened; fame came overnight. In view of his position as a Canon of St Paul's and other dignified livings in the Church, Barham had decided to write under a pseudonym, Thomas Ingoldsby. But his breezy nature blew through that disguise as freely as it had done through St Paul's Churchyard and the Garrick Club. His own inventive imagination was augmented by a fund of stories and anecdotes offered him by his friend, the old Mrs Hughes, and her now famous son, a one-book man.

The first three *Legends* were ghost stories, one of which had been told the Hughes by Lady Eleanor Butler, one of the two Ladies of Llangollen; another by Sir Walter Scott. Barham was fortunate in being able to glean material from the wide circle of his friendships. His geniality now paid dividends. So did his marvellous memory, his facility in rhyming and making use of foreign languages and the various jargons of the legal and other professions, particularly his own, the Church, which he contrived to exploit with a humour that never over-stepped the mark. No Victorian prude or religious zealot could be shocked, even when Barham tended, in his convivial manner, to greet even Satan himself on back-slapping terms, as in one of the most popular of the Legends, *The Lay of St Cuthbert*:

> The Saint made a pause, as uncertain, because
> He knew Nick is pretty well 'up' in the laws,
> And they *might* be on *his* side—and then, he'd such claws!
> On the whole, it was better, he thought, to retire
> With the curly-wigged boy he'd pick'd out of the fire,
> And give up the victuals—to retrace his path,
> And to compromise—(spite of the Member for Bath).
> So to old Nick's appeal, as he turned on his heel,
> He replied, ' Well, I'll leave you the mutton and veal,
> And the soup *à la Reine*, and the sauce *Bechamel*;
> As the Scroope *did* invite you to dinner, I feel
> I can't well turn you out—'twould be hardly genteel. . . .

It should be noted that this Sir Guy de Scroope, who inadvertently, in a fit of anger at the lateness of guests whom he has invited to a banquet, finds himself entertaining the Devil, is introduced to the reader by a footnote preceding the poem:

There is every reason to believe that the gentleman who plays, though passively, so prominant a part in it, had Ingoldsby blood in his veins. This conjecture is supported by the fact of the arms of Scroope, impaling Ingolds-by, being found in one of the windows, and by a very old marriage-settlement nearly, or quite, illegible, a fac-simile of the seal affixed to which is appended to this true history.

The joke may be too long-drawn-out for modern taste, for the Legend of St Cuthbert fills 14 pages, and ends with a colophon reproducing the sup-posed 'seal attached to an ancient deed *penes* Thomas Ingoldsby Esq., pre-served in the archives at Tappington Everard'. As for the moral of the Lay; that is offered as blithely as the narrative preceding it.
'For this be assured, if you "go it" too fast,
You'll be dished like Sir Guy
And like him, perhaps, die
A poor, old, half-starved, Country Parson at last!'
Such was the genial character of this remarkable Man of Kent, who never lost his love for his native county. It haunted him and his writings, and drew his imagination back to its past history, its myths and legends, and its folk. He spent much of his adult life in London, busy with his res-ponsibilities as a Canon of St Paul's Cathedral and his two parish livings in the City. His last years were financially more easy, for in 1842, three years before his death, he acquired a third living, St Faith's Church, together with a Divinity Lectureship, which increased his income by £400, a good sum in the mid-nineteenth century.

He remained, as he began, a sound Tory, but this did not prevent an unbroken friendship with Sydney Smith, also a Canon of St Paul's, a famous wit and emphatically a Whig. No hint of rivalry appears in the record of their parallel careers. The only touch of criticism that may be construed as slightly acid, comes from Dean R. W. Church (famed by posterity not for his position in the hierarchy of St Paul's, but for his re-telling for children's reading of the tales from Greek mythology). The Dean is said to have 'hoped that Barham would be preached to death by wild curates'. It was, however, said of Barham after his death that 'he never lost a friend; he never met with coldness or neglect'.

He had never been physically robust. In addition to the crushed arm due to the accident when the stage coach overturned as he was on his way back to St Paul's School, he suffered chronically from a tendency to bronchitis, the disease which killed him on 17 June 1845, in his fifty-seventh year. He continued to write to within three days of his death, and even the sadness of the last two stanzas of that poem is lightened with a happy fancy, touched by his unquestioning religious faith, but still conveyed in verse shaped behind the mask of comic form.

> As I laye a thynkynge, a-thynkynge, a-thynkynge,
> And sadly sang the Birde as it perched upon a bier;
> That joyous smile was gone,
> And the face was white and wan,
> As the downe upon the Swan
> Doth appear,
> As I laye a-thynkynge—oh! bitter flowed the tear!
> As I laye a-thynkynge, the golden sun was sinking,
> O merrie sang that Birde as it glittered on her breast,
> With a thousand gorgeous dyes,
> While soaring to the skies,
> 'Mid the stars she seemed to rise,
> As to her nest;
> As I laye a-thynkynge, her meaning was expressed:—
> Follow, follow me away,
> It boots not to delay'—
> 'Twas so she seemed to saye,
> *'Here is rest !'*

Index